ON BEING RIC[...]

Christianity in a Time of Economic Globalization

JACQUES ELLUL

Compiled, edited, and translated by Willem H. Vanderburg

One of the most original thinkers of the twentieth century, Jacques Ellul (1912–1994) was a French law professor, sociologist, lay theologian, and self-described "Christian anarchist." *On Being Rich and Poor* is a collection of Ellul's prescient reflections on some of the most important theological questions of the modern age. In these lectures, which follow on those presented in *On Freedom, Love, and Power*, Ellul asks how it is that Christianity can justify the abandonment of the poorest, weakest, and most vulnerable members of society, the marginalization of youth and the denial of a liveable future for the next generation, and an unprecedented wave of environmental destruction.

Ellul observes that some of the harshest language in the Jewish and Christian Bibles is reserved for those who are rich and powerful, and thus able to bend others to their will. Through his analysis of the prophetic book of Amos and the letter of James, Ellul exposes the gap between the principles of Christian life and the practices of secular mass society. Criticizing a world that values domination over collaboration, he offers an alternative path.

Transcribed from the original audio recordings and translated by Willem H. Vanderburg, a student and long-time colleague of Ellul's, *On Being Rich and Poor* is a thought-provoking look at how one of the twentieth century's foremost thinkers grappled with some of today's most challenging issues.

WILLEM H. VANDERBURG is a professor emeritus at the University of Toronto, where he was the founding director of the Centre for Technology and Social Development. He was a NATO post-doctoral fellow under Jacques Ellul from 1973 to 1978 at the University of Bordeaux.

On Being Rich and Poor

Christianity in a Time of Economic Globalization

JACQUES ELLUL

*Compiled, edited, and translated
by Willem H. Vanderburg*

UNIVERSITY OF TORONTO PRESS
Toronto Buffalo London

© University of Toronto Press 2014
Toronto Buffalo London
www.utppublishing.com
Printed in Canada

ISBN 978-1-4426-4854-8 (cloth)
ISBN 978-1-4426-2626-3 (paper)

Printed on acid-free, 100% post-consumer recycled paper
with vegetable-based inks.

Library and Archives Canada Cataloguing in Publication

Ellul, Jacques, 1912–1994
On being rich and poor : Christianity in a time of economic globalization/Jacques Ellul ;
compiled, edited, and translated by Willem H. Vanderburg.

Includes bibliographical referencess and index.
ISBN 978-1-4426-4854-8 (bound).   ISBN 978-1-4426-2626-3 (pbk.)

1. Economics – Religious aspects – Christianity.   2. Globalization – Religious aspects –
Christianity.   3. Economics in the Bible.   I. Vanderburg, Willem H., editor of
compilation, translator   II. Title.

BR115.E3E46 2014   261.8'5   C2013-908548-3

This book has been published with the help of a grant from the Canadian Federation
for the Humanities and Social Sciences, through the Awards to Scholarly Publications
Program, using funds provided by the Social Sciences and Humanities Research
Council of Canada.

University of Toronto Press acknowledges the financial assistance to its publishing program
of the Canada Council for the Arts and the Ontario Arts Council.

 Canada Council   Conseil des Arts
for the Arts   du Canada

University of Toronto Press acknowledges the financial support of the Government
of Canada through the Canada Book Fund for its publishing activities.

Contents

Translator's Introduction

Much has been written about the influence Christianity has had on the emergence of an industrial civilization in western Europe and North America during the last 200 years. Today, Christianity continues to exercise a considerable influence on the economic, social, political, and moral life of the American and Canadian nations. With that influence comes enormous responsibility. How would we explain our role if there was an economic meltdown, a breakdown of our civilization, or an environmental collapse? To dismiss these possibilities out of hand is seriously to ignore the power of our scientific and technical means in the hands of the nation-state and the transnational corporations. How would we account for our individual and collective actions when brought before a commission investigating how and why such a catastrophic event caught us off guard? What would we say to God if he asked us why we could not understand what was happening until it was too late?

Since I am neither such a commission nor a prophet, the reader owes me no answer. However, it does not mean that you can close this book and be off the hook. Reading it may convince you that the course of events in North America during the last few decades might have been very different had the Christian community paid a little more attention to what God has to say, via the prophet Amos, about a time of considerable economic expansion and military success that made many people rich and many others poor as they were left behind. This message was further reinforced by James, who struggled with the implications of rich people's joining the Christian community. Some of the harshest language in the Jewish and Christian Bibles is reserved for those who are rich and powerful and thus able to bend others to their will. Moreover, their ways are held out as the symbol of everything that is antithetical to the ways of the Christian life.

Included in what is symbolized by monetary riches is being rich as a consequence of having received the good news. It is worth more than all other forms of riches. It is riches par excellence, riches that can also be turned into a certain superiority over others. We know where we are going, and it is too bad for everyone else if they do not wish to come along. Bring on the rapture and let us be done with it, and whatever else may happen is not our concern. It is these greatest riches that have been turned into a kind of economic, social, political, and moral capital that is every bit as real as financial capital. As a result, what we need to think about is what it is to be rich *and* poor instead of being rich *or* poor.

Another reason why we may be in for some surprises is that, as we live out our lives and thus influence the world around us, this world simultaneously influences us. The generally accepted plasticity of the brain implies that each and every experience is symbolized by neural and synaptic changes to the organization of our brain-minds that help us to evolve our lives, adapt, and subtly change who we are. This kind of reciprocity also applies to the reading of our Bible. We seek to understand it with our languages, ideas, values, and cultures, with the result that we cannot avoid imposing something of our lives on what we read. In this sense, we influence our Bible as we hope it also influences us. If the former influence is more decisive than the latter, our understanding will be aligned with our life and our society, while if the opposite is the case, we may get a glimpse of how its message is *entirely other* than our life and our society. We cannot dismiss the former possibility out of hand because many studies have shown that, apart from a few issues, Christians by and large appear to have little trouble fitting in and going along with the ways of our society. Even if we admit that this may be a possibility, we are likely to see ourselves as more or less faithful and thus not fitting into that pattern. We then confront another dilemma. How could we have received a message earlier in our lives which is so radically other that it pulls the rug out from underneath our feet? Would this not have produced a great deal of anxiety and stress on top of all the other tensions of our busy lives? In such a case, we may have been very tempted by what Devereux has called a countertransference reaction, which takes the form of an involuntary adjustment to how we interpret something in order to make it less threatening to who and what we are. A reduction in our anxiety level is one of the obvious benefits. In this case, we are back to the above possibility that our own influence on our understanding of the Bible is greater than the influence the Bible has on our understanding. From a sociological perspective, it would appear that in North America, the messages of Amos and James have insufficiently called this into question and have not convinced us to alter the course of our lives in an age of economic globalization.

Where does this leave the reader who has given up on institutionalized Christianity or who is not exactly attracted by what it says and does? For many of us, Jacques Ellul is among those who have opened the door to something different. I would almost be tempted to say, for those Christians who are comfortable in their churches, that this book is probably not for them. In any case, it offers a very different perspective on how human life was intended to be lived in love, and how one day it will be lived again.

Let us prepare ourselves then by inquiring into the kind of mental images, values, and commitments we inevitably bring to the reading of these texts as people of our time, place, and culture. We cannot avoid these influences, but we can take responsibility for them by critically examining the "cultural glasses" through which we are about to begin reading these texts. We cannot take these "glasses" off, but we can make ourselves more aware of how they may affect our reading of the Bible.

What I have in mind is that in North America, and probably beyond, Christians appear to know that there is a growing gap between their daily lives and what they read in their Bibles. At the same time, many of us feel helpless in the face of global forces that shape and reshape our lives and communities. Must we accept as necessary, inevitable, or normal that our society sacrifices the livelihoods of our neighbours? It does this by exporting their jobs, by making it more difficult for people to take care of themselves when they become old or unable to work, by economically marginalizing many youth in denying them the meaningful employment necessary to participate in our communities, by making higher education unaffordable for a growing number of youth, by excusing corporations from paying their fair share of taxes for the running of our communities and nations, by agreeing that basic public services should be handed over to corporations that are less and less accountable under free trade, and by turning those who work into just-in-time labour – in sum, by participating in the creation of a "system"[1] that works very well for products, capital, and technical experts but does not work for people and the biosphere. Of course, we all have our explanations of how and why we fit into this picture the way we do. Nevertheless, I suspect that all of us will find that this will not stand up to a responsible reading of Amos and James. Let us begin by taking a more careful look at what we so easily take for granted.

We live in what are called mass societies. Elsewhere, I have shown that in pre-industrial traditional societies people built and lived their lives by symbolizing their experiences as moments of their lives lived in a community embedded in the biosphere. In contrast, mass societies rely extensively on discipline-based approaches to knowing and doing, which are separated from daily-life knowing and doing. The result is a desymbolization of the lives of the members of these mass societies. These are therefore characterized by highly weakened and desymbolized traditions, values, and religious commitments. Their inability to sustain individual and collective human life through these traditional cultural means has been largely offset by the bath of images in which the mass media and the Internet submerge us. Collectively these images tell us how to fit in, belong, and "go with the flow." They reassure us that most of our private opinions more or less coincide with public opinion, and that our private moral convictions closely follow what has been referred to as a statistical morality. What this means is that what most people think and do is considered to be normal, and what is normal has become normative.

The bath of images in which we find ourselves submerged informs us as to what to eat and drink, how we should dress and groom ourselves, what we ought to possess and which vehicle to drive, how we can have a good time, what we should ask our doctors, what we should leave to scientists, how we should plan for retirement, how to make sense of what is happening in our world, and much more. A certain lifestyle is thus portrayed as a substitute for what has been lost with the break-up of traditions and the desymbolization of cultures. Advertisements connect this lifestyle to particular products without which it cannot be enjoyed. These advertisements are remarkably free from information about the products. Initially, advertisements bonded these products to the new lifestyle by means of its cultural symbols. Later, as a consequence of desymbolization, technical alternatives such as corporate logos were substituted. In this way, products and services have been endowed with capabilities they do not possess. The consumption of material things is transformed into the participation in all the good things the "system" has to offer. Many non-material needs thus appear to be satisfied by material things, which is a necessity in a mass society in which so much depends on mass production, mass consumption, and mass advertising.

At the same time, the mass media inform us about the difficulties and crises we face. Our concerns are managed by placing them in the context of what really matters, namely, that we are travelling down the road of progress and history, that economic growth driven by free and global markets can cure all our woes, that democracy can overcome tyranny, that medicine can save us from disease, that education will keep us in the global race, that the consumption of the goods and services that the system has to offer is the gateway to everything good, and that human nature continues to improve. The mass media incorporate every event into this destiny by means of pre-judgments, stereotypes, ideologies, and myths. Such an approach leaves us with no other direction or reference point for our lives. We are swept along by these currents of information grafted onto myths.

Apart from these mental images of our lives and our world, we have a need for values and profound commitments. These provide us with existential roots in an ultimately unknowable reality. What we are looking for are the kinds of entities in our lives and in our world that are so fundamental and essential that it is impossible to imagine who we would be, how we would live, and what our world would be like without them. To put it in religious language: they have made us and our world who and what we are. It is almost as if such creating and sustaining entities have no limits and are good in themselves. In our present world, such entities clearly include science, technology, the nation-state, and history.

We live as if science has no limits. We find it very difficult to come up with things that science can never know about our lives and our world. It would appear, then, that in the domain of knowing, we live as if science is essentially omnipotent. We have become completely unaware that a discipline-based science, which studies human life and the world one category of phenomena at a time, can be applied only to those situations in which one category of phenomena dominates all the others, so that these can be neglected. As I have shown elsewhere, such an approach to knowing is most appropriate to everything technological but not to any living entities such as human lives, communities, and the biosphere, where everything is related to everything else. As a result, a science organized on the basis of disciplines has a strong anti-life bias. Yet we live as if our discipline-based approach to knowing can be used to study anything and everything without limits. This constitutes a secular religious attitude towards science, one that obliterates the obvious fact that, as a human creation, the discipline-based approach to knowing is good for studying certain situations, irrelevant to others, and a distortion of still others. The cult of science (scientism), like all cults, has done tremendous damage, which could have been avoided by treating it as just one approach to knowing as opposed to the god of all human knowledge. In sum, in contemporary mass societies, science has become a secular myth in the sense of cultural anthropology, that is, a god-like entity.

The technical doing that advances contemporary ways of life is almost entirely given over to discipline-based approaches, which have replaced traditions and cultures. We are mesmerized by the technical virtuosity achieved through efficiency. Everything in our lives and our world is unthinkable without the relentless pursuit of efficiency. How would we deal with anything other than through a discipline-based approach and the expertise gained from it? If so, such approaches appear to have few, if any, limits and thus are treated as omnipotent in the domain of doing. However, improving human life and the world one category of phenomena at a time again presupposes (as was the case in science) that all other categories of phenomena may be neglected. In turn, this implies that the fabric of human lives, communities, and the biosphere, in which countless categories of phenomena intermingle and help constitute the context in relation to which these phenomena function and evolve, plays no essential role. Our relentless pursuit of performance and efficiency has created a "system" that slices through every connection. This system began as the phenomenon of rationality (observed by Max Weber), which evolved into that of technique (examined by Jacques Ellul). Simply put, technique treats everything in human life and the world the way technology deals with machines. As a result, we are almost entirely unaware that the economic growth that was achieved with discipline-based knowing and doing has created a triple economic, social, and environmental crisis. All living entities are in decline. We are now treating every situation as a technical problem to be solved through discipline-based approaches. It has placed our civilization in a situation in which this approach to doing is our only tool. Would we hire a contractor to repair various things in our homes if he or she was convinced that a hammer could do everything? As a result, our leaky toilet, binding door, cracked window, and much more would all be "fixed" with hammer blows. Surely, this is the summit of secular religious idolatry on our part. The cult of efficiency ignores the fact that the output-input ratios by which this efficiency is measured have nothing whatsoever in common with traditional cultural values, which have always measured things in relation to everything else. Once again, we have turned technique (the discipline-based approach to doing) into a myth, in the sense of cultural anthropology.

When it comes to politically organizing our affairs, we live as if everything is political. This implies that the nation-state, whose business it is to deal with everything political, has no limits. All our difficulties thus have political solutions, and all of these solutions must come from the nation-state, whose powers must therefore be considered to be unlimited. The nation-state has taken over the role traditionally provided by cultures in terms of organizing, directing, and sustaining human lives and communities. Of course, we know full well that today's government leaves a lot to be desired, but we hope all this will fundamentally change with the next election and that a better tomorrow lies just around the corner. Moreover, everyone's political priority is the all-out use of discipline-based science and technique in order to stimulate economic growth. This growth must be made to produce as much wealth as possible, and from it we must pay our bills and distribute the rest to the things we value: education, health care, social security, or environmental clean-up. It has led to a stunning political reversal, which amounts to suspending our aspirations and putting our political, moral, and religious convictions on the back burner until the time comes to distribute the wealth created by economic growth. The nation-state arranges everything in support of this growth as the very fountain of our future. Democracy has become the cult of the nation-state and the limitless power of politics. Again, we live within the myth of the nation-state.

All this flies in the face of our conviction that we have come of age and live in a secular mass society. It fails to recognize that we, like those who went before us, have to create points of orientation in an ultimately unknowable reality by absolutizing those entities without which our lives and our world would be unthinkable. This brings us to another myth, namely, that of history. Only one future appears to remain open to humanity now that all alternative ways of life and cultures have been destroyed or decisively weakened. As a consequence of this single historical path, "time will tell," and the future will judge everything in relation to it. Everything that is "entirely other" has been excluded, as we have entrusted everything in our knowing and doing to discipline-based approaches and the economic growth derived from them.

This is but a brief sketch of the kinds of mental images, values, and commitments we acquire by growing up and living in a contemporary mass society. We internalize them by virtue of the fact that each and every experience is symbolized by neural and synaptic changes to the organization of our brain-mind, which in its entirety symbolizes each person's life in the world. Consequently, as we shape and evolve science, technique, and economic growth, these human creations simultaneously shape us. If the influence we have on our creations is greater than the influence they have on us, we are free; but if the opposite is the case, we have become "the newly possessed" (the literal French title of Jacques Ellul's *The New Demons*). From the perspective of cultural anthropology, our struggle to make sense of and live in the world also involves the establishment of the cults of idols, although these have now taken on a secular form. As a result, the stories of the Old Testament take on a whole new meaning for so-called secular societies. In particular, we approach our reading of Amos and James with the kinds of mental images, values, and commitments derived from our way of life, and we cannot expect our way to have much of a resemblance to God's ways. On the contrary, we ought to expect major counter-transference reactions as we read these books; and this is likely to be the case for both Christians and non-Christians.

At this point, it is essential to bring religion into the picture. The original meaning of this concept refers to a binding together, and such a binding together of the members of a community can be effective only if they make sense of and live in the world by means of a shared culture. We have observed that, in contemporary mass societies, much of this is accomplished through the mass media and information technology. As a result we all, to varying degrees, wish for a share in the good things the "system" has to offer; and we have little difficulty being rooted in public opinion and statistical morality, even though these are all signs of being "newly possessed." The presence of Christianity in our midst appears to make little difference. For example, our growing reliance on the box stores implies that we have little concern for the livelihood of our neighbours, a growing number of whom have lost their jobs, which continue to be exported as the stores gain larger market shares. Yet, the problems of underemployment and unemployment are among the most devastating forces of destruction of people's individual lives, their families, their communities, and nations. Few, if any, moral or religious barriers appear to exist against voting for politicians who allow this to continue. Apart from illness, I have difficulty imagining anything that robs our neighbours as effectively of their dignity, self-respect, and ability to take care of themselves and others. Yet on a regular basis, we are informed by mind-numbing statistics about the number of jobs being shipped offshore, and about the loss of the kinds of jobs on which one can actually live and feed one's family – jobs to be replaced by part-time work with few if any protections against illness or old age. We can hardly claim that we are ignorant of this massive destruction of people's livelihoods. Nor do we appear to connect this to the statistics about the way poor people are becoming poorer and the increasingly fewer wealthy people are becoming enormously wealthier. How can a system that utterly fails to provide people with the essential necessities of life be democratic? How can we elect governments that do not act to protect the common good but simply bow to economic necessities? Apparently, the Christian community has other occupations than loving our neighbours as ourselves.

As far as the spiritual binding together is concerned, the presence of Christianity frequently boils down to essentially two things: adding some spirituality to the American and Canadian ways of life (to which we are religiously bound), and having ecclesiastical bodies pass statements on various topics such as social justice, abortion, or sexual orientation, with little or no input from the rank and file. All this seems to have little effect on the way Christians conduct their lives, with the result that their being "newly possessed" remains essentially unaffected. In many quarters, however, there is a great passion to confront others with their sins. These people appear to forget that the biblical model for sin is slavery to something or someone, with the result that you are not free to engage in what you are called by God to do. Bathed in God's love, we have been set free, which means that we have permission to enjoy whatever is truly good, to think what is just, and to behave not by morality but by love. Instead, by attempting to meet the moral and religious needs of our societies, counter-transference reactions have created an incredible measure of incompatibility between our way of life and God's ways, as far as our daily-life behaviour is concerned. It may well be as great as that described by Amos and James. We are no longer aware that our secular societies have their own idols, immersed as we are in our cult of efficiency and Mammon.

All spirituality, morality, and religion have essentially become a private affair. I have spent a great deal of my life teaching large classes of engineering, social science, and environmental studies students in a city with the most incredible religious and cultural diversity. However, when I pass out an assignment, every single student will use appropriate discipline-based methods and approaches (guided by output-input ratios), which put their own convictions in the background. It is the perfect reflection of the dualism of our societies. The public sphere is given over to discipline-based knowing and doing and economic growth, while in our private lives we can have religious freedom since it has little or no bearing on our way of life. It appears that we trust and belong to the "system" in our professional and working lives as well as in much of our private lives, and we can claim to love God and belong to him in whatever is left. This is certainly not a situation of which Amos and James would have approved.

In a first volume of Bible studies, Jacques Ellul argued that, in the opening chapters of Genesis, we encounter an attack on morality, religion, and magic. These warnings against serving false gods and surrendering our freedom to morality continue throughout the Jewish and Christian Bibles, but this message has become largely incomprehensible since Christianity was split into its "horizontal" (love of neighbour) and "vertical" (love of

God) dimensions. The so-called "liberal" Christians emphasize the former, while the so-called "fundamentalist evangelical" Christians emphasize the latter, to the point that each group transforms inseparable dimensions into separable aspects. This division of Christianity greatly facilitated its assimilation into our secular way of life. The evidence is plain for all to see: the majority of Christians have little or no difficulty aligning themselves with political parties and governments in the belief that this may advance their cause. It may come as a shock to us, but in the book of Amos this is radically condemned. As in the days of Amos, this trust in political power will have devastating consequences for the poorest and weakest members of society. The politicization of Christianity in North America is a clear sign of how it has turned itself inside out and upside down, reinterpreting the call to freedom and love and turning it into a slavish submission to the American and Canadian way of life. God has been re-created into an image that stands directly behind certain "principled" presidents and prime ministers. The only way this is possible is by our convincing ourselves that we have made our way pretty close to God's ways. Be prepared for another shock as Amos and James deliver us from this illusion.

I would ask my non-Christian readers to engage in the same kind of preparation by questioning how secular we have really become. If we expect more from science, technique, and economic growth than they can possibly deliver, we will sooner or later be caught out with terrible consequences for our children, grandchildren, and the planet. Perhaps entrusting our lives to all this in a secular religious manner should be avoided by carefully examining what our own creations can really do for us, what they can never accomplish, and what they will simply destroy. Not to do so is to allow our secular religious attitudes to go unchallenged as we entrust all life and the planet to these creations. In other words, we have not solved or escaped the problems that are as old as humanity itself – we have simply re-created them in a secular religious form: putting our trust in things that will never deliver. We think there is one and only one way to meet our material needs, share our lives, and relate to the biosphere. We are attempting to fix our problems and strive for a better world by banging away at everything with "hammers" that we deem to be omnipotent. The freedom and love offered by Amos and James may turn out to be something we all badly need. However, I must warn you from the beginning: their messages are extremely harsh and almost unendurable unless we bear in mind that much of it is a scolding we receive from the One who loves us and has given up everything to win us back. The endings of these books make that abundantly clear.

The consequences of what I have been arguing are straightforward. If, during the last half-century, Christianity had been faithful to the one and only God, it would have rejected the temptation to make science the secular god of knowing, technique the secular god of doing, the nation-state the deity that organizes life, and history the deity of time presiding over all this goodness. In such a case, Christianity would not have been anti-science, anti-technique, and so on. Instead, it would have traced the limits of what science can know, what technique can do, and what the nation-state can organize in order to find alternatives to take care of what has to be done beyond these limits. Perhaps our societies might not have created the deep structural economic crisis that has turned economies from wealth creators into debt creators. This happened because discipline-based approaches have built a "system" that deals with the problems it creates in an end-of-pipe fashion by adding compensating technologies and services, thereby making it top-heavy and eventually reaching a point where the creation of costs exceeds the creation of wealth. Science and technique might not have dominated this kind of economic growth because their limits would have made it possible to regulate them according to our values and aspirations by means of negative feedback control. These are some of the practical consequences that could have occurred if Christianity had been faithful to its calling, that of being a yeast in the dough or a salt in the food. Instead, its idolatry permitted the unleashing of some of the most destructive forces in all of human history. We still have no idea how this will end. I hope we are now a little more ready to hear what Amos and James have to tell us in this age of economic globalization and planetary destruction.

For readers unfamiliar with Jacques Ellul, I would like to briefly introduce him with the following remarks. I believe a strong case can be made for his being the most important Christian thinker of the twentieth century. It has always astonished me that, in the social sciences, we do not assess concepts and theories on the basis of their ability to describe and predict the evolution of human life in our world. We jump from one intellectual fashion to another without ever putting them to the test. If we did, we would quickly discover that Jacques Ellul's concepts and theories accurately predicted almost all the important events of the second half of the twentieth century, as has been documented by a French journalist. As someone who has devoted his entire life to the understanding of where we are taking science and technology as our most powerful creations and where these creations are taking us through their vast influences on human life, society, and the biosphere, I know of no other thinker of whom this can be said (with the possible exception of Max Weber).

Jacques Ellul's Christianity was also unique. Having become aware of a Presence in his life, he had to rethink everything and find new bearings. In his search for kindred spirits and fellowship, institutionalized Christianity proved to be of little help. The result was neither a theology nor a philosophy but a walking with the Light in the world of his day. He had a profound critical awareness of the "cultural glasses" with which he read and interpreted the Bible. An inevitable dialectical relationship was thus established between these glasses and the ways of a transcendent God. Much of this found expression in his written work, which can be divided into a sociological, political, and historical component on the one hand and his study of the Bible and the role of Christianity on the other. Any escape into disciplines such as theology, philosophy, or history was thus cut off by the dialectical tension established between these two components.

Jacques Ellul warned us that technique was the "wager of the twentieth century." In another book, I have argued that the desymbolizing effects of technique on human life and society have unleashed *Our War on Ourselves* and that, barring a global catastrophe, this war will mark much of the twenty-first century. The American and Canadian ways of life are desymbolizing individual and collective human life, thus weakening and destroying what has made us human until now and putting nothing in its place. It is the consequence of the reciprocal interactions we have with our own creations: as we change them, they simultaneously change us. As a theory this explains much, particularly in relation to the influence of information technology and the Internet; and we will have to see if subsequent events bear this out.

If the light of Christianity is not to disappear from North America, the kind of Bible studies undertaken in this work will have to become more commonplace. As Jacques Ellul points out in these studies, we need to read the Bible communally. Collectively, we must confront what we bring to the reading of the Bible with what we encounter within it. In turn, what we learn must confront our lives and our world. Doing so will not be easy. It will require members who know the original languages well enough to point out the many translation errors and theological adjustments that have been made to make our Bible translations more readable and acceptable. It will also require members who have thought about what we bring to these studies as people of our time, place, and culture. We will all have to decide how we are then to engage ourselves in our lives and the world. All these contributions must somehow be meshed together. One thing is certain: I know of no current Christian institution or ecclesiastical structure that will tolerate such Bible studies, because they would turn the Christian religious establishment upside down.

Finally, my readers may find it helpful to understand how this book came about. I recorded on tape Jacques Ellul's studies of the letter of James during the nearly five years I spent with him as a NATO post-doctoral fellow between 1973 and 1978. They mostly represent his formal presentations made as an integral part of our reading the Bible together. A number of us had approached him with existential questions as our professor or colleague at the University of Bordeaux. We came from very diverse backgrounds and represented (in roughly equal numbers) Protestants, Catholics, Jews, and agnostics. Into this study of James I wove a significant amount of material from a later study that he conducted for the local congregation of Pessac, with guests from the twin congregation of Merignac and from the local Catholic church. The studies of the book of Amos and the letter to the Romans were recorded during Bible studies Jacques Ellul conducted in Pessac for the same group. Jacques Ellul started the former congregation, which initially met in his dining room and later in the adjacent facilities purchased and renovated for this purpose.

I owe an enormous debt to Burney Médard, who carried taped copies of the biblical studies I did not have to a U.S. airport, where I collected them. It turned out that the recordings of two of the sessions of Amos were missing, and these were provided by Philippe Louiset. For many years I urged Jacques Ellul to publish these Bible studies, but it was not until a year before his death, when we met for the last time, that he gave me permission to do so, realizing that he would not have the opportunity. It turned out that transforming these studies into a written manuscript was rather difficult, and I was unable to do a French version. I have taken the liberty of adding references wherever this appeared appropriate. I thank his children, Jean, Yves, and Dominique, for their support in this labour of love. These Bible studies constitute an important complement to the writings of Jacques Ellul. The reader may find the first volume helpful for understanding the present one. For this reason, I have included a number of references to it where these appeared to be essential. Any clarifications Jacques Ellul made during the discussions were incorporated into the body of the text as much as possible, and where this was not possible they are prefaced by the phrase "In response to your questions ..."

As always, I also owe an enormous debt to my wife, Rita, who contributed greatly to making this work as readable as possible. It is not always easy to work with a blind author who easily gets frustrated with his inability to do certain things on his own. I am also indebted to my daughter, Esther, who worked with me during the summers when she was compelled to go back to school to start a second career. It is another sign of our time that our children become "just-in-time labour" for the "system" and have to accept the fact that a normal life-long career has become virtually impossible. I thank my son, David, who helped me finish up when Esther was busy with her studies. I also wish to thank a number of readers who provided feedback and suggestions for additional clarifying notes but who, for various reasons, will have to remain anonymous. Thanks also to Craig Bartholomew, who provided the Hebrew and Greek transliterations, and to Hannah Wong, who developed the index. May all this work contribute to the maintenance of a faithful remnant in North America and beyond.

Toronto 2013
Willem H. Vanderburg

PART ONE

Amos

Chapter One

Introduction to Amos

By way of introduction, I will deal with the following three themes: the role of a prophet, the historical background of Amos, and what we know of the person and life of Amos. I will begin with the first. In Hebrew there are three words used to designate a prophet. Amos employs all three words without any apparent distinction. The most common word is *nabi*, essentially referring to God's servant. There is also *roeh*, meaning seer. The third word is *hozeh*, which usually refers to a professional prophet.

Some common misunderstandings must be avoided. A prophet is not someone who foresees the future. Nor is a prophet a holy person or someone we might refer to as being possessed by the spirit. One of the more common and recent interpretations is that a prophet is a general preacher of the Word. It arose out of the distinctions Paul draws between the different ministries such as apostles, deacons, and those who worked miracles. Included in this list were the prophets, and people have speculated about who they were in Paul's days. Some people have concluded that the closest we come to prophets in today's Protestant churches are those who preach the Word. However, there is little or no correspondence between their roles and actions and those of the prophets in the Old Testament. Based on different texts, others have concluded that the prophets were those who proclaimed God's judgments, condemnations, and punishments. It is true that the prophets announced these kinds of things, but that does not mean this was their primary role.

An analysis of the prophetic books of the Bible shows that the roles played by the prophets were a great deal more complex. To begin with, they knew and understood the social, political, and international events as they affected Israel in their time. In this context, they evaluated the actions taken by Israel's political leaders as well as those taken by its enemies. They were therefore thoroughly familiar with the developments all around them. These included actual and potential dangers, crises, and wars. They politically and morally judged the situation in which Israel found itself. However, there is as yet no question of a spiritual judgment, or a relating of their own judgments to God's revelation.

Based on these judgments, the prophets would always proclaim the following things. They would announce what would be the outcome if Israel chose to continue to go down its current path. They thus predicted wars, deportations, or other catastrophes as integral to the "logic" of the course of events. The prophets discerned the fact that, barring any interventions, this is what would happen. Such "normal" unfolding of events continues to occur. The Second World War was a certainty in 1939, but it was essentially predictable in 1933. Permitting things to run their course would make the war inevitable. I would say the same thing for so many dangers we are creating today. If we allow them to unfold, we will face incalculable risks.[1]

The prophets then warned God's people that they ought to interpret the coming events and catastrophes as judgments pronounced against them by God. Although these events and catastrophes were the normal consequence of the course of events, they were to be discerned as God permitting history to run its course. This announcement transformed the political and moral interpretation of what was happening into a judgment and warning of a spiritual kind. If the Jewish people were to discern the course of events in this way, we as Christians must surely do the same thing.

The prophets would also announce that if the people repented and changed direction by appropriate actions, God would forgive them, intervene in the course of events, and nothing would happen to them. In other words, it was not God who triggered the events and catastrophes, although he was the one who would prevent them if the people repented in time. These are the elements contained in every prophecy. In reading the prophetic books, this becomes evident only if we read the entire book instead of a few verses isolated from their context. In this way, we keep together what belongs together: the political and moral interpretation of events, the catastrophes to come, discerning the judgment, and the call for repentance. All these elements are integral to the prophetic message as well as to the role of the prophets.

This understanding of the prophets may be deepened by examining when and why these prophets began to play a role. They began to appear in Israel almost as soon as the creation of the monarchy. During the reigns of Saul, David, and Solomon, there were the prophets Samuel, Elijah, and Elisha. These were the first prophets. Their appearance can be related to the time when God informed Samuel that Israel could have a king. He also told Samuel that the people were not rejecting him but God himself. A human king would apparently now replace God as the head of his people Israel. However, it was not as simple as that. God cannot be replaced by a human king. God therefore decided to have this king be counterbalanced by a man of God who would exercise no direct political power but who would judge the actions of the king and do so in the name of a revelation from God. In other words, the prophet would have no power but that of the Word. In order to make such judgments and discuss them with the king, the prophet needed to discern what was happening politically and spiritually. This required an incredible human insight and a great deal of courage. The prophets thus constituted a kind of counter-power to the king. This represented a highly democratic principle, a recognition that every form of power should be confronted by a counter-power.

It should come as no surprise that these prophets were not well received by the kings, since they endlessly warned them about the wrongs they were doing, and what the consequences would be. In some cases, these prophets were vigorously persecuted, as was the case with Jeremiah. The interventions of the prophets were relatively rare and always timely. During the creation and evolution of the monarchy in the tenth century before Christ, there were not only the three great prophets I have just mentioned, but also ecstatic bands such as the Nazirites and others such as the Rekabites, who strictly organized their moral life around three tests. These kinds of bands of prophets expected salvation to come from living a simple and ecological lifestyle, as it were. They desired an elimination of all power, and a return to a very basic life. In the tenth century there were many such bands, but over time their numbers dwindled. John the Baptist was one example, living off locusts and wearing a camel's hair coat.

The kings and priests were not at all in agreement with these prophets and bands of believers. In order to reduce their influence, they conceived of the idea of creating schools for prophets. These schools were to train people in a ministry, just as was done for priests and Levites. These prophets were taught the techniques of ecstasy, the trance, speaking in tongues, and the language of prophecy. Of course, these trained prophets were under the orders of the king. It explained why Amos declared that he was not a prophet, or the son of a prophet, which meant that he was never a student in these schools for prophets. As a result of creating these schools, there was conflict between the true prophets, whose writings have survived, and what they refer to as the false prophets. This latter category included the prophets trained in schools as well as the Nazirite and Rekabite bands. None of them were taken seriously because they knew absolutely nothing about the social and political situation of the Israelites even though they said beautiful things that had little to do with real life. The conflicts between the real prophets and the false prophets under the control of the king lasted for centuries, and were from time to time extremely intense. These conflicts tended to be resolved historically in one of two ways. One way is illustrated by the conflict between Elijah and the false prophets of Baal, who built separate altars and waited to see which one would be lit from above. The other kind of resolution came when a true prophet announced that this or that would happen, and where the course of events settled who was right. The false prophets always turned out to be wrong, and their writings have not been preserved.

From a Christian perspective, the true prophets were a part of the covenant as the prophets of the Messiah. Many of them announced that the only possible solution to the situation in which Israel found itself (the break-up into two kingdoms, the deportation, and more) would be the coming of the Messiah; and the portrait they provided of him corresponds very well with Jesus Christ. All this is part of how we are to understand the prophets. Amos was one of them.

Let us now turn our attention to the time of the prophecy of Amos. It emerged shortly after Israel's break-up into two kingdoms, one in the north and the other in the south. The events leading up to this break can be summed up as follows. The religious idolatry of Israel grew enormously during the reign of Solomon. He began as a very wise king but allowed himself to be seduced by numerous wives and concubines. These brought with them all kinds of pagan religions, which he more or less adopted, thereby producing a Greek or Chaldean-like pantheon of gods. At the same time, he levied a heavy tax on his people in order to support these and other endeavours. Following his death, the elders of the people approached Solomon's son Rehoboam to ask if he would consider substantially reducing the taxes. The son arrogantly threatened to double the taxes and to punish the people with scorpions instead of the whip. The majority of the people rebelled under the leadership of Jeroboam I to form the kingdom of Israel, while the kingdom of Judah remained faithful to the house of David.

The tribes of Judah and Benjamin remained faithful to the descendants of David and Solomon, and so Rehoboam founded the kingdom of Judah in the south. It included Jerusalem, and thus the temple, and this turned out to be a big problem. The citizens of the kingdom of Israel in the north could no longer visit Jerusalem and the temple, which created a religious dilemma. Jeroboam took an old temple of Baal (a local god), rebuilt it, and named it Bethel, which means *house of God*. However, the worship of Baal quickly returned. There is an important ambiguity in some of the names. Since God's name could not be pronounced, the Jewish people had substituted Adonai for YHWH. Adonai means *lord*, as does Baal. The latter was a Phoenician god, but the Jewish God was the One who had revealed himself.

The worship of Baal continued until the year 850, when a general by the name of Jehu killed the members of the royal house and the priests of Baal (in the story of Jezebel). He returned the kingdom of Israel to the service of the God who had delivered them from Egypt, but he maintained the temple at Bethel. He also attempted to reach an understanding with the kingdom of Judah. However, his power base was a military aristocracy, with the result that it was essentially the army, which allowed one of its generals to rule. The kingdom of Israel became technically and economically so successful that its artefacts were traded all around the western Mediterranean. Some have been found in Greece and Egypt, for example. With this commercial success came a great deal of wealth, resulting in more rich people but also many more poor people. It ushered in a time of enormous social inequality.

Two of the descendants of Jehu were moderate rulers who allowed things to run their course. However, they were succeeded by Jeroboam II, who around the year 800 began an all-out pursuit of power. In addition to a further economic and commercial expansion, he also sought to conquer the kingdom of Judah. Wealth continued to accumulate near the top, thus creating a kind of plutocracy of the rich. Along with it came social and moral degradation. Moreover, Jeroboam II was completely indifferent with regard to the worship of God that his great-grandfather had attempted to restore. It was around this time that the priests of the Baals denied that it was the God of Abraham who, through the hand of Moses, had led his people out of Egypt. They declared that the people had escaped because of their extraordinary military and political skills. It was also during this time that Amos appeared, and he did not accept any of this. However, Jeroboam II was largely indifferent to what Amos had to say, and as we will see, we do not know what happened to Amos as a result. Not surprisingly, the king was supported by the prophets who had graduated from the schools under his control.

I suggested that we read Amos together, in part because he is the first prophet whose prophecies have been preserved in the Bible. The prophetic books in the Bible came about either by a prophet writing down his prophecies, or because he had a secretary who wrote them down (as was the case for Jeremiah). These writings ended up in the Bible because the people discerned them as a Word from God. It was neither the priests nor other qualified persons (including theologians) who made these choices, because almost without exception they were on the side of the kings. It was God's chosen people who made the discernment regarding these prophecies against the kings and the priests. How this may have happened remains somewhat of a mystery to me, but it is an attestation that the people were truly chosen.

In his preaching, Amos based everything on the Torah and the covenant. Whatever the people had become, they remained the people of the covenant.

Finally, I propose to briefly review what we know about Amos as a person. He was the first prophet whose writings were included in the Bible, preceding Hosea by roughly ten years and Micah by about twenty years. Amos's appearance was rather spectacular. The power of the kingdom of Israel was at its peak, and yet he prophesied the disasters to come. The first to be announced was an earthquake in Jerusalem, which occurred two years later. He also announced that Uzziah, the king of Judah, who was at the height of his power, would be struck down. Uzziah contracted leprosy, from which he died. The fulfilment of these two prophecies made a deep impression on the people.

There is one thing that has surprised and stumped every historian. Amos came from the kingdom of Judah, and yet all his prophecies were announced in the kingdom of Israel. How was this possible at the height of the tensions and conflicts that existed between the two kingdoms? We do not have a good answer to this question. Some historians have concluded that Amos must have been from the kingdom of Israel and not that of Judah. This simply cannot be true because Amos was born in Tekoa, which is a town located in the Judaean desert next to Bethlehem. Amos raised sheep in this desert. He was more than a simple shepherd because he owned these sheep. He also planted or cultivated sycamore trees, whose figs were used as cattle feed. These trees had to be split at some point during their growth in order to mature. This work was done by specialists, and Amos may have been one such person. In any case, he also had a hand in this cultivation of sycamore trees.

As noted, Amos's first prophecies regarded Jerusalem and the king of Judah. He was denounced to this king as being a dangerous agitator, and he may have been banished as a result. He found himself in the mountains of Israel, where he received his inspiration and did his prophetic work. Up to this point, everything had gone very well for the kingdom of Israel. Its enemies, including the Philistines and the Moabites, had been defeated. Moreover, the Assyrians, who were its most powerful and dangerous enemies, were busy fighting a people from the north. During this time of commercial and military success, a farmer began to call into question the society in general, and the king and the priests in particular. It is important to recognize that the earlier prophets had always spoken about specific events such as the murder of Uriah (the prophet Nathan) or the appropriation of Naboth's vineyard and his murder (the prophet Elijah). A prophet would go to the king in order to tell him that because of this or that event, he was unjust. With Amos, the character of the prophecy changed. It no longer primarily involved the king but applied to the entire society. This was possibly the first time in human history that someone had called into question his entire society. Amos also challenged the wealthy living in luxury, the military, the wise, as well as the religious establishment. In the case of the latter, he attacked almost every aspect, including the beliefs of his time, the sacrifices, and the feasts. He also criticized people's daily lives. He posed the astonishing question of whether morality becomes a consequence of faith, or (inversely) whether faith is the result of a particular morality and conduct of life He accused Jeroboam II of amalgamating God and the Baals as well as God and the nation. Without hesitation, Amos proclaimed that the only true master above the king was Yahweh, and further declared that he, Amos, was the only representative of Yahweh in the kingdom. He also reminded the king about the past, including the Exodus, the covenant, and justice. The God who revealed himself in Egypt was a universal God and the Lord of all nations; and to show that he was not a local god (of the mountains, for example), Amos began his prophecies with those against the neighbouring peoples before he attacked Judah and Israel. In doing so, he demonstrated that he was not unpatriotic, because the judgment of God fell on all peoples.

I would like to make four more observations. First, all exegetes agree that the discourse of Amos is a whole and not bits and pieces gathered together and edited, as is the case for some of the other prophets. There is also agreement that Amos's ministry lasted for six months. Following these six months, Amos disappeared, never to be heard from again. We have no idea whatever, from any source, as to what happened to him.

Second, Amos's prophecies, which were not acted on by the people, were fulfilled within a time span of fifty years or so. This included the famine, the fall of the Jehu dynasty, and the exile of the people of the kingdom of Israel around the year 700. It is generally assumed that Amos prophesied somewhere between the years 780 and 750.

Third, Amos presents a model of human life and society as God wills them. As a result, some commentators have concluded that Amos proclaimed what social justice was. However, this is a reinterpretation arrived at through the lens of our ideas. The condemnation of the rich in favour of the poor is not necessarily all about social justice. Those are our ideas. In Amos it is a question of the harm done to the poor being a harm done to God's people. What counts is not that people are poor but that they belong to the people of God. When the poor are persecuted, God himself is attacked. The evil is not so much a question of poverty, wealth, and injustice, but of a lack of faith in God, a lack of obedience in observing the covenant, and a lack of love for one's neighbours (otherwise there would be no poor). It is these things that are at the very heart of the problem rather than only social justice. The very existence of the poor is a revelation of a deeper evil. It reveals a lack of faith, obedience, and love. It calls for a reorientation of society in general, and a decision not to permit money to dominate it in particular.

Finally, I have noted that, possibly for the first time in human history, we have here an affirmation of respect for the poor and of the roles of faith and love in society, even in politics. This dates from around the years 780 to 750! Buddha appears around the year 560, and the Greeks begin their thinking around the year 550, which means that Amos's reflections on society, including the behaviour of its members, its organization, and its injustices, occurred before the others. Amos also reminds everyone that the face-to-face meetings between God and his people that had begun in the Sinai desert with Moses as intermediary had been broken for some 500 years, and that it was high time that the people went back to the covenant. This covenant, which for a very long time had been a dialogue between an individual person and God, should again become the face-to-face meeting of God and his entire people. Amos says this explicitly when he declares that the people must prepare for the encounter with their God.

In answer to your questions: Claims have indeed been made that the biblical prophets were not the only ones. For example, the birth of Jesus was supposed to have been announced in the writings of Virgil. I also recognize that Augustine held Virgil to be a prophet. As I have attempted to explain, I do not believe that prophecies are first and foremost a question of predicting events. Instead, at the centre of any prophecy is the bringing of the Word of God to his chosen people. There is therefore a close tie between the person who does so and these chosen people. This Word is proclaimed in relation to a particular historical setting and contains a double element: if you continue what you are doing, this is what will happen, but if you repent, God's love will forgive you.

I do not believe that prophetic work is limited to the prophets in the Bible. For example, consider the way in which Israel transformed the legends from Babylon and Egypt in relation to God's revelation in order to make them into a Word of God. There is little question that parts of Job are based on an Egyptian poem. It was rethought through Jewish faith to become a Word of God. We see the same thing with Paul, who takes stoic philosophy and rethinks it in relation to the revelation of Jesus Christ in order to create a Word of God. I strongly believe that this kind of work should continue in the Christian community, with the important difference that the results will not end up in our Bibles.

A great deal of work needs to be done. If we continue to produce greenhouse gases, if we continue to destroy the great forests, along with many other destructive actions, there will be inevitable catastrophes. If the Christian community discerns this as the destruction of God's creation, and if this discernment does not lead to repentance, we must not be surprised if God becomes angry with us and allows events to take their course. It could result in a great deal of suffering. The Bible frequently reminds us that our God is the One who is all-powerful as well as being the God of Jesus Christ.

There is another aspect to our destruction of the creation about which the Bible has a great deal to say, namely the acts of de-creation. When humanity split the atom, I could not help thinking of it as an act of de-creation of one of the constituent elements of matter in order to transform it into energy. Is this possibly a sign of our ability to destroy the entire creation; and if it is discerned as such, what ought we to do? Much the same kind of thing is now occurring with the constituent elements of all life. Are we to discern this frontier as one of de-creation? Some observers are convinced that soon we will be able to manufacture life; and we ought to ask ourselves what God might say about this. In any case, these kinds of developments will bring their own inherent catastrophes.

Chapter Two

The Prophecies against
the Six Surrounding Nations

The book of Amos begins with his prophecies against the six nations surrounding the kingdoms of Judah and Israel (Amos 1:2–2:3). I will begin with the second verse because the first was largely dealt with in the Introduction. When we read that the Lord (YHWH) roars from Zion, we may well wonder what this could possibly mean. The verb used here refers to the roar of a lion. It is an expression used by many other prophets. Despite this, some commentators have concluded that it does not mean very much. Others have pointed out that the Hebrew verb can also designate the thundering of a storm that is about to burst over Israel. The text refers to a God who roars and not one who reveals himself. Consequently, I believe that the expression refers to the existential shock Amos received when he encountered God. It reminded him of the roar of a lion. Following this encounter with God, he became the bearer of his Word with a power like that of a lion's roar. Moreover, the frequent use of this expression may indicate that the people could readily identify with such an experience: hearing the Word of God has the same effect as meeting a lion and hearing it roar.

The prophecy that follows is direct and concrete. There is no explanation of who God is, how he speaks, and how he operates. It is very different from the way the people met God at Sinai. The Word is directly concerned with the historical circumstances at that point in time. God appears as speaking in the present moment. We have become so accustomed to thinking theologically in terms of a God with metaphysical characteristics, as it were, that we have difficulty grasping that God speaks here and now. In contrast with the false prophets, the prophet uses no mysterious language or inexpressible ideas. The use of these things also troubled Paul when people spoke in tongues, leading to his recommendation that

it is better to be clear. In this sense, God speaks clearly, and not in eso-
teric or secret ways, as we hear so often today. He speaks in order to be
understood.

God roars from Zion, meaning Jerusalem. That this is so was perfectly
clear to any Jew, because the temple in which God resided was located in
Jerusalem. Next, the text refers to the pastures of the shepherds and the
summit of Carmel, which indicates that God speaks to Amos where he is,
namely, in the pastures in the mountains. These pastures and mountains
are in mourning, which means that there is nothing there. Once Amos
has received God's prophecy, his herds and the fields have fallen away, as
has the mountaintop of Carmel. This mountaintop, which was the highest around, symbolizes the heights – everything that is raised up in the
world. Once God has passed, nothing of the life before remains un-
changed, including the landscape of Israel. Similarly, once God's Word
has intervened in Amos's life, his former life pales in comparison. It is as
if this life has dried up.

Amos, seized and stunned by God's presence, feeling crushed as by the
roar of a lion, does not turn mystical. What God says has to be clear, and
he immediately turns to what must be done. Doing so engages him in a
struggle with the powers and authorities of his time, including the king
and the priests. There is nothing abstract here, and this characterizes the
work of all the prophets. They immediately go from the shock resulting
from their encounters with God to what must be done. Amos was the first
to give a central role to prophecy in the political and historical life of his
time. His mission, and that of the other prophets as well, was to destroy the
false gods and false values in order to restore the truth of the living God.

The history of the people of Israel appears to alternate between periods of peace, stability, and development, and periods of turmoil, crises,
and war. The latter periods appear to be more frequent than the former.
During periods of stability, the priests and Levites exercised the most
dominant influence over society. During periods of crisis, they had little
to offer. They did not know how to fight, and they usually lacked the courage, with the result that no one listened to them. It was under these circumstances that the prophets appeared. This pattern is exactly what we
find during Amos's time as well. In the growing disorder, the influence of
the priests and Levites almost disappeared, although at one point there
was a conflict between the high priest, who was on the side of the king,
and the prophet Amos.

When we reflect on the above situation, it is difficult to believe that
Amos's coming down from the mountains had such an enormous influence

in such a short time. It is easy for us to say that he was bringing God's Word, but that explains very little. This brings me back to what I said in the Introduction, namely, that what Amos said resonated with the people, who discerned it as a Word of God (also shown by its incorporation into the Bible). Of course, there were factors that facilitated all this. We are dealing with a population size and density that was extremely small by modern standards. We are talking about scattered villages of about one or two thousand inhabitants; it did not take long to cover the entire country. Besides, news spread very rapidly in these kinds of societies. All this does not take away from my astonishment that the people discerned what was happening.

Each curse pronounced on the people that surrounded the kingdoms of Judea and Israel begins with the phrase "For three transgressions of ... and for four I will not revoke the punishment ..." It tells us that each of the neighbouring peoples had committed some very serious sins. There have been three crimes that God has forgiven, but the fourth time God decides not to forgive but to punish. We must remember that numbers in those days were treated very differently. It is not a question of counting: 1, 2, 3, and then 4, but of starting the count all over again with the number 4, reaching a total of 7, a number symbolizing a totality. However, God no longer tolerates the fourth time, which, with this way of counting is the last of seven. God responds by sending a fire, and allowing it to burn. God only takes account of one crime, which is the last one. For Amos this means that God's patience is limited.

The expression "three and four times" occurs frequently elsewhere in the Bible. For example, it is found five or six times in the book of Proverbs. Some exegetes have assumed that Amos simply borrowed this expression from Proverbs. The problem is that the book of Amos was written well before many other biblical books. As a result, some of its expressions later found their way into the Pentateuch (also called the Five Books of Moses). In any case, Proverbs was written well after Amos. I believe this is true for a number of expressions in Amos.

The opening phrase designating seven times is followed by "I will not revoke the punishment." I have found seven other ways of translating the original Hebrew expression, which indicates a difficult translation problem. Alternative translations include "I will not answer"; "I will not come back"; "I will not bring them back," and so on. Although I am moderately competent in Hebrew, after reviewing the arguments for translating the expression one way or another, I prefer Neher's translation: "I will not answer."[1] Another very similar way of translating this expression is, "I will not give a reply." In other words, God refuses to be called on by anyone. This somewhat curious expression corresponds to an ancient part of the worship of God, namely, consulting Yahweh by the Urim and the Thummim. We do not know exactly what was involved. We think that it was a kind of drawing of lots by using these items, which were carried by the high priest in a small pouch. What we do know is that it was a way of consulting God, and it was widely used even by neighbouring peoples who came to the temple to consult the God of Israel. Our text announces to these peoples that all this is finished and God will no longer answer. There will be no more consultations.

This expression corresponds exactly to the one that came later, where God turns his face away. This act of God is what the Hebrew people feared the most. Over and over in the Psalms and the prophets we read that it is better to endure God's anger than to have him turn his face away from us. This would mean that God no longer bothers with us, and that would be unendurable. However, this is exactly what is announced in our text.

In each one of the prophecies in our text, God sends the fire and allows it to burn and destroy. As we have already discussed, God launches a development and allows it to run its course. He no longer intervenes. Another translation is that God does not bring things back. He will not bring back a people from a destiny that has now fallen on them and to which they have been attracted through their sins. This further clarifies the phrase "three and four times."

When God no longer speaks, his silence reveals the sins of humanity. We have always been tempted to turn this around by arguing that if God doesn't speak, it is because he does not exist. Amos shows that this is not the case, because God's silence is the result of our having committed too many mistakes. Through his silence, God calls for repentance. After all, it is God who says that he will no longer speak to us. However, in saying this he has spoken to us. He then allows the unfolding events to speak in his place. It is now history that speaks for God, as it were.

Amos reveals that the God of Israel is not a local god. In the books of Samuel and Kings, we are told that all people have their gods, who are all local ones. The God of Israel is referred to as the God of the mountains. In fact, in the second book of Samuel, we find the belief that since God is the God of the mountains, all that you need to do is to go down to the plains and he will not follow you there. Amos proclaims the opposite, that the God of Israel is a universal God. He is the first to show that this God is master of the world, the nations, nature, and history. The nations

may not recognize him, but that doesn't change anything. It is this same
God who can trigger natural events. For example, compare this teaching
to what we read in the story of Naaman the Syrian, who came to Israel to
be healed from his leprosy. When he is healed, he asks Elisha to be permitted to take some soil from Israel back to his home country so that on
it he can worship its God. In other words, Naaman is entirely convinced
that this God of Israel is a local god associated with a certain territory. As
a result, he needs to take four bags of soil to create a tiny plot of land
which will now be part of the territory of this God, thus making it possible for him to worship. For Amos, all this would be a waste of time because the God of Israel is the God of all nations, including Naaman's.
Wherever Naaman goes, he will be able to encounter the God of Israel.

Amos also reveals that God does not make history. He does not dictate
what will happen in history. However, he is free to intervene in it. For
example, in the texts we are told about the various wars in which neighbouring peoples are engaged. God allows these peoples to go about their
business without intervening. However, he can do so at any time in accordance with his sovereign decisions. This revelation regarding the relationship between God and human history flies directly in the face of a
providential God who arranges everything. Instead, history unfolds, but
God is free to intervene when he decides to do so. For example, when
the people of Babel decided to build a city with a tower, God came down
to see it and decided to do something about it. In the same way, God intervened in our history through Jesus Christ. There is therefore a kind of
dialectical relationship between an evolving human history and the God
of Israel, who intervenes according to a sovereign decision.

All the sins described in the prophecies against the peoples surrounding Israel are contained in the Hebrew word *pesha,* which means a revolt.
Amos clearly sees all these people as under God's authority, yet everything they do is a revolt against him. It is this revolt that is their sin. Of
course, this raises the question as to how these people could possibly
know the good that God wills for them when it had not been revealed to
them. In order to answer this question, we need to remind ourselves that
all these people were descended from Noah. As his descendants, they are
therefore all party to the covenant God established with Noah and his
descendants. The terms of this covenant are clearly described in Genesis
9. In it, we find no credo and no theology, which means that God does
not reveal himself as Yahweh. As a result, to live by this covenant, people
do not need a Jewish or Christian belief, as it were. It is a covenant that

God made with everyone who descended from Noah. Its sign, that of the rainbow, makes this clear.

The covenant God made with Noah and all his descendants contains three elements. First, there is a relative appeasing of the forces of nature. The rainbow guarantees a measure of cosmic stability. Second, this covenant was made with Noah, who is the father and ancestor of all of humanity. It is not Adam who is the ancestor of humanity. All nations and races are thus related to each other, having descended from the three sons of Noah. In other words, these relations are not the result of humanity's having been created by God, as we are in the habit of saying. The implications are far-reaching. The humanity descended from Adam was separated and in revolt against God. People lived their lives independently from the help God could have brought. The humanity descended from Noah benefits from the covenant God decided to make with it. This covenant includes God's decision to create a unity of all humanity as a fraternity of all races related to each other. The third element of the covenant uses this unity as the basis for a requirement that people live in peace together, and for affirming the unique value of the human person. God will demand the lifeblood of any person who spills the lifeblood of another human being.

Based on this affirmation, Amos is the first to declare that there is a kind of universal morality in the simple sense that everyone is descended from the same ancestor whether we like it or not, and that the human person is protected by God and loved by him. (I am not saying that the human person is sacred.) This simple universal morality is not based on nature, or on a human nature, making it very different from the United Nations' universal declaration of human rights. Its foundation of a supposed human nature is difficult to take seriously. As Jews and Christians, we should think of it as being based on God's alliance with Noah, but this would not go over very well with the United Nations! In any case, Jews and Christians can accept this simple universal morality as founded on the covenant God established with Noah, and thus with every human being. As a result, each and every sin and mistake that we are about to study in the prophecies of Amos, and that he considers as a revolt against God, derive from this unique value of the human person.

Amos, however does not develop his prophecies in relation to the entire world. For example, he did not bother with the Assyrians or the Babylonians, who are not far away. The reasons for this are related to who a prophet is, and what he does. A prophet is immersed in a particular history and acts in relation to it. In other words, he does not bother with what happens in America, Africa, or Asia. That is not the role of a prophet. A prophet is concerned with the situation in which he lives. In this case, this meant that he was concerned with what was happening in the kingdoms of Judah and Israel, and how the surrounding nations were about to destroy them. Amos spoke to this political problem, which he knew was about to disturb his whole world. The same is true for all the other prophets.

The last similarity between all Amos's prophecies against the surrounding nations is that, except for one, all the sins of these nations have been committed against the kingdoms of Judah and Israel. For example, Gilead is one of the twelve tribes of Israel. All these sins are related to a long period of anarchy and conflict that followed the reign of Solomon and occurred during the reigns of Jeroboam II in Israel and Uzziah in Judah. We will also see that, in some cases, a condemned people are punished by another people who are also condemned. For example, Edom is condemned; but Moab, which has massacred its [Edom's] people and burned its king, is also condemned for doing it. Moab was an instrument for punishing Edom, but it went too far. This is an instance of something that occurs frequently in the Bible and that is rather important. God launches something through a person or a people, but he expects a certain respect and wisdom on the part of this person or people. This is clearly explained in Isaiah 10:5–8, which condemns the Assyrians, who were the instrument of God's anger, which he launched against other peoples. However, the Assyrians were not humane. They did not respect the other peoples. As victors, they took themselves for God by carrying out a judgment. This is why God condemned the Assyrians. They were chosen to punish God's people by war and pillage but not by complete extermination and destruction. They went much too far, and that is why God condemns them. The text shows that Jeremiah, as a prophet, understood the gravity and importance of being chosen by God. Those chosen must be all the more moderate and respectful, whether they are the bearers of God's anger or the bearers of God's Word. They may not claim these [responsibilities] for themselves and use them for their own purposes.

This reminds me of what Paul says constantly: It is not I who do this, because I am nothing. What matters is what I have been given and what I must do, no more and no less. Moab may well have been launched to punish Edom but did it in a completely unacceptable manner.

It is important to understand that the Assyrians did not have a mandate from God. They could not claim that God had sent them. Such a thing never happens. God alone knows what the Assyrians are really doing, and he expects them to behave with respect towards the other, even in war. We must remember that in those days, wars could still be fought with a great deal of respect for the other. [Today,] the power of our weapons has made this completely impossible.

The prophecies we are examining concern six nations, which together completely encircled the kingdoms of Judah and Israel: Damascus (the Syrians) to the north, Gaza (the Philistines) to the southwest, Tyre (the Phoenicians) to the west, Edom to the southeast, Ammon (the Ammonites) to the northeast, and Moab (the Moabites) to the east. The latter was the closest country to Jerusalem. As noted, Amos's attack on these six nations shows that he is not simply against the kingdoms of Israel or Judea. He upholds the Torah for them as well as for Israel and Judah. Visscher[2] notes that the storm of anger raged around the six nations before it burst over Israel, the seventh nation. He also points out that all six nations were conquered and annexed to Israel by King David, who allowed them to retain their own cultures and independence. They were not integrated into his kingdom. We may think of this arrangement as a kind of commonwealth or federation of nations.

Damascus (Syria) is accused of the crime of using iron harrows to lacerate prisoners. It is not the war in itself that is condemned but the extremity of the measures, including the torture of prisoners. The punishment for this crime, which is roughly the same for all six nations, is on two levels. It involves the king, who will be burned along with his palace, and the people, who will be killed or led away as slaves to Kir. All this happened fifty years later by the hand of the king of Assyria. Some historians have pointed out that the nation of Kir was formed after this event. The probable explanation is that the text of Amos was not completed until after the event took place. We encounter a similar issue with regard to the Gospels and the destruction of the temple in the year 70 A.D., because some of these accounts were also completed after the destruction took place.

Gaza is the territory of the Philistines, who were the oldest inhabitants of that area along with the Canaanites. They lived along a strip of coastal land. Their crime was to have sold prisoners of war as slaves. There is a nuance in the Hebrew term that indicates this. We must remember that at that time slavery was common and not forbidden. The only biblical text that forbids the slave trade is Deuteronomy 23:16, but it post-dates Amos. Therefore, Amos is the first to announce that the selling of prisoners of war is a crime worthy of severe punishment. In this case, we happen to know reasonably well what went on. The Philistines were a warlike people who captured many prisoners of war. These were sold to Edom, which was an important centre of the slave trade. Many of these slaves were sold to Ionia, from where they were transported to Greece. The punishment for selling prisoners of war into slavery was fire, the death of the king and the people, as well as the destruction of their three main cities. However, this never happened, making this a prophecy that, as far as we know, was never fulfilled.

Tyre (the Phoenicians) is also accused of slavery, but the situation was different from that of the Philistines. There was an alliance (referred to as the covenant of brotherhood) between the Phoenicians and the Hebrews. This agreement was broken by the Phoenicians when they began to sell into slavery the members of the small Jewish communities that lived in their territory. Once again, God sent his fire against Tyre to destroy her strongholds.

Edom is a very particular case because its people were the descendants of Esau. Edom means "the red one," named after the dish of lentils for which Esau sold his birthright to Jacob, according to the Hebrew text in Genesis. As a consequence of this event, the descendants of Esau never ceased to claim that Israel occupied the place Jacob had stolen from them. Although the two brothers kept up a reasonably good relationship after their reconciliation, the nations of Edom and Israel had been at war for a very long time because of the grudge the former bore against the latter.

Ammon is condemned for having cut open the bellies of the pregnant women from Gilead in the war they waged in order to enlarge their territory. Not only was this a horrible crime in itself, but it was compounded by the decision to eliminate as much as possible all the descendants of Israel who lived just beyond their territory. Because this territory was very small, pinched, as it were, between Israel and Assyria, the Ammonites had decided to empty out the Israeli lands across their borders by killing Israel's children and future children. Amos declared that, because these people wanted to conquer more territory, even by destroying unborn children, they would learn what war is all about. This prophecy was fulfilled when the Ammonites were conquered by the Assyrians and sold into slavery. There is an important detail in this text – namely, that the king does not have the same title as in the other prophecies. Here, the king is referred to as Baal, with everything this implies, including the confusion between Baal as lord and God himself. Their god was the bull, which the Jews ironically referred to as the golden calf. It was a Jewish irony because the

Ammonites worshipped the bull as a symbol of fertility. Of course, during the time of Amos, the Baals represented a constant temptation for the Israelites. During the kingship of Jeroboam II and Uzziah, the worship of Baal symbolized by this bull became the dominant religious force. This religious temptation is also condemned by Amos.

This leaves us with the prophecy against Moab. Moab is condemned for burning to ashes the bones of the king of Edom. The seriousness of this crime is not so much that it was the king. At the time, burning someone's bones to ashes was a common practice for dealing with the bones of people killed in war. The ashes were made into lime water, which was used as whitewash on all the houses. What this meant was that these dead could not be buried with the appropriate religious ceremonies. The importance of this is made very clear in the book of Deuteronomy, which tells us that if a dead person is burned, the bones must be saved so that they can be buried with the appropriate religious ceremonies. Consequently, the absolute evil in this case is the complete obliteration of a person.

When we examine these prophecies, we get the impression that they enumerate almost every possible crime against humanity: torture, enslavement, deportation, the elimination of offspring (genocide), and the annihilation of human beings. Once more, Amos is the first to declare that the will of God requires respect for the human person – for any other human being. In other words, we are dealing with something more than condemnations of specific peoples. Together, the prophecies show how the general alliance between God and humanity must be respected. It is about time that the church takes this teaching to heart, given what is happening in the world today. If the church has any prophetic role left, let it at least repeat this teaching over and over again in the face of what is happening around us.

I continue to be amazed that these hard-hitting prophecies were scrupulously transmitted in an oral society, discerned as a Word of God, and eventually recorded in our Bibles. All of this did not come about by God's imposing himself. As Deuteronomy tells us, he places before us the good and evil, life and death; therefore choose the good in order to live. God is with us so that we will choose the good. However, if we choose evil and death, he cannot and will not prevent us. When we think of God's power, we must always consider God's freedom, which respects the freedom of humanity. When we understand this in a context in which these kinds of prophecies were discerned by a people as the Word of God, I must confess that we can only marvel. It shows how God's revelation is progressive in the sense that he brings us what we are capable of understanding given our time, place, and culture. It involves an extraordinary pedagogy on God's part that respects our freedom within his own. This strongly reminds me of a text in Jeremiah that essentially acknowledges that some laws were given to their fathers even though these may have been unjust, because they were the only ones the people could understand. Paul says something similar when he tells us that we were given milk because we were as yet children; and when we have managed to become adults, we will be given the food of adults.

With regard to these prophecies, it is also important to understand that God produces earthquakes no more than he produces historical events. There is a planet; it has a structure; there are bacteria and viruses, and so on. All this and more functions and evolves. What these and other texts tell us is that, in our role as Christians, it is possible that we can from time to time discern a Word from God.[3] When we do so, we cannot impose this on others, or use it as a means for judging others. For example, when a war or catastrophe occurs, we as Christians must ask ourselves if God is possibly telling us something. However, as Jesus says very clearly, we may never say that the victims were punished by this war or that catastrophe, or that they were somehow more evil than those who survived. In fact, he warns those who are not affected to repent and change their lives so that evil will not befall them also.

Chapter Three

The Prophecies against Judah and Israel

Overview

The first six prophecies against the people who surrounded the kingdoms of Judah and Israel were based on the covenant God had made
with humanity through Noah. The prophecies against Judah are based
on a different covenant, which gives them a different character. There
are three themes in this text: the prophecy against Judah (2:4, 5), the
prophecy against Israel, beginning with the account of what God had
done for Israel and the sins it had committed, followed by the second
part of this prophecy, which includes the reaction of the prophet Amos
and the prophesied punishments (2:6–16).

The Prophecy against Judah

The prophecy against Judah begins in the same way as the previous six.
Because of a seventh crime (a limit to transgression decided by God),
God will no longer listen to his people when they call on him in prayer or
invoke his name. However, Judah's crime is not against human beings but
against God, and it involves two elements. The people have not observed
the Torah (the law) and they have been led astray by idols and by a lie.
When we look ahead to the prophecy against Israel, an important distinction emerges. Judah's crimes are against God, while those of Israel are
against other human beings. We may interpret Judah's sin as the transgression of the first great commandment to love your God with all your
heart, and Israel's sin as the transgression of the second commandment
to love your neighbour as yourself. All this makes sense when we remember that the kingdom of Judah retained Jerusalem with the temple, thus
making it the guardian of the revelation. Moreover, the kings of Judah

were the direct descendants of David, and were thus, like him, the ones sent by God. Consequently, the central issue regarding the two tribes that constituted the kingdom of Judah was their relationship with God through the covenant.

Given the way things evolved, this posed the following dilemma for the people. Should they follow the king, who was a messiah sent by God, in which case they would join in his disobedience to the covenant, or should they follow the Levites as the guardians of the Torah? The Levites had not dared to accuse the king, and thus had remained silent. They had become conformists, which is exactly what Amos would say later on.

Amos faced the same dilemma. Was he to uphold the king despite everything because he was the descendant of David, with everything that involved? Or was he obligated to affirm the pre-eminence of the Torah? Amos clearly chose the latter; hence the accusation of having broken the law and the statutes.

We do well to remind ourselves of what the Torah was. The Torah is usually translated as the law, but that is not a good translation. The Torah means teachings. This distinction is even more important during Amos's times, because this Torah was not the one we know today. Levinas,[1] one of the greatest contemporary Jewish theologians, has shown that the Torah comprises four elements. First, there is the Levitical Torah, which we find in part in the books of Genesis, Exodus, and Leviticus as we know them today. This is the written Torah. Second, there is the oral Torah comprising all the recollections the Hebrew people had of their history. These were handed down from generation to generation and, in an oral culture, we know would have been extremely precise, accurate, and reliable. Third, there is the revelation people have of God through nature. Although this may be shocking to some people, David's Psalm 19 informs us that the heavens tell us the glory of God. It does not mean that if you do not know God, all you need to do is to look at the stars, the clouds, the mountains, and the ocean and you will know him. What it means is that if you know the true God, you may discover something of his glory in nature. Nature is one expression of God's glory. Fourth, the Torah also includes what the parents teach their children in the family setting. During that time, it was the fathers who had the primary responsibility for this. The complete Torah is made up of these four elements. It existed in Amos's time, although the Torah in the written form we know today did not yet exist. It was these teachings, which included remembering the entire history of God's dealings with the Hebrew people, that Judea had abandoned.

By and large, we misunderstand what the Torah was for the Jewish people. It was not a set of commandments that were more or less abstract, theoretical, and general. The Torah emerged out of and was inseparable from the historical experiences of the Hebrew people. For example, we must not understand the Decalogue without the long historical experience of the exodus from Egypt, the travels in the desert, and the arrival in Sinai. It remained inseparable from these and other historical events. What this implies is that the Torah is not similar to a morality constructed by an intellectual or a philosopher in a more or less abstract fashion. It is the reflection of a certain history, and it was this history that the kingdom of Judah had abandoned.

Moreover, the commandments of the Torah had a very different character from what we think of as laws or rules. We must not read the Decalogue as a set of commandments. It is a promise and a future: there will come a moment when you will no longer need to steal, commit adultery, murder, and more; which means that if you respect this law, it is possible to live, but if you transgress it, you will enter the domain of death. The Torah thus describes a domain within which life is possible and permitted. When you transgress these commandments, you leave this domain to enter into that of death. It is perhaps helpful to explain that in Hebrew there was no present tense as we know it. The Hebrews regarded an action that begins in the present as something that continues, with the result that the present is the beginning of the future. Each moment begins something new, but not in the sense of an imperative, but of an opening up in hope. As such, the present is a continuing hope. It is for this reason that all the commandments of the Decalogue are generally translated in the future tense. The other Hebrew tense is that of the past: things that have happened but that are now finished. As a result, in the Old Testament, and especially in the Pentateuch, the verb tense is in the past when the subject concerns evil or some form thereof, because evil is finished. What the people now have before them is the future in terms of what is possible to undertake. All this goes much deeper and is much more hopeful than our common understanding of commandments.

The text also tells us that the kingdom of Judah was led astray by the *idols of the lie.* This goes well beyond our usual notions of idolatry. The Hebrew word for idol in the plural is, with the exception of one vowel, identical to the Hebrew word found in Ecclesiastes, which is usually translated as vanity, or vanity of vanities. The common root signifies that idols are not so much false gods as they are a lie, a smoke that disperses, or a vanity in the sense of being nothing. To follow these idols of lies is to be seduced by an appearance of something, be it an apparent power, beauty, success, or anything else that is really nothing of the kind. It is this nothingness that is at the very heart of the role idols play in human communities. Following these idols is an abandonment of the One who is alive in favour of such an appearance. This helps us to understand why God is frequently referred to as a rock of solidity because he is not like a smoke that disperses and disappears into nothingness.

It is in this context that we also need to understand the biblical references to God as jealous. For example, in the Decalogue, God describes himself as a jealous God. This jealousy has nothing in common with what in human relationships of love we refer to as jealousy. God is jealous because he loves humanity and knows full well that if humanity detaches itself from him, the living One, it will die. When human communities follow idols, these vanities, and this "smoke," they do not understand what they are really doing. However, God knows where this will end up. He is jealous because he cannot tolerate competition from these idols and these false gods. God is the only one who can say, "I am." He is that being in full. The tetragram of the four sacred letters YHWH derive from the Hebrew verb that is the equivalent of "to be." For example, when God sends Moses to Pharaoh to deliver a message, Moses asks in whose name he will be speaking. God answers him, "I am the One who is." However, this tetragram also means "I will be the One who is," "I am the One who will be," or "I will be the One who will be," bearing in mind that Hebrew knows no present tense. In sum, God's jealousy is aimed at saving humanity.

As punishment, God will send his fire on Judah, and it will destroy the strongholds of Jerusalem. This is exactly what happened in the year 734. Once again, some may object that this prophecy may have been written down after the fact, but personally I do not see any reason why that would change anything related to Amos's role as a prophet.

The Prophecy against Israel

The prophecy against Israel begins with the same statement: after the seventh crime, God will no longer hear the people. As we have noted, their central crime, from which all the others derived, was not directly against God but against other human beings, and thus indirectly against him. Israel is accused of sinning against the second great commandment.

The account from chapter 2:6–16 may be divided into three themes: the sins of Israel (2:6–8 and 12), the actions of God on behalf of Israel (2:9–11), and their punishment (2:13–16). I will begin with the second theme.

Amos reminds the people of what God did for them: "Remember O Israel …" This is a very important phrase that we ought to take to heart. Today we have the feeling that God is silent and that he is no longer intervening; and at that point we ought to remind ourselves of what God has done for us. Doing so is as important for us as it was for the Israelites. It is also true for individual lives, in which God has revealed himself at one time or another, following which there may be a silence, even a long silence. During these times, I must remember what at that earlier time has been the presence of God in my life. I must not expect that God constantly and permanently reveals himself and accompanies me every moment of my life. The remembrance of the moment in which we met God in our lives is something fundamental from which we must live.

The people of Israel are reminded of three things God did for them. God made a covenant with Abraham, promising him a land for himself and his descendants. When Abraham died, the only part of this land he had was a tomb he had purchased to bury his wife Sarah. The land belonged to the Amorites and the Canaanites. Joshua conquered the land of the Amorites, who, according to the text, were a mighty people. Nevertheless, God destroyed this people in order to give their land to the people of Israel. In the ninth verse, there is a detail that requires clarification, namely, that God destroyed their fruit above and their roots beneath. It refers to a complete victory. Their roots were their fathers, who were killed, and the fruits were the children, who were also killed.

The people of Israel are next reminded of their liberation from Egypt. In Hebrew, the word for Egypt is *mitsrayim,* which means the land of the double anguish. According to a rabbinical commentary, this refers to the anguish of living and the anguish of dying. God did much more than deliver his people from slavery. This liberation was much more comprehensive. It provides a much deeper meaning than God reminding his people that he is the One who liberates.

God led his liberated people for forty years through the desert. He did so in a completely non-authoritarian manner. His people were invited to follow him; and his presence was marked by a pillar of cloud by day and a pillar of fire by night. To be sure, life in the desert was not easy, but God accompanied them. In the same vein, in our lives God does not leave us to wander aimlessly. There always is an indication of some kind, but it is never constraining. God never mechanizes human life by a set of rules. Amos is the first to use the phrase "forty years in the desert." The duration of the journey in the desert had never been mentioned before. Following Amos, this phrase became accepted as inspired by God and was adopted in Exodus, for example.

The third event the Israelites are invited to remember is God's revelation through the prophets he called. These included the Nazirites, who were witnesses to the good and to virtue requiring self-control. We frequently find references to this in Paul, who refers to it as moderation. This does not appear to mean a great deal, and yet it is rather important. For the Nazirites, this self-control took the form of abstaining from sexual relations and from alcohol. The people God longs for are those who can control their passions and thus temptations, in which case the good is possible. Hence the importance of the Nazirites and God's reason for raising them up. These are the three events God asks the Israelites to remember. Amos cites seven sins committed by the Israelites. They are accused of selling the just for money, and the poor for a pair of sandals. Doing so transforms people into merchandise. The Hebrew words translated as the just and the poor are related (*tsaddiq* and *ebyon*). It is likely, therefore, that we should associate the just with the poor. Of course, this does not mean that all the poor are just, but it is certainly true that the just are poor. The consequence of this is important, as we will see in a moment.

The second sin committed by Israel was their desire to have the dust of the earth cover the heads of those who live in misery. It was the custom of the time to cover your head with dust when you no longer saw any way out and were led to despair. When things went catastrophically wrong, people would tear their clothes and cover their heads with dust. In the kingdom of Israel, people desired that those who lived in misery be as miserable as possible, and they pushed them into extreme despair.

The third sin involved the people of Israel depriving the miserable ones of their rights. Translations to this effect are not very helpful. The Hebrew is better translated as follows: "they cause the humble to deviate from their ways." The translation difficulties stem from the fact that in our language we do not really distinguish between those who are poor and those who are miserable or unhappy, which appear to us as more or less the same thing. In Hebrew this is not at all the case. The Hebrew word sometimes translated as those who are miserable is *anawim,* which refers to those who are poor by their own choice. When they were well off, they gave away what they had, and they now deliberately remain poor. The choice of not wishing to be rich is another kind of witness rendered to God by completely entrusting your life and future to him. Some of you here will know of Sister Antoinette and the small community at Pomeyrol. This sister never devoted even one second to ensuring that the community would have the cash it needed. She was entirely convinced that the money would come when it was required. She lived this way her whole life. In the beginning, the Asiles Jean Bosque were run in exactly the same manner. This is the kind of thing the Hebrew word *anawim* means. What the Hebrew text tells us is that attempts were made to have these kinds of people change their vows and vocations. The people of Israel are accused of interfering in the lives of these people.

With these first three sins, Amos reminds us that in the kingdom of Israel, which was a society full of injustice, there were the *tsaddiq* (the just) as well as the *anawim* (the voluntary poor). Hence, everything was not lost. There remained the just, as well as the people who confided in God in a complete and total way. It is what in the Bible is referred to as the remnant. It designates those people in Israel who remained faithful. The grace and work of God will continue through this remnant, and this will happen over and over again in the history of the people of God. Things go very badly, but there remains a faithful remnant. When Elijah complains to God that he is the only one left in Israel, God answers him that there are seven thousand people left who have not bowed their knees before Baal. Despite the condemnations announced by Amos, the work will continue.

The fourth sin of which Israel is accused is commonly translated as father and son going in to the same girl so that God's holy name is profaned. This kind of translation creates the wrong impression. The girl in question is *naarah*, a word used for slave girls attached to the clergy of certain gods of that time. Their duty was to submit to any man; and through a sexual coupling and eroticism the aim was to reach an exaltation which was taken to be an access to the god whom the woman served by this act. If we translated the word as a sacred prostitute instead of a girl, it would not quite capture the deeper purpose: to achieve communion with a god. The Hebrew word usually translated as "girl" is *quodeshet*, which has the same root as *quodesh*, which means the holiness of God. We can understand the problem of the translator, who may not want to mix the holiness of God with prostitution even if it is considered sacred. However, it is now possible to understand the second part of the description of this sin: in order to profane God's holy name; this would make little sense if the sin was a matter of incest in families. In contrast, if it is a question of a religious and sacred union between a man and a woman to reach the glory of God and the name of God, then there is a clear profanation of his name. All this makes this sin an even more serious matter than what the usual translations imply.

The fifth and sixth sins involved lying down beside altars on garments taken in pledge, and drinking wine bought with fines these people had imposed on others. We are again left with the impression that this is not something we would get excited about. Nevertheless, it was a violation of a law described in Exodus 22–4, which forbade keeping pawned clothing

for longer than a day. This was deemed essential so that the people compelled to pawn their clothing out of sheer desperation would have a covering for the cool nights. The heart of the matter was not the keeping of
the clothing but the explicit transgression of the Torah. The drinking of
the wine bought from levied fines refers to the fact that it was commonplace at that time to pay a fine with wine. What was going on was that
those in authority to render judgments would drink the wine with which
the people had paid the fine they imposed. This wine was supposed to be
used as a libation to God in the temple, but instead it was drunk by them
in the house of their god. The seventh sin (2:12) was to make the Nazirites
drink wine and to order the prophets not to prophesy. The accusation
was aimed at the king, who was very authoritarian and who compelled his
administrators to carry out his orders, which led to these things. By cor-
rupting the Nazirites and forbidding the prophets to do their work, Israel
sought to destroy what little was left of what was holy and forbade God's
word to be proclaimed by the prophets. Together, these seven sins represent a totality of ways in which the second commandment of love and
respect for neighbour was not followed.

By way of historical context, we must remember that Israel was a small
people in the midst of many others. They all had impressive deities, among
which the Baals are mentioned, but there were many others. These were
very seductive in the eyes of God's people because they were not permitted to have any visual representations of their God, to whose presence
only words could testify. We saw the people's desire for a visible and tangible god in the desert. The same problem occurred with God being
their king. For this king to send them a judge once in a while appeared
to the people not nearly as practical as a permanent king who would
have the authority and the organization to get things done. It was the
great temptation to be like everyone else, where things seemed to be so
much easier. In a sense, the seven sins of Israel were an integral part of
this endeavour to make life easier and more practical for themselves.
Indirectly, this meant that they distanced themselves from God and his
Word by taking over the practices of their neighbours, or by transforming their own ways in imitation of such practices. Some of the religions
of the surrounding peoples, such as those of the Chaldeans and the
Assyrians, were based on a vast mythology with a great many gods, much
as we find later with the Pantheon of gods of the Greeks.

We will now turn to the last part, which contains the reaction of Amos,
who announces God's Word and the punishments to come. We have
seen that the society organized as the kingdom of Israel was undergoing

a profound mutation in the eighth century. Solomon had set the stage by encouraging commerce and creating commercial banks. All this was further sustained by the existence of many Jewish communities throughout the eastern basin of the Mediterranean. The result was an enormous influx of wealth but also a substantial impoverishment of another part of the population, whose traditional agricultural methods were being displaced and whose products were less in demand. Wealth was now primarily produced by means of commerce, and those who did not participate in it were left behind in a variety of ways.

Four categories of poor people are named in the text. There were the *anawim*, who were the voluntary poor. There were the *anaw*, who were the people that were oppressed; then there were the *ebyon*, who were the beggars. Finally, there were the *dal*, who were the vagabonds. Together they were what we might refer to as a kind of proletariat who were completely idle, with nothing to do. They had no way out of this condition other than by selling themselves into slavery. When a family became deprived of everything, they would usually sell their children; then the husband would sell his wife; and finally he would sell himself. Some people thought this was preferable to becoming a vagabond or a beggar.

Greek texts dated from the time of Amos show that most of the slaves in that part of the world came from Palestine via Edom, which traded these slaves with Greece. It is not difficult to imagine the social upheaval that accompanied all these transformations, and along with it came a radical change in customs and habits. Until the century before this time, the poor were greatly respected and considered devoted to God. They had now become merchandise. Superimposed on the mistreatment of others was a growing immorality and idolatry. All this implied a change in the roles prophets played in that society.

Before Amos, prophets such as Elijah essentially confronted specific religious problems. For example, Elijah battled against the worship of Baal and the priests associated with it. As a result of the changes described above, the prophet Amos had to intervene on the religious level (as we saw with Judah), and on the socio-economic level in terms of the relations between people and people's conduct. It was now a question of God and the idols, as well as of God and wealth. As a result, the prophetic message became concentrated on the way people dealt with others (the second great commandment). For the first time, Amos shows that those with power placed themselves above the Torah, and that this revolt of the people against God manifested itself in contempt for, and ignorance of, the other (what the New Testament refers to as the neighbour). This contempt for the other is a negation of the covenant with God. As the New Testament explains, the second great commandment is like the first, in the sense that disobeying the second commandment amounts to disobeying the first commandment as well. Whoever scorns others excludes God. It is therefore not a question of what today we call social justice. I know that many of the texts of Amos have been interpreted along these lines, but these interpretations have little to do with Amos's thinking. Amos does not say that what is happening is unjust but that the contempt for other human beings is also contempt for God himself.

The age of wealth has produced a devaluation of the human person and, along with it, the impossibility of loving and serving God. As von Rad[2] put it, In order to restore the Eternal One, the neighbour had to be restored as well. For Amos, the neighbour is always present and related to the love of God. For Amos, God is everywhere, but first and foremost in the other. These insights fundamentally change the role of a prophet. Beginning with Amos, all the great prophets have recognized that the way people treat others is a sign of their love, or lack thereof, for God.

Israel's Punishment

Through Amos, God announces that there will be war and that his people will be punished. From then on, he will no longer protect them. Those who live to see it should remember this prophecy and interpret the military disaster that fell on them as an act of God. All the power and armaments in the world will not be able to save them. Neher[3] notes that, in parallel with the four categories of poor people we have noted above, there are a corresponding four categories representing those with power: the strong, the heroes, the archers, and the cavalry. Together they will face a much greater power.

We have now reached the very heart of what is at stake. God asks his people to remember what he has done for them. "I brought you out of Egypt by my power, and I led you into the Promised Land by my power. Israel has forgotten all of that. It no longer has any confidence in that power: they now have their own king, army, wealth, and much else that they desired. They are confident they no longer need God." He respects this by no longer helping them. The terrible punishment is God's withdrawing himself from Israel's history. In a sense, we can say that this is their own desire implied in their actions. The people of Israel broke their communion with the God who protected them, and now, having been given over to their own strength, they will be conquered.

The pattern is very different from the judgmental thinking we have become accustomed to, of communities sinning and God punishing them. This is absurd reductionism because it does not take into account that God loves and respects his creatures and allows them to go their own way, although doing so will have its own consequences. Living with God in the covenant made with Abraham is one thing, and breaking it and going on their own is quite another. Through it all, God remains faithful in his love. He came to save his people, he came to help them and sustain them, but they did not believe in him. Now that the people will be conquered and crushed, they may remember that God warned them, and return to him. In the good God did for them, the people of Israel did not recognize him, and now in the evil encountered away from him, they may return to him. It is the "logic" we find in all the prophets.

These prophetic teachings were not at all those of the priests in Jerusalem. The prophet's words rested on the historical experiences and traditions (the Torah in the second sense) that the tribes had handed down from generation to generation. As such, Amos was the spokesperson of Israel's memory, which Israel could once again embrace and conserve as remembrances.

This eighth prophecy of the destruction of the kingdom of Israel occurred in the year 734, when the king of Assyria conquered Judah. Israel attempted to defend itself, but was destroyed in the year 724, along with Bethel and Samaria. It may strike us that this was a long time after the prophecy was made, but we must remember that to God a thousand years are like one day.

We may well ask ourselves what happened to those people in Israel who were just. In this context, we ought to remember Abraham's prayer to God not to destroy Sodom if there were fifty people left in the city who were just. When there were not that many, he asked for forty-five, forty, thirty, twenty, and finally ten people who remained and who were just. When this was not the case, he dared to go no further. We must also remember that we are talking about historical events through which Israel was punished, and this has nothing to do with damnation. If just people died in that war, it was part of the condemnation of Israel as a people. God appears unjust to us because we are always thinking in terms of our individual futures. However, we also are inseparable from a society in which we play a role, and that [connection] brings with it the possibility that we may fall victim to what happens to our people. Difficult as this may be for some of us, in the final analysis, none of God's punishments are for eternity. They are always within the history of a people.

Today we may be overwhelmed by the problems we continue to create. However, we must always remember how Jesus fed the multitude. The people contributed what they had in terms of bread and fish, and God did the rest. If we do not do anything, God will not do anything either. We must be faithful in what little we can do and have confidence that God will do the rest.

Chapter Four

Intertwining Themes ...

Overview

This part of Amos is complex because it involves intertwining themes. There are those of accusation and condemnation, and also themes revealing the evil done by Israel. In an attempt to clarify this intertwinement, I will first deal with chapter 3:1–8. Next, I will discuss chapter 3:9–11 and chapter 4:1, 4, and 5. The third part we will examine includes chapter 3:12–15 and chapter 4:2 and 3. This reordering of the text is simply my attempt to facilitate its explanation, because in the end, we will see that this text is extraordinarily coherent. I am well aware that an exegete following a structuralist approach would proceed differently by attempting to understand the structure of the intertwining themes, but I am not a structuralist, and thus feel free to exercise some pedagogy.

The Role of Prophecy

This text (Amos 3:1–8) begins with the election of God's people from among all the other groups on the earth. This election has something fearsome about it. Once again, we do not encounter the stereotypical God full of goodness, nor are we reading the Sermon on the Mount. It is a matter well explained in the letter to the Hebrews, namely, that it is a terrible thing to fall into the hands of the living God, not because he is mean but because he is demanding. Many of the parables convey the same message, such as the one about the talents and the vineyard, for example. When God returns, the people involved have to account for their actions. Moreover, those who have received more than most are also expected to have done more with it. God did not liberate us to do whatever comes up in our

heads. We did not choose God; he chose us to do something, and he is
demanding in this respect. In the same vein, God chose Israel, and not
the other way around. As his chosen people, God has high expectations
of them.

To make sense of this text involves a number of difficult translation
problems, and we immediately encounter some of them in the first two
verses. God tells his people that they are the only ones he chose. The
corresponding Hebrew verb is complex in terms of its meaning and its
verbal form. It designates two things we do not find in the usual translations. The first is that God chose in love. The form of the verb implies the
persistence of the act of choosing. As a result, a more adequate translation would be: I have chosen you and I continue to choose you in love.
The text also tells us that the knowledge God has of his people, his love
for them, and their election endure forever.

There is another translation problem in the opening phrase of the
second verse. The Hebrew meaning is very different from what is usually
translated, to the effect that God will punish you. It really means that God,
on an ongoing basis, preserves the remembrance of what you have done.
This remembrance may bear in mind the possibility of punishment. As a
result, we could describe the Hebrew as follows: on an ongoing basis, I
(God) preserve the remembrance of everything you have done, with the
possibility of punishing your sins in the back of my mind. In any case, the
Hebrew does not say outright that God will punish his people.

The overall thrust of the text which opens chapter 3 is that the covenant and the Torah that God gave to his people are not only still in force,
they continue to be given in love. However, if you (the people) will not
follow this law out of love for me (God), it can only be applied through
the force of justice, and I will be compelled to judge. I will not be turned
into this judge unless you, my people, abandon your love. In either case,
you will remain my chosen people. You will always be my people of Israel.
This is as close as I can come to the meaning of the Hebrew text corresponding to the first two verses.

In the six verses that follow, we find a progression of images up to the
first half of the sixth verse. In each we find a relationship that exists between an event and the explanation of that event. Two people walk together because they have agreed to do so. The lion roars because it has
captured its prey. A bird is caught because there is a trap. A snail comes
out of the ground because it has found something. There is terror in the
city because its people have heard the trumpet announcing war, or the
arrival of the anointed. In each case, the explanation confirms the event.

All these events and their explanations appear to lead up to the question of whether a disaster can strike a city without God's having done it. The problem is that this question has no relationship to the text that preceded it unless all that text is referred to by "it." If this is the case, then everything fits perfectly together because there is an event and an explanation of that event given by God. There is a catastrophe in a city and an explanation of it by God. It does not mean that God did it, but that he explained it. To put it more generally, every historical event is accompanied by its proclamation. If there is a catastrophe in a city, would God not have announced it? The catastrophe does not happen because God spoke it and it is, but he speaks of it as a warning. God warns us of a coming catastrophe, and tells us what it means. Here Amos speaks of the prophet, who explains to Israel the meaning of certain events. He is the intermediary between the God who speaks and his people.

Some historians believe that these six verses were part of a public discussion. Amos undoubtedly encountered a great deal of resistance to what he said. Some contested his being a prophet, and others did not believe him at all. In verse 7, Amos defends himself by declaring that God first revealed his secrets to a prophet; the prophet would then transmit this to the people, and only after this declaration would the foretold catastrophes come to pass. When a prophet hears a revelation from God, he has no choice but to speak, faced as he is with an irresistible constraint. It is not a question of Amos seeking to demonstrate that he is a true prophet. In fact, he says very clearly that he was not a prophet, but God told him to prophesy to his people Israel. In any case, it is not his argument that counts. What will settle the issue one way or another are the historical events to come, because they will confirm or deny the explanations of these events. When the chosen people heard this Word of God, they became responsible. The same is true for us. Those to whom God has revealed his will by his election are entirely responsible; that is, they will have to answer for it. We also have been chosen and elected in God's love, which makes us fully responsible as well. There can no longer be anything that can be considered a necessity, a destiny, that is, a tragedy, or a chance. These exist only in the dramas of the daily lives of those who are not called to serve.

We are faced with a choice. If we are free, there are catastrophes, which we provoke in that freedom. If, instead, we would rather have everything running like a well-oiled machine in which we are only the cogs, we would have to confess before God that this is all we can ever be. There are no other possible hypotheses. If we claim to be free, even when we claim that this freedom does not come from God, as was the case with Adam, we should realize that this implies the possibility of making mistakes and doing harm. Closely related to this is a fundamental difference between Jews and Christians. For the Jews, the Messiah is one who comes in glory. When he comes, all Jews will return to Israel, the world will end, and the new world will be created. Since Jesus did not put an end to this world nor create a new one, he cannot be the Messiah. As Christians we believe that Jesus created a new world, beginning with our hearts. It makes us fully responsible. I am thinking of all the pastors, priests, and missionaries who believed that converting others was something entirely positive but did not realize that once people recognize Jesus Christ, they become responsible and can no longer do whatever they like. They become witnesses, with all the responsibilities that come with it. At the same time, we cannot claim that we have faith, as if we can have and possess it, as it were. Faith is given to us. God chooses certain people to bear his Word among all peoples, and he gives these people faith. That faith changes everything, and it is to this they must bear witness from generation to generation. Everything depends on it. Remember our studies of the parables of the kingdom of heaven.[1]

The Crimes

Ashdod was a town located in the extreme south of the kingdom of Judah; and since it faced Egypt, the king had transformed it into a considerable fortress. However, during Amos's time, this fortress had been taken by the king of Assyria, which gave him a bridgehead to invade Egypt and Judah. This historical detail must be borne in mind when we read, "Proclaim to the strongholds of Ashdod [in Assyrian hands] and to the palaces of Egypt, and say 'Assemble yourselves on Mount Samaria, and see what great confusion there is within it, and the oppressions that are within its midst.' " Through his prophet, God appeals to the Assyrians and the Egyptians to come and see all the injustices and inhumanities occurring in Israel and Judah. It is absolutely incredible that God appeals to those who are not his people to come and take note of the evil his people are doing. It means that the non-Jews, and later the non-Christians, have to come and see and judge what is happening. It has happened all too often that others have been entirely correct when they have judged what happens in our churches today. According to our text, what was happening at the time of Amos was a great confusion. The Hebrew means that no one could trust anyone else. There were no longer any true and healthy relations between people. Violence reigned because the shared order of daily life had broken down. Verse 10 tells us that they no longer knew how to do right. However, the Hebrew word translated as "right" is complex. There are two possible translations. It can mean they no longer knew how to act face to face, or they no longer knew how to act with justice. Hence, the best possible translation of this phrase would read, "They no longer knew how to act with justice, the one face to face with the other. They were no longer just with one another." The Hebrew word used here, *neko-hah*, was invented by Amos. Following Amos, it occurs a number of times to refer to justice, one face to face with the other. This behaviour included stealing from the very poor and enriching oneself by means of violence. The prophet appeals for awareness.

In chapter 4, we encounter the cows of Bashan, which has been traditionally interpreted as referring to the rich women of Israel. It turns out that these cows from Bashan were extremely rare, purebred animals that were highly pampered and extremely valuable. These animals were not exploited in any way and were very well fed. When these heavy animals settled down to sleep, they would crush any small animals that were near to them. Our text also tells us that what they drank was brought to them by their *adon*, which has a rather ambiguous meaning. It could be a husband or a servant; but since this word is the singular form of *adonai*, it can also mean the Lord God. What our text means therefore, is that these cows from Bashan were the model of what the people of Israel had become. They were the people on Mount Samaria.

These cows of Bashan were involved in rituals of the worship of the Lord. These rituals appear to have been sensual, possibly involving alcohol. In addition to all the crimes we have seen already, what Amos denounced here is the sin of hypocrisy. We must remember that this is the reign of Jeroboam II over Israel, the king who had officially shut down the worship of Baal. Officially, this left only the worship of the Lord God of Israel. What Amos claimed is that despite this, the people had many masters or lords whom they worshipped in secret. Amos later names some of these lords, including Ashema and Shicouti. The people had Baal in their hearts, while officially the nation was committed to the worship of the One who revealed himself. This hypocrisy manifested itself in the behaviour of the people. The betrayal that Israel had committed in its heart would be fully revealed thirty years later during the reign of Uzziah. However, during the days of Amos, we encounter what has been called a Baal complex. The evil started with worship in the hearts of the people, without as yet being an official worship. This worship was of a god who

was not yet named officially but who brought a variety of sensual gratifica-
tions. The nation celebrated at the same time that they crushed the poor.

The people of Israel therefore were engaged in a double violation, of
the first great commandment (you will love the Lord with all your heart)
and of the second (you will love your neighbour). Our text speaks about
the ambivalence this created. The people worshipped other gods, and as
a result, the people stole from and crushed their neighbours. Or conversely, the people stole from and crushed their neighbours, which signified that they worshipped other gods. In other words, these things can
happen only when people worship other gods. This explains the relationship Jesus establishes between the two great commandments by saying
that the second is like the first. It is impossible to separate the one from
the other. We are called to consider our spiritual orientation, beginning
with our orientation towards others, by moving from the latter back to
the former, as it were. Once again, this teaching is hardly limited to the
people of Israel. It applies equally well to the churches and the Christians,
who have often behaved in ways that showed that they obey other gods,
including the state and the associated secular political religions.[2] We worship them while officially we confess the God of Jesus Christ.

In chapter 4, verses 4 and 5, we encounter seven issues that are taken to
their extreme: go to Bethel and sin, and go to Gilgal to sin even more; and
this is followed by a list of rituals. Bethel and Gilgal were the two places of
worship in Israel that no longer had access to Jerusalem and the temple.
Officially, God was worshipped there. Neher[3] observes that when the people ascended to go to Bethel, or when they descended to go to Beersheba,
in either case they would geographically turn their backs towards
Jerusalem, symbolically distancing themselves from the temple. Our text
tells the people to go to their places of worship where they officially
adored God, and sin even more. The reasons are explained by the list that
follows. The Hebrew word translated as sacrifice specifically refers to the
lamb slain for Passover. From Exodus we know that this lamb was slain the
evening before the Israelites departed from Egypt. However, our text specifically says that they made this sacrifice every morning. It also tells the
people to bring their thank offerings made with yeast, which was specifically forbidden, as noted in the book of Exodus. The people were to use
unleavened bread. The people were acting as if they were bringing the
sacrifice of Passover and the offerings of unleavened bread, but these
were not at all what had been prescribed. In the same vein, to proclaim
and publish their free-will offerings refers to the people's practice of solic-
iting recognition for what they were about to do. In sum, the ceremonies

performed at Passover and described in these two verses were the exact opposite of what God had requested. The people obviously no longer understood the meaning of these sacrifices, and they had forgotten Israel's deliverance. They took pride in their offerings and generosity, and thus showed themselves to be pious for the spectacle it brought. Once again, the crimes against the poor and the oppressed are linked to the crimes against God. As a result, God rejected these sacrifices and offerings. They meant absolutely nothing since the people had forgotten everything. They continued to act as pious Jews, but it meant absolutely nothing.

This condemnation must be a warning to us, also. We had better be very careful in what we do when we join a worship service, and especially when we celebrate communion. We had better know exactly what it is that we are doing. At one point it was common to read the texts warning us to discern the body and blood of Jesus Christ. Otherwise we eat and drink our condemnation. Today we rarely bother with this. The reasons are readily understood, but it does not take away our obligation to know what we are doing. It must never become a shallow or empty ritual. These are the crimes of which Israel is accused, and we must take them to heart as well. If we decide not to obey God, at least we should not act as if we are. If we do obey God, we must be faithful in every detail, just because they are details. The question of the Pentateuch is whether we are capable of obeying the small things, which altogether envelop our whole life. For example, for the Jews, whether the celebration of the Passover sacrifice is in the evening or the morning is a rather important detail. For them, the day begins at sundown, with the result that celebrating the Passover sacrifice in the morning (the middle of the Jewish day) robs it of its significance. In Jesus Christ we are liberated from these small things, but that does not mean that we can despise them. Here we are still very far from being free in Jesus Christ.

The Punishments

The punishments announced in our text (Amos 3:11–15 and 4:2 and 3) are, as it were, political and military as well as religious in character. There is an element of ambiguity. They begin with, "Thus says the Lord God," followed by a description of the historical events to come: "Your enemy will destroy your power." It is a Word of YHWH, transmitted by the prophet Amos, describing how certain events will unfold in the course of human history. There is another kind of situation where God himself decides to intervene in history. God tells his people that he will destroy, and that he will punish, and so on. There is a difference between God's warning of historical events to come and his sovereign decision to intervene in the course of historical events. Our text begins with the former kind. The people have stored up the products of their violence and robbery in their palaces; and God tells them that they will be surrounded by an enemy and their power will be destroyed. This power refers either to that of the people as a whole, or (since there is a reference to palaces) to that of the king himself.

The other kind of situation is described in verse 14, where God himself intervenes in order to punish transgressions of a religious nature. God tells his people that he will strike the altars of Bethel, and the horns of the altars will be broken. Traditionally, these horns had symbolized the power of God, and officially they still did, but in reality they now symbolized the powers of the gods being worshipped at these altars. People were in the habit of suspending offerings from these horns in order to transfer to themselves a little of their powers. These altars had thus become a manifestation of the religious sins of the people of Israel.

Verse 15 may refer to luxury, symbolized by the houses for winter and summer. These double residences already existed back then. Another interpretation has also been made. The summer house may symbolize Israel, and the winter house Judah. If this is the case, then this prophecy was aimed at both kingdoms. We do well to remember that although Amos was a citizen of the kingdom of Judah, he prophesied in the kingdom of Israel.

The punishment pronounced on the cows of Bashan is that they will be taken with hooks, which means that they will be treated as beef cattle on the way to the slaughterhouse. Alternatively, they will be led out through breaches in the wall to be put into a harem (this is the correct translation of the Hebrew word).

We will now go back to take a close look at a rather curious verse, namely, chapter 3:12, where we find a shepherd rescuing two legs and part of an ear from the mouth of a lion. In this whole military and religious catastrophe, something is going to be retrieved. That this is the case must be heard and declared to the house of Jacob, because the entire house is involved. What this prophecy deals with is the remnant that will be left after the greater part is devoured by the lion. That this must be declared to the entire house of Jacob refers us back to the beginning of chapter 3, where the children of Israel are addressed, meaning both peoples: Judah and Israel. The two legs symbolize what will be saved from each one, and both remnants will have a part of an ear left with which they can hear the Word of God. Amos thus has not only brought Judah into the punishments, but also into the remnants that will be retrieved from the catastrophes to come. Together, these two remnants will form the house of Jacob once again. Who will do all this? Will this house of Jacob be constituted out of what remains within the two remnants in terms of good will, virtue, or anything else? The text tells us that the answer is a clear "no." It is the shepherd who rescues the two legs and what is left of an ear. The shepherd of Israel can be no one else but God himself. This image occurs throughout the Old Testament – we find it in Psalms 23 and 80, for example. In the parables in the gospel of John, Jesus is referred to as the good shepherd. Once again, through these calamities, God will save a remnant from Judah and Israel and remake them into a unified house of Jacob.

Some historians have raised the question as to whether these prophecies are eschatological in character, having to do with the gathering together of the two remnants at the end of time; or whether they are historical in character, having to do with events in the history of the Jewish people. The difference is rather important, because if these prophecies are apocalyptic, there was little the people of Amos's time could do. In contrast, if these prophecies were historical, so were the punishments, which would make them avoidable. If the people had listened to these prophecies, taken them to heart, and repented, God would have forgiven them. On the other hand, if they had ignored them and continued in their ways, the prophecies would stand. We are back to the role of the prophets. They warned the people that certain historical events would happen if they continued in their ways. They also told them that if they repented and made their ways just, God would change his mind.

The conversion of the people of Israel would have had enormous ramifications. The time of Amos was a period of wealth, power, and fame. As a people, they were extraordinarily successful, thanks to an expansion of commerce, rising standards of living, military triumphs, and an official return to the worship of God. I believe there is a message here for our contemporary civilization. We are having an almost unlimited expansion of science, technique, and economic development, with one success following another. It is exactly at this juncture that the churches ought to be bringing the message of Amos. In addition, we should carefully re-read the history of the kings in the books of the Kings and in Chronicles; when we do, we see that the ones we would consider to be great kings because they were economically or militarily successful are all condemned for their idolatry. In contrast, the kings that we would probably regard as good, honest, pious, and faithful kings who lived by the will of

God were politically and militarily weak, ineffective, and sometimes even conquered. I recognize that these stories of the kings are not an easy read, yet they hold an important key for understanding certain things that are particularly relevant for our day.[4]

In conclusion, I hope that by slightly rearranging the text I have been able to convince you that the intertwining of the various themes of accusation, condemnation, and the possibility of repentance and change forms a well-structured and extremely coherent text.

Chapter Five

God's Pedagogy and the Evolving Revelation

Overview

I would like to make two brief remarks before we discuss this text (Amos 4:6 to 5:7). It is difficult not to be overwhelmed by all the punishments and catastrophes. Nevertheless, we can discern what may be called God's pedagogy. With this discernment, however, comes the difficulty that it is not the same in all circumstances. God changes his pedagogy from time to time. These changes give rise to the texts that tell us that God repented of the harm he intended to bring about. God had decreed a particular punishment, but in the end he decided against it. These changes in pedagogy also raise the theological problem referred to as a progressive revelation. It means that God does not reveal himself all at once in his totality. He never does this other than in Jesus Christ. I believe that the notion of a progressive revelation is incorrect insofar as we could establish "stages," which would imply that the Israelites of the second century had a better understanding of God's revelation than the Israelites of the eighth century. There is a progressing revelation, but not in this sense. There is an ongoing revelation of God that at times moves forward and at other times retreats, to get at things with a kind of flexibility, as it were. We began with a pedagogy based on the plagues, which we still need to explain. It was followed by a pedagogy based on the announcement that God was coming and that the people must prepare to meet him. This pedagogy was followed by a third one based on a call to responsibility: the all-powerful One tells the people to seek him out. There are three phases, as it were, resulting from three very different pedagogies.

The Five Scourges

The text (Amos 4:6–11) describes a series of five scourges, with each one becoming harsher. They all have a material character. The first one brings famine. The second one brings either rain or drought: one city receives rain and another does not. One field receives the water it requires while another withers. People go to where there is water, but they are unable to satisfy their thirst. Jesus expressed much the same thing in the Sermon on the Mount when he said that God made it rain on the just and the unjust, and made the sun shine on both good and bad people. To us, and to the people of that time, it must have seemed an injustice. Moreover, they appear not to have understood the meaning of this injustice.

The crops are struck next with blight, mildew, and locusts. Traditionally, people regarded the locusts as a scourge sent by God. Also, a certain parallel with the plagues in Egypt is gradually becoming perceptible. It is also important to note that the gardens, the vineyards, the fig trees, and the olive groves were, for Israel, the signs of the covenant of grace that God had established with humanity. How important this is becomes apparent near the end of this prophetic book, in the conclusion of chapter 9, where we find exactly the inverse of what has just been said. An abundance of crops from fields and vineyards will be restored. It is a symbol of a political, moral, and religious resurrection of the people of Israel. It confirms the terms, as it were, of the covenant that had been established.

Next, God sends the plague (the disease), which is explicitly likened to one of the plagues of Egypt. It is followed by a rain of fire, as in Sodom and Gomorrah. These five scourges pose the following problem. They are not punishments, but signs that must be discerned in faith and received as such. This is indicated by each of the five scourges, since each ends with the statement that despite this catastrophe, the people did not return to their God. We must be very clear to avoid misunderstandings. Our text does not say that when the people suffered they should have called on God for help and deliverance. He is not the kind of God on whom you call whenever you are in trouble. Instead, this all-powerful God who struck the people with these scourges appears to express disappointment that once again he failed to bring his people back to him. Why was it so important that the people return to their God? The reason is that if, as a people, they had lived out their history with that God and continued to be in communion with him, and if they had truly remembered what their slavery in Egypt was like and what Sodom and Gomorrah were all about, they would have come back to the God who had done all these things for them, and they would have done so with humility and in repentance. They would immediately have recognized these scourges as an urgent appeal addressed to them, just as God had done throughout their entire history with him. After all, in the Talmud's commentary on the Torah, these plagues were clearly indicated as the five plagues characteristic of God's actions. If the people had lived by faith in their Lord, they would have recognized what was happening, abandoned their idolatry (described in the verses immediately preceding this text), and repented. However, they no longer knew and lived with their history and their God, and this is what triggered the warnings and appeals to begin with. It was a matter of faith and the discernment made possible by it. The five plagues should have been five signs, and not five punishments. Without its being a question of faith, a punishment would simply be a punishment, no more and no less.

All this has far-reaching implications for the churches today. In this regard, I would like to share a personal experience with you to illustrate the problem. I had written an article in which I posed the following problem. AIDS is clearly a disease of our societies, related as it is to drugs and sexual behaviour. AIDS does not call into question individual people but the general behaviour and practices of our societies, extraordinarily dependent as we have become on drugs and on erotic images and practices. It reflects what it is to live in mass societies or in traditional societies that have lost their moral and spiritual direction.[1] Should Christians in faith perhaps discern AIDS as a sign that we must repent and change the way we live together? How can we do this and thereby enormously diminish our society's need for drugs and for erotic experiences, and so on? How can we get back to healthier and more normal sexual practices, particularly among our young people? In any case, I wish to be utterly clear that those who contract AIDS are not the people who are guilty of the problems of our civilization. I regard this as absolutely fundamental. The people who suffer from AIDS are not struck by a punishment directed at individuals.

We confront the same problem posed to Jesus. Were those who were slaughtered by Pilate guiltier than the survivors? Were those killed by the collapse of a tower more sinful than the survivors? Jesus' answer is very clear: It is none of your business, but take care that the same thing does not happen to you. It must be interpreted as an appeal for repentance; and never can it be taken as a judgment of others. My article developed these kinds of reflections in greater detail, and I would not have believed the polemical storm it would unleash. How did I dare suggest that perhaps AIDS was a sign and an appeal addressed by God to us Christians? I recognize that in part this is a reaction to a past when God was portrayed as vengeful, brutal, and a stickler for justice. Theologically, we have now gone to the other end of the spectrum with our emphasis on God as love, and our liberator. Hence, it is unthinkable that this God could possibly send a plague our way. Nevertheless, the Bible shows us that this God of love also warns us, and sometimes with terrible consequences. Our text makes this plain enough. We appear to have lost our fear of falling into the hands of a living God. The current stereotypes of a good old man and a harmless Jesus have done us a great disservice.

Our text goes much farther than our current stereotypes and theological distortions. Here is this all-powerful God who deeply regrets that his people did not return to him. It is a moving text of a Father who gradually exposed his children to a variety of experiences in order to help them grow up and in the end was not appreciated and even rejected as a parent. The entire history of the Jewish people is full of meaning for us and can help us understand many things. To use a scientific term, it is a paradigm for us. If we do not live in freedom and in love (God's will), the events of our individual and collective lives will run their course in a way that will bring a great deal of harm. God as our Father accompanies us and intervenes from time to time, and we must attempt to discern this.

In answer to your questions, I believe that the almost unlimited exercise of power and violence shown by the Nazis was a clear warning to us. So were the concentration camps in the Soviet Union. These and other developments are warnings against our almost unlimited appetite for power. In every area of human life today, we seek to increase our control and our power. We have plenty of warning signs showing where all this will lead. In saying this, I wish to make it quite clear that I have always told my students about the positive aspects of what the Nazis accomplished. In six months, Hitler resolved the problem of unemployment, which affected three million German people. He also overcame the economic crisis that was crippling Germany. With equal rapidity, he took care of the monetary crisis. Hitler did all this and more within a year, and he was widely admired for it. The only problem was that most of these admirers did not ask about the price that would inevitably have to be paid. With hindsight, we know it all too well. The concentration camps were only one of the signs. I can say the same thing for the unlimited search for power and efficiency in our civilization today. A terrible price is already being paid, and there will be more to come. Insofar as Jews and Christians remind our civilization that there are limits, and that there are consequences of ignoring these limits, we stand in the way of our civilization's goals, and that will have consequences as well. As the history of the Jewish people shows, we cannot expect to be protected more than everyone else just because we believe in Jesus Christ.

God's Pedagogy

Amos 4:12–13 and 5:1–3 describe how God has now changed his pedagogy. Because the people did not recognize his behaviour as that of a father, they will now have to encounter him as God. It is clear that God would have preferred a return to faith, which would have permitted Israel to discern the signs as coming from him. This relationship between God and his people through faith, trust, and repentance would have been preferable because it would have permitted an all-powerful God to relate to his people in love. Since this did not happen, the text announces that this is what God will do. Most translations of verse 12 are problematic. The literal translation would be, "Here is what I am going to do Israel, yes, immediately I will do this to you." After this, nothing more is said. What follows is a call for the people to prepare to meet their God. In other words, we are told nothing about what God is going to do. There is a discontinuity in the text. Every possible hypothesis has been advanced to explain it. Some have suggested that a piece of this text was lost. Others have speculated that what God was going to do was so terrible that Amos did not dare to write it down. All this is pure speculation. In any case, we are not told what God had in mind.

Next, the people of Israel are told to prepare themselves to meet their God. It is he who is all-powerful, totally just, and absolutely pure. The text gives a number of examples of his power, including the formation of the mountains and his walking on the heights of the earth. This latter expression means that God dominates everything that has power on earth. He is the one the people are going to meet. God once again gives the name first revealed to Moses and Elijah, namely, YHWH. To this name is added what is commonly translated as the God of the armies, or the Lord of hosts. The former translation is correct insofar as we do not interpret "the armies" in a military sense, because it refers to the innumerable elements that together form the creation. The meaning of the Hebrew phrase is "the creator of everything," as the Talmud puts it. To get a sense of this, we only need to think about the infinitely large numbers of galaxies and stars, which are all included in this Hebrew phrase. It is this God the people are now going to meet instead of God the Father. Neher[2] makes what I believe is an astute observation. Where can an individual person or the entire people of Israel meet this God? There is no possibility of doing so in heaven. The Creator (the Everything) is going to meet the people in his own creation. They will recognize how small they are before God, and this is the key point of the text: this God, overwhelmingly powerful and inspiring as he is, remains absolutely faithful. The text leaves no doubt whatsoever. The people are going to meet *their* God. Despite everything that has happened, he remains their God, which means that he is the only possible God they can have, and that he is the one who has decided to belong to them. We often overlook this double element when we speak of "my" or "our" God. This God, who is terrible in his power, is intimately related to our being. His faithfulness is further emphasized by his once again giving his name, with everything that implies.

Our text tells the people of Israel to prepare themselves to encounter their God. It is not a question of waiting around for it to happen. They must prepare themselves, but the text is completely silent on how they are to do this. Are they to prepare for a celebration? Are they to cover themselves in sackcloth and ashes? Once again, there is the same silence encountered in the previous verse related to what God was going to do to them. A little farther on in our text, we will encounter some elements of a possible answer. For now, we can simply conclude that even when God comes to meet us, we cannot meet him without making a deliberate preparation on our part. In the first three verses of the fifth chapter, the tone of the text is completely different. Amos no longer speaks in his capacity as a prophet proclaiming the Word of God; he now speaks personally about what a disaster all this is going to be for Israel. We find the same kind of interjections in the writings of Paul. From time to time, he makes it clear that he is now speaking for himself.

Amos laments that the house of Israel has fallen, and that she who was a virgin has been violated. This latter phrase was the traditional way of saying that the temple had been taken. No one has any love for this virgin of Israel, the people will be decimated, and their power destroyed. Israel's real power was its alliance with the Lord of the armies. Now it will have to rely on the power of its own army, and the results of the war will be catastrophic. Of one thousand men going into battle, only one hundred will survive, and of one hundred, only ten will survive. The army, now the only power of Israel, will be destroyed. Then God begins to speak again.

God Awaits His People

We now come to the third stage of God's pedagogy. Following the signs, and the announcement of an encounter with him, God declares that he waits, telling the people to seek him. This declaration is rather surprising because God had just told his people that he would come, and now he tells them that they have to come (seek me). How were they to do this? According to verse 5, they had to start by freely giving up their places of false worship – namely, Bethel and Gilgal – which they had substituted for the temple in Jerusalem. We have examined in some detail everything this involved in terms of perverting the meaning of sacrifices and everything associated with them. Seeking God would involve a spiritual decision to go to the temple in Jerusalem and resume the true worship. Since Jerusalem belonged to the kingdom of Judah, which was their enemy, it also implied a political decision to reconcile the two kingdoms of Israel and Judah, and to reunify the Promised Land. I believe Amos had all this in mind. This reunification had already begun in his own life since, as a citizen of the kingdom of Judah, he resided in the kingdom of Israel, where he also did his preaching. All this was surely implied in God's call to the people of Israel: "Seek me and live."

This latter phrase corresponds to a Hebrew one which is very difficult to translate. It cannot be translated as "seek me and you will live" because this creates an act (seek me) and a consequence (you will live). This translation in effect says that you will live because you have sought, but that is not the Hebrew meaning. The Hebrew word translated as "seek" is a very particular term that expresses the intention and the will to enter into contact with God. This has a clear and precise meaning: contact with God comes by means of prayer and the accomplishment of the Torah.

We can now begin to understand the meaning of preparing for the encounter with God. The people had to abandon their idols and their hypocrisy, pray, and *live* the Torah. As we have already discussed, the latter does not mean following the law in a legalistic sense, but following the teachings. I must say, I find it quite amazing that when God says, "I come," he also says, "and you the people, come to me." Israel had to come towards their God. I do not believe this is contradictory in any way or form. It reminds me of the text which tells us, "Do not ascend toward heaven in an attempt to find God. Do not descend to the very depths of the oceans to find him there. It is entirely pointless because he is there, in your heart, in your mouth, in the words you speak. This all-powerful God who is so distant, he is the One close to you." All this makes sense because God does not impose himself. He calls us to seek him so that we come. We must want this for God also to want this, because he will not impose himself. He remains the one who is faithful.

"Seek me and live." This clearly has a very broad meaning. If we seek God, it is possible to live. When God tells us to seek him, we know that he is the God of the multitude of galaxies and more, and at the same time the God who is near us. We must not tell ourselves that it is impossible to meet this God. Pascal put it beautifully when he said that we should console ourselves because we would not be looking for God if we had not already found him. The will to search for him is the attestation of having found him.

"Seek me and live." It also reminds me of a text in Ecclesiastes: "Why would you die before your time?" (Ecc. 7:17).[3] When God has spoken to you, and you seek him, you will continue to live. If you turn away and you stop seeking and loving God, you will die before your time. We are not dealing with a general law that applies to everyone.

There is another dimension as well. When we seek God, we begin to live more fully. I am not simply speaking of a spiritual life. It affects the entire thrust of our lives. We are told to get fully engaged in everything our hand finds to do, with all the strength we have. It strongly reminds me of something Paul wrote in 1 Corinthians 16:13 and 14 based on a text of Isaiah: "Be men and women, strengthen yourselves and do everything in love." It is a matter of the fullness of our lives. We have become so accustomed to thinking of the Christian life as being extremely limited by all the things we must or must not do. In part, this is the result of our interpretation of the commandments as delimiting our possibilities rather than being a liberating grace. If we place our complete confidence in God, we will learn to live more completely, and the future opens up. We no longer need to be afraid. We must always remember that the fear of God is something entirely different from being afraid of him. The fear of God designates a reverence and obedience with regard to God, which excludes all other fears. When we fear God, we no longer need to fear anything else in the world.

We have now examined the three stages of God's pedagogy, beginning with dire warnings and ending with the strong commandment "Seek me and live." I believe this is how this text plays itself out. In any case, this is what I hear in it.

Chapter Six

Justice and Related Themes

Overview

This passage (Amos 5:4–27) is full of passion and anger, with the result that the themes are intermingled to such a degree that I am unable to explain them without adopting a different approach. I cannot discern a plan in this text. For example, one of the themes is that of justice, and we find it in verses 7, 12, 15, 24, and 25. In the same way, all the other themes weave in and out of this text. Consequently, I will proceed in a way that I really do not like very much because it involves rearranging the verses into coherent groups in which each corresponds to a particular theme. The result will be a three-part study. The first will deal with the contrast that exists between the official worship and the social conduct of Israel, which includes the question of justice and the sins of Israel. In a second part, we will examine the power of God and the day of the Lord. In a third part, we will study the appeal that God launches, and the situation in which the prophet finds himself.

The book of Amos is the outcome of a certain preparation leading up to Amos's preaching, and possibly further years of reflection as his prophecies were turned into a written manuscript. Amos kept a close watch on what was happening, events about which he knew a great deal. Undoubtedly, all this led to much going back and forth between the various themes of this book, his preaching, and the course of events. We do not know whether Amos himself wrote it all down, whether he was assisted by friends or followers, or whether he had a secretary, as some prophets did. It is somewhat similar to the situation of Jesus: his disciples eventually wrote things down, sometimes well after the fact. This helps to explain why this book does not have a clear overall plan: it is a summing up of the work and thoughts of Amos.

Justice

The official worship of God is dealt with in verses 5:21–6. What is described in these verses are the traditional feasts and rituals of God's people, but practised in a manner that was completely wrong. It does not concern other idolatrous celebrations. For example, the Passover meal was celebrated with bread made with yeast, while it should have been done with unleavened bread (made without yeast); and the lamb was to be slain at the beginning of the day, and not in the middle. The true symbolic meaning of these rituals was no longer respected, with the result that they had lost their intended significance. Nevertheless, Israel claimed that it was maintaining the traditional feasts and rituals while it was doing no such thing.

When it came to making sacrifices, other prophets had accused Israel of offering to God animals that were often not in very good condition, such as thin cows. Amos tells the people that God did not even look at the fatted animals they offered because they were not living as the kind of people who could come before God to give thanks by means of these offerings. It reminds us of the parable Jesus told us regarding the Pharisee who gives thanks to God for not being like the others, who were sinners. Jesus tells the people that he will not be justified, and his thanks will not be accepted. In Amos we encounter the same thing. The offerings of thanks coming from a people who commit and tolerate so much injustice and violence mean nothing and will not be accepted. God tells the people the same thing regarding their songs and the playing of their harps. What is required for all this to be acceptable before God is that justice flows like the waters, and righteousness like a running stream.

This judgment ought to make us think about our own services of worship. For them to be acceptable to God, and for him to be present, the participants must be believers who are genuine. We cannot cover over our mistakes by holding services and making gifts unless we come before our God as people who know that they have fallen far short of his will; otherwise all our services and offerings will be no different from those of the Israelites described in the text. The services God loves and accepts are the ones from people whose justice flows like water.

Verse 26 provides us with an example of the justice God has in mind: Do away with the tent of your King, the pedestals of your idols, and the star you have made of your God. The tent refers to the one the people had made and which unified them with their God and protected them. They made it into a tent for a god whom they could possess, and this god

is not the one who is now speaking to them. Rejecting the pedestals of
their idols refers to much more than simply rejecting these idols. The
people had to get rid of everything that served as the foundation for
them. For example, there clearly was an idolatry of money. Getting rid of
its pedestal involved the rejection of wealth and the coveting that had led
to its accumulation. If they (and we) reject coveting, then the limitless
accumulation of wealth will disappear with it. "The star you have made of
your God" refers to the Star of David, which was already in use during
Amos's time. God reminds his people that they had made it for themselves and that he would no longer accept it.

The evidence that God did not ask for these feasts and offerings follows
in verse 25. God asks the house of Israel whether they made any of these
sacrifices and offerings during the forty years they wandered in the desert. We know very well that during that time the people did not behave in
an exemplary manner. There was even an occasional revolt. However,
and this is the critical difference between that time and that of Amos, the
people were not hypocritical. When they complained about not having
enough to eat, or threatened to abandon their God along with Moses,
this was exactly how they felt. There was no pretence of obedience or piety, while in the meantime they did what they pleased. They accepted
being led out of Egypt and into the desert by a pillar of cloud by day and
a pillar of fire by night, but that did not mean that they were always happy
about it. This kind of behaviour was the complete opposite of that during
Amos's days, when the people were play-acting. They had settled down,
built themselves beautiful stone houses, and at the same time had permitted the development of enormous social inequalities and injustices. In
verses 11 and 12, we see that the real problem was not the social inequalities per se but the injustices they produced. The poorest, weakest, and
most vulnerable people bore the burden of all of this prosperity, as taxa-
tion and other measures crushed them.

I believe that it is this contrast between the behaviour of God's people
in the desert and that during the days of Amos which provides the key to
understanding the last verse in this chapter (5:27). At first glance, this
verse appears to be a rather strange conclusion to the preceding issues.
God reminds his people that in the desert they did not make the offerings and celebrate the feasts as they did now. He then tells them to get rid
of all idolatry, and this is followed by the threat of their being led as captives north of Damascus. This does not make any sense, unless we bear in
mind the contrast between people's lives during the Exodus and during
the days of Amos. If this is the case, God tells his people that he once

liberated them from Egypt, but now they will become slaves in Assyria north of Damascus. It is as if God says, "We will have to start all over again. You will be living once more as an enslaved people, and I (God) will decide when to liberate you. In this way, the history of the people of Israel will once again become the history of a holy people." Along with the punishment comes a promise, and this is how I personally make sense of this last verse.

All this brings us to the very difficult question of justice. I will try to make it as clear as possible, but I cannot promise success. Justice in the Hebrew Bible does not correspond to any of our ideas about justice. It is not a juridical justice, a social justice, a metaphysical justice, a moral justice, or a retributive justice. The Hebrew language has two words for justice: *mishpat* and *tsedaquah*. The former comes from the root *spt* and the latter from the root *sdq* (the Hebrew language has only consonants, and each word has a root of three letters). The translation of these words presents many difficulties. I will take a look at their etymology, and at some of the texts in which they occur. *Mishpat* is pronounced by someone referred to in Hebrew as a *shopet*, whom we would call a judge. In the book of Judges, we encounter the acts of these judges, who were God's representatives on earth, who led the people, and who told them the will of God in a particular situation. In a sense, they were the forerunners of the prophets, but the prophets never had their political power. In this context, *mishpat* means justice in the context of judging and leading. However, this may be interpreted in two different ways. For some, this judging and leading gave birth to customs, laws, and justice in the human sense of that word. For others (including Neher, one of the great Jewish commentators), *mishpat* presupposes a knowledge of justice anterior to permanent settlements and the emergence of the people of Israel, which was a justice that contained both the tone (manner) and the pardon, that is, the decision as well as the forgiveness.

Tsedaquah is associated with a person referred to in Hebrew as a *tsadoq*, who is weak (lacking any power) and just, or poor and just. Its root is the same as that of the Hebrew word for grace and justification. With *tsedaquah* we encounter the same duality of justice and grace. The condemnation is tied to the pardon. It is this relationship that makes this kind of justice and law very difficult to understand for us, because it implies the notions of both pardon and justification. This explains why, in some texts, God is said to judge according to *mishpat*, while in others according to *tsedaquah*. In any case, whether God judges according to the one or the other, he does not judge unto death but unto life, as Ezekiel says. He judges to make life possible and not to end it. The ambivalence of these two terms comes out in a remarkable manner in Deuteronomy 1:16–17. The human judges referred to at the beginning of this text must judge by the *tsedaquah*, while the reference to God's justice near the end of this text is the *mishpat*. As a result, what we are tempted to understand as human justice is rendered by God, while what we are tempted to understand as God's justice is pronounced by human judges. Almost every text dealing with justice has these kinds of issues. God acts, but it is the human justice that he pronounces.

However, human justice cannot be independent because it always involves a choice between one thing and another. Either a person is just or unjust, guilty or innocent. In contrast, God's justice, whether it is *tsedaquah* or *mishpat*, always involves both possibilities together. Someone is both guilty and innocent, both sinner and blameless. I hope it is a little clearer now why every text involving justice is so difficult.[1] I believe that we are not forcing these texts when we say that all this is accomplished in Jesus Christ. He was at the same time the one who was condemned and innocent, cursed and just. From a Christian perspective, the texts about justice in the Hebrew Bible all point towards this realization of justice in Jesus Christ.

In answer to your questions, the biblical meaning of human justice, as we saw with *tsedaquah*, is that it aims at protecting those who are weak. It has nothing to do with incarnating some kind of theoretical justice or set of abstract principles. Instead, it aims to re-establish an equilibrium, as it were, to the benefit of the weakest and most vulnerable people. Doing so is not necessarily a social matter; it can just as well be an issue of age, or illness, or any other kind of weakness. Human justice must be rendered to these kinds of people.

I recognize very well that this very much relativizes what human communities create as law, and the entire system of justice. All such efforts are useful as long as we accept them not as expressions of justice but as rules of the game, so to speak. In order for people to live together, it is necessary to have these rules, but we must not have any illusions about justice. The real issue here is that we make certain mental images of justice for ourselves. In the course of human history, these images have varied enormously; examples are those of Greece and Rome, which have both profoundly influenced our Western civilization. The contents of these two sets of images have nothing in common; and I am saying this as someone who has considerable knowledge of this very issue. Simply put: the Romans never understood Greek philosophy in general, and what they

meant by justice in particular. They developed a system of justice that
worked very well for themselves. In contrast, the Greeks had developed a
highly intelligent theory of justice, but they never managed to success-
fully apply it to anything. I am simply pointing out that we all have our
ideas about justice. They come from a variety of sources, including philosophy, our political convictions, our socio-cultural context, and more.
What we must avoid at all cost is to judge God's actions by our ideas of
justice, which we have gathered from many different sources. We are always tempted to do this. At a time when many people were convinced that
it was quite normal to execute criminals even for relatively small offences,
Christians frequently judged God's actions that involved the loss of human life as normal. Now that we have a different concept of justice, many
Christians do have problems with these actions. The churches certainly
have to do some work here as well.

Many of the difficulties we have with what the Bible calls justice come
from the interpretation of texts in philosophical rather than existential
terms. The same is true for many other issues. For example, Luther's
expression to the effect that we are always sinners and always justified
means very little. We often have difficulties with these kinds of issues,
where we cannot separate things in order to classify them.

The Power of God

In order to discuss what Amos tells us about God's power, we need to
include the text from chapter 4:13. It is also discussed in chapter 5:8–9.
This power is manifested in God's creation by all its elements, from the
very largest to the very smallest. The description of the diversity of God's
power is quite remarkable. He calls the waters of the sea and pours them
out on the surface of the earth. This latter expression refers to the limits
God imposed on his creation as described in Genesis, when he separated
the waters from the land, for example.[2] It means that God is not bound
by the limits he imposed on his creation. His ability to change day into
night refers to the same thing. It also means that he is the master of time.
God's power manifests itself in his creation of the Pleiades and Orion,
but this means much more than that he made these stars. The Pleiades
and Orion were demigods for the Greeks, and also for the Canaanites.
What the text is telling us is that, despite whatever in our surroundings
are considered to be gods, or demigods, it is the God of hosts, your God,
who has created them. This same God is able to transform the shadow of
death into the morning. It means that with God, death simply becomes

a beginning. To this extraordinary diversity of power, the verse from the previous chapter adds that God created the mountains (as one of the most majestic elements of creation) and he walks on their heights.

One more aspect of this enormous diversity of God's power is mentioned in the last verse of chapter 4. It tells us that God created the wind. The Hebrew word translated as wind is the same as that used for breath, and for spirit. The text appears to have these in mind because of what follows, namely, that God reveals to human beings their thoughts. He knows us better than we know ourselves. Psalm 139 tells us the same thing: that God already knows our thoughts before we think them. I do not believe that this means that our thoughts are but the expression of a kind of inspiration from God. We are the master of our thoughts, but these thoughts come from the breath or spirit that God has created. I am almost tempted to say that if we believed this revelation, we would not say, "I think, therefore I am," but "I think, therefore God's spirit is." It corresponds to the whole concept of creation: God blew the breath of life into the nostrils of Adam, and he became a living being.[3] What this means for the relationship between this breath of God and human thinking is that we think our own thoughts, but God unveils our thoughts to us, thereby making human consciousness appear. I myself think, but God reveals that I do so, thus making me aware of it. What the text refers to is our becoming conscious of our thinking. Altogether, this is what is revealed regarding God's power. Beyond this revelation we must not go with our questions and speculation, as if we could learn more by ourselves.

Following this revelation regarding the power of God, the announced encounter between him and the people of Israel will be terrible. We learn this by examining chapter 5:16–20. It is remarkable that in the first two verses of this passage, we are not told that disasters are about to happen. The crops are not ruined, and the vineyards are not destroyed. Instead, the people will be struck with a terrible fear. It is not provoked by material disasters because the farmers do not wail over their ruined crops. The fear people experience results from God's presence, and nothing else. This is a first aspect of what is so terrible.

Immediately following, we read, "Alas, for you who desire the day of the Lord." For the people of Israel, this day of the Lord was very different from what we as Christians think of it, namely, a day that comes at the end of time when history is interrupted and the kingdom of God will appear. They expected a happy ending to a long and progressive evolution of humanity, almost in the sense of the kind of thinking we find with Teilhard de Chardin. It would bring a kingdom on this earth inaugurated by the

Messiah. The justice of Israel would burst forth, and its glory would be borne by the Messiah. This expectation of the day of the Lord continues to be a point of difference between Jews and Christians. For the Jews, Jesus clearly was not this kind of Messiah: he did not end human history to usher in the kingdom of God.

Amos contradicts this vision of the day of the Lord, the accompanying mystical hopes, and all the millennialist tendencies found in Christianity of establishing the kingdom of God on this earth right now. When God comes, what will he find? How can anyone have the audacity to await and long for this coming, given our behaviour and what is happening all around us? Amos warns the people to think about what will happen, since they are fundamentally unjust, do not really believe in this God, and behave like hypocrites by claiming to long for the day of the Lord. If indeed this day were to come right now, it would not be the fulfilment of your aspirations of glory but instead the coming of the all-powerful Lord, who expects something very different from the kind of behaviour and practices you engage in. Under these conditions, all you can expect is a terrible judgment from this all-powerful God. You will not be able to escape this judgment, constrained as you are by the limits he imposed on his creation. Those who are present on the day of the Lord will meet him face-to-face, and the confrontation between his justice and their injustice will bring nothing but darkness and calamity.

This prophecy regarding the power of God and the fearsome character of the day of the Lord puts an end to any idea of progress in human history, as if today we are better than our ancestors were one or two thousand years before us. It should also make anyone think twice about helping to usher in the millennium.[4] It is important to recognize that in the description of God's power, nothing is automatic, as it were. We are reminded of all the things he is able to do, but that does not mean that he will change day into night, for example. These are all images of God's power, and not a description of a reality that will happen. This text also tells us that God has the power of death in his hands, and that he is able to transform it into a morning for us. However, there is nothing automatic about it. From the Resurrection of Jesus Christ we learn that death has been overcome, but we must not infer any speculative ideas of our own, including whether after dying we are resurrected immediately, at the end of the world, or any other ideas we may have. It simply is none of our business. We must stick to what we have been promised, and know that we can count on it. For example, objections to the effect that if everyone were to be resurrected at the same time, there simply would not be enough room for them to stand shoulder to shoulder on this earth are completely idiotic in my view. God will do the resurrecting in the way he intends to do it, and that is all we need to know.

These prophecies (and the same is true for the entire Bible) are bound to be very disturbing for religious people. We are religious animals. We need religion. Every community creates what is religious. However, what every human community and civilization creates as a religion is completely contradictory to the revelation that comes from God and thus is not made by us. God destroys what is religious, and as religious animals, we do not like this one bit. We only need to take a look at the many volumes written by Christian mystics, who in a sense want to complete the Bible with their visions and all the rest. It has always put Christians in a very difficult position. In order not to feel superior towards others by virtue of knowing the revelation, we have always been tempted to be conciliatory, and without exception this has always turned into a disaster. There are endless historical examples. Adopting parts of Greek philosophy, including elements of Islam during the ninth and tenth centuries; making accommodations for National Socialism by the German Christians and communism by many Christians everywhere; and lately, trying to include Buddhism (even though its non-violence brings it close to Christianity) – all these attempts and more have turned into disasters.

God's Appeal

God's appeal is set out in chapter 5:14–15. Its opening phrase to do the good and not the evil raises the question as to what this good is. We can immediately reject a metaphysical good, or some entity that exists on its own. It is the same kind of issue as we saw with justice, which does not exist of itself, but as an act of God or a human community. In the same vein, there cannot be a good in itself, because we would then be able to use it to judge God's actions, as in the wars described in the text, for example. This good would then be superior to God. Doing the will of God as expressed in the Torah is not the good either. The text provides us with the answer immediately following the call to do the good: "and thus God, the Lord of the armies, is with you." The good is being with God, because he desires to be with us (Emmanuel: God with us). Being with God does not mean to execute the will of a master who is all-powerful, but to love his will. It is exactly what we ask for in the Lord's Prayer, that your will be done because we love that will. The Hebrew verb used in this context makes this very clear. "Seek the good" should really be translated as "seek through love the good." In Hebrew it is neither a legalism nor a moralism. It is loving what God loves (the good), and hating what God detests (the evil). It is as simple as that. Seeking the good in this manner is the way in which we can live through love. If we abandon the good, it means the triumph of death.

I believe this applies to each and every society, because God's appeal is both individual and collective. Our churches should recognize this. They are churches only insofar as the members are alive and love God. They do the will of God not out of duty and obligation but purely out of love.

A second aspect of the good is also explained in the text: "make justice reign in the gates." The gates were the customary places where justice was administered in the cities. In Amos's time, a tribunal was made up of free people who were citizens but not specialists. These citizens would make themselves available at the gates, and anyone who had a problem or a conflict to deal with could go to them for a judgment. It is highly proba-ble, given his interest in justice, that Amos himself may have participated in these tribunals. Justice was rendered according to an oral tradition, possibly with some written elements. In this way, the people had to ren-der a genuine justice, which is the service of God. Personally, I believe that this double aspect of the good, namely, to love what God loves, and to render justice at the gates, corresponds exactly to the two great com-mandments: to love your God with all your heart, and your neighbour as yourself. I believe this to be true for the second commandment because the kind of justice to be rendered brings with it a pardon and an absolu-tion, which implies a love for the accused person. It also implies a hatred of evil – this of course does not mean evil persons. It means evil in the sense of nothingness, the void: as everything that destroys life. Moreover, when the Hebrew text talks about hating, it is not merely a question of the action of hating but above all of not carrying it in your heart. It is exactly what Jesus explains in the Sermon on the Mount when he says, "You were told not to commit adultery, but if you look at a woman with desire in your heart, you have already committed adultery." Hating evil is therefore a matter of rooting it out of your heart.

In closing, our text tells us that perhaps God, the Lord of the armies, will have mercy on the remnant of Joseph. In the Hebrew, the word trans-lated as "perhaps" is very important because it has two meanings. It also has the meaning that it can be so, but there is no guarantee of anything. If you love the good, and if you render justice and hate evil, perhaps God may be gracious. We cannot take it for granted, as if it would automati-cally happen, because then we could claim to be able to determine God's liberty by means of our own decisions. However, the prophet Amos moves forward and commits himself with a promise.

In chapter 5:10 we are told that those who criticize in the gate and those who speak the truth are hated and despised. Verse 13 continues by telling us that a wise person will keep silent in such a time because it is an evil time. To render justice then was obviously very difficult. The power was in the hands of evil people, and the people as a whole were idolatrous in their ways. If you dared to proclaim justice in the gates, you were not well regarded and more likely to be despised and hated. This is what happened to people who told the truth about what was going on. If you did not want to be persecuted, you needed to keep silent. Personally, I am very pleased with what follows in the text, namely, that the wise will keep silent. The Hebrew word here translated as the "wise" has also been translated as the "philosopher"[5] or as the "intellectual."[6] Regardless of the translation, the point is clear. These people know very well what justice is all about, and what should be said, but they prefer not to be persecuted.

The only one who confronts all this is the prophet. As the bearer of God's revelation, he has an obligation to speak. This refers back to the text in which God asks, "Who will prophesy?" (3:8). When the prophet is seized by the Word of God, he cannot do anything else but prophesy, whatever the risks and consequences may be. We will soon see that Amos did run into some trouble. The times were bad because there were no solutions at hand. Idolatry was widespread, God's people were divided into two kingdoms that were bitter enemies, and there were a host of other problems. Failing any obvious way out, there was nothing else to do but to proclaim God's revelation, and this is what the prophet does, regardless of the consequences. Perhaps something else may happen, and this is what Amos hopes for.

Chapter Seven

The Five Visions

Overview

The book of Amos contains five visions. The first three are described in Amos 7:1–9; the fourth vision is recorded in Amos 8:1–10 and the fifth in Amos 9:1–4. As we have noted, we know very little about the duration of the ministry of Amos, but what has been transmitted to us was originally proclaimed over a certain period of time. We do not know whether these five visions were delivered in the order they occur in our text or whether they were spoken together. I will first attempt to explain these five visions and then turn to their theological significance.

The Five Visions

The words of Amos delivered in the first six chapters are sustained and complemented by these five visions. In the first, locusts ate the second growth of wheat without touching the first growth, which was destined for the king. It is surprising that only this second growth was devoured, which was intended to satisfy the needs of the people. What is equally surprising is that only after this was eaten, everything else was devoured right down to the grass in the fields. Amos prayed to God for forgiveness; God repented and informed Amos that the destruction would not take place. In other words, this was a vision of the future and not of what was really happening, and this future catastrophe would not, after all, come to pass.

The next vision was of a judgment by fire, which had been the judgment of Sodom. This fire devoured the great abyss as well as the field. I have not been able to find any commentator who claims to understand what this means. However, the best three I know of think that the great abyss may refer to the people or all the nations. The field, which is distinguished from this abyss, may possibly refer to the king himself or to the people of Judah as the direct descendants of David. In any case, the field as opposed to the abyss represents something like an elite or at least something of more than ordinary importance. Whatever it stands for, the situation was certainly very serious since, once again, the prophet Amos intervened by asking for a pardon. Visscher's[1] translation is rather beautiful when he asks how Jacob can withstand this since he is but a little boy, incapable as yet of making the necessary judgments. It goes well beyond the acknowledgment that Jacob is so small. Once more God relented, and we are told that it would not happen.

These pardons show that the relationship between God and his people was not founded on laws, rules, or something else whose application is perfectly rigorous and inflexible: it is a genuine relationship. God announced what he was going to do. The people reacted and, through Amos as their representative, pleaded for forgiveness for being like a small child. In response, God changed his mind. This shows the reciprocity that occurred in the relationship between God and his people.

Beginning with the third vision, Amos no longer dared to intervene through prayer. What he saw in this third vision was God standing on a wall with a level or a plumb line in his hand. He was going to check whether the wall was straight. God was measuring the rectitude of his people Israel to see if they conformed to the covenant and the law. If the people were righteous, they would stand like a wall that is straight and level. If they were not, they would be like a leaning wall. What is gripping in this vision is that, sooner or later, a wall that leans will fall down by itself. No one needs to give it a push. If Israel was like a crooked wall, it would eventually collapse without God's intervention. The level or plumb line thus "measured" Israel's future.

The second gripping aspect of this third vision is revealed through a play on words. In Hebrew the word translated as level or plumb line is *enak*. When the vowel *i* is added to the end of this word (recall that all vowels need to be inserted in Hebrew), it means *myself*. Hence, when God asked Amos what he saw to which he replied that it was a level, it can also be *anoki*, which would mean God himself. Beneath the image of a level or a plumb line is hidden the reality of God himself. He is the level and the plumb line of his people. It is his very presence that reveals whether Israel is level and plumb, and thus whether Israel will stand or fall.

Through this text Amos confronted a common idea of his time. The Israelites were in the habit of perceiving God's presence only in their

times of happiness and prosperity. They had thus made an idealistic image of their God as the one who brought them everything that was good,
such as wealth, well-being, and a good life. God was indeed free to bring
them these things, but he was also free to do otherwise. Even if this involved suffering, God would still be present. This is further clarified in
what may appear as a strange announcement from God: never again will
he pass his people by. What this means is that from here on God will stay
so close to his people that there will be an identity between the people
he has chosen and the Eternal One's presence on earth. The boundaries
of his people will now coincide with the circle of God's justice. We will
encounter this expression again later in an even more gripping manner.
The New Testament clarifies it still further: in Jesus Christ, God takes all
our suffering upon himself, with the result that when we suffer he suffers
as well.

In the fourth vision, God again asks Amos what he sees. He replies: a
basket of summer fruit. This involves another play on words because the
Hebrew word *kayits* refers to ripe fruit. However, the Hebrew word for the
end, namely *kets*, is the same except for one letter. This vision of a basket
of fruit which is ripe, if not overripe, is an image of the destruction of
Israel. Following this, God declares once more that never again will he
pass his people by. This declaration is now even more important because
it identifies both the end of Israel and God's presence in Israel. However,
as Karl Barth[2] has pointed out, this must be understood in a double sense.
When the Jews believe that they can take hold of God, they cause their
own end. Simultaneously and reciprocally, wherever and whenever the
Jews reach the end and believe that it is all over, it is God himself whom
they will have reached. It develops the previous play on words of a basket
of overripe fruit that symbolizes the end of Israel. When God promises
that he will no longer separate himself from his people, he identifies this
end of Israel with his presence there. This amounts to a dialectical reversal so typical of the interpretations of Karl Barth: when Israel thinks it has
God, what it actually has is its own end; but when it believes that everything is lost, it will meet God. It is an explanation of the text that is not
very obvious on a first reading.

God could no longer forgive what had been going on in Israel, and
what follows (Amos 8:4–10) is a series of judgments against it. It reminds
us of what we read earlier. There was a double disregard for the two tablets of the law as the two great commandments. For example, as far as
their relationship with God was concerned: At the beginning of the new
moon, three days were consecrated to God. During that time the Israelites

removed their sins by sending out a scapegoat into the desert and by the offering of sacrifices. During these three days, all other activities were halted. The people could hardly wait for this time to pass so that they could resume their commercial activities. They had more or less the same attitude towards the Sabbath. This should give us cause to reflect on how we spend our Sundays. Are we any different from the Israelites when we can hardly wait to do something more interesting than worshipping God? We should also remember that these three days at the beginning of each month represented the celebration of the creation. These sins against God show that the Israelites observed the law much like the previously discussed observation of the Passover, by doing all kinds of things that were completely contrary to what God had intended. They observed the rituals, but it went no further than that.

As far as the sins against other people were concerned, we encounter much the same attitudes: tampering with the weighing scales to cheat others, raising prices, buying the poor with money to make them little more than slaves, and so on. All this ends with a kind of reminder of what was dealt with in chapter 5 with respect to the day of the Lord, the sun going down at noon and the earth darkening in broad daylight. Because the people no longer know or respect the meaning of their feasts and celebrations, God will turn them into mourning, he will turn their songs into dirges, and more. In verse 8 we read that the land will rise and retreat like the river of Egypt: a clear reference to the flooding of the Nile and the subsequent lowering of its level. In other words, the people may rise like a soufflé and then collapse like one. All this is a reference to the successive judgments God renders of his people, followed by the verdict brought via the intermediary of the prophet: God will make it like the mourning for an only son, and the end of it like a bitter day.

What is also important about this fourth vision is that Amos did not intervene. He did not pray for the people or ask God for anything. He only transmitted the message of this prophecy on behalf of God. As we shall examine more closely later, the vision of the basket of overripe fruit is the beginning of the spoken prophecy, which follows in verses 4 to 10. It is its opening and introduction.

The fifth vision shows God standing beside an altar, presumably in the place referred to as the Holy of Holies in the temple. He speaks a series of commands, but to whom? There are two interpretations: he is addressing Amos, but since Amos is unable to carry them out, he also has to be addressing an angel responsible for bringing about destruction and death. The angel must be the one who delivers the blow that destroys the temple, who strikes the capitals until the thresholds shake, and shatters them on the heads of all the people.

There are also two interpretations as to which temple is destroyed. One suggests that it is the temple at Bethel, but the difficulty is that this temple was not actually destroyed. The other indicates the temple in Jerusalem, which was destroyed by an earthquake in 749 – a few years after the prophecy of Amos. We have already seen that this earthquake had been associated with King Uzziah's reign. Consequently, this vision represents a judgment against Jerusalem and against the kingdom of Judah, which shows once again that the prophecies of Amos were aimed at both kingdoms.

This judgment is so comprehensive that no one could escape it. We have seen much the same thing in our discussions on the day of the Lord. Escaping is impossible: if the people descend to the abode of the dead, they will be taken. If they mount up to the heavens, they will be brought down. If they hide anywhere in nature, be it on a mountain or in a forest or the sea, they will be found out. If they shelter among other nations, they will be caught. Even if they suffer captivity by their enemies, they will be found and killed. The people God has chosen will no longer be able to escape him. To be so chosen is therefore both a blessing and an enormous responsibility. It defines everything, and there is no escape. In Western Christianity, we have made all kinds of images to the effect that the poor are Jesus Christ; but we forget that they also face God's demands and will be judged like everyone else. Hiding out in a spiritual or a demonic world will change nothing. The latter possibility is represented by the sea with the serpent as the power of hell. Even suicide as an escape into death will not succeed.

Faced with this ultimate dimension of the prophetic judgment, Amos is unable to utter anything on his own. Of course, we are dealing with a prophecy in which God announces beforehand what he threatens to do in the hope that those to whom the prophecy is addressed will repent, change their behaviour, and become worthy as a people to bear God's Word. We have encountered this in our discussions of chapter 4. This is the overarching message of these five visions.

I can well understand that you may feel out of your depth in attempting to contribute to a discussion of these texts. There are many difficulties related to translating the Hebrew texts, especially where a play on words is involved. We have lost the habit of reading these texts together in our congregations. We have become accustomed to reading them by ourselves for our personal spiritual edification. However, they are not intended for our personal satisfaction. They must be read in company, and it is here where the different ministries are so essential. We have noted that the ministry of the doctor (of the Word) who knows how to explain these texts and who masters the many technicalities is essential, but it must remain a service rendered to the community; and among all these services it must remain one of the most humble ones. After all, knowing certain interpretations of the text is but the beginning of our response to it.

I would also like to emphasize that we have grown used to underestimating God's presence among us. His relationship with us is "existential," as it were. It is not simply a question of God's deciding and our accepting. Throughout the Old Testament, we often see God orienting events in a certain direction, and when that fails he attempts something else. He suffers when he sees that his people prefer their idols over him, or when they are brought low by what they get themselves into, or by his efforts to get them to repent. Our images of God frequently lack the kinds of elements so fundamental in the Hebrew Bible.

Vision and the Word

Throughout the Bible there is a radical opposition between seeing the world and hearing the Word. God does not show himself. He speaks to us. There is no such thing as a theophany (appearances by God). There are only three instances in which a person could claim that he had seen the Eternal One: once by Isaiah, once by Ezekiel, and once by Amos. In other words, it is not by means of vision that God reveals himself. There is in fact a radical opposition between vision and the Word.

It is by means of seeing that we establish a certain kind of relationship with what surrounds us, which constitutes our reality, but it excludes what that reality means.[3] Its meaning comes from language. Seeing is of the domain of what is exact or inexact, while language is of the domain of what is true or false. Consequently, an image must be explained by means of language. God will not tolerate any image of himself, nor does he tolerate any idol. Every image of God that human beings make for themselves is radically false, and this is the case for both physical and mental images.

All this is very difficult because we cannot escape making some mental images of God, and these usually depend on the kind of milieu in which we grow up and live. Although we cannot avoid making such images, we must become critically aware of them. For example, one important aspect of the "God is dead" theology was not the claim that God was actually dead but that the way we had come to represent him during the eighteenth and nineteenth centuries was finished. For example, Nietzsche was entirely correct when he claimed that *this* God was dead, but he was mistaken when he claimed that *God* was dead. In the same vein, we also have mental images that do not correspond to who God really is but that may correspond to the truth of what God allows us to know.

Why has God chosen the Word over the image?[4] There are many possible reasons. First, the Word is a relationship. It implies a dialogue. When I look at something there is no such relationship. Moreover, the choice of the Word is related to what is unique to humanity. Recall that the first thing God asks people to do is to give a name to all the animals he brings to them. What sets people apart in creation is that they speak. God thus places himself on their level: people speak and God speaks to them. It is not a matter of anthropomorphism but of God bringing himself within the reach of human beings. This is fundamental.

God also chooses the Word over the image because it is a means that is weak. It requires an interpretation and multiple meanings, and as such it mediates. If God revealed himself in his real being (his reality), we would disappear entirely. Instead, the mediation by the Word requires an interpretation on the part of the listener that permits different ways of understanding or misunderstanding. It is a means that is weak enough to respect the listener and permit a relationship. No such relationships are established by seeing.[5] Images take hold of us in a different way, especially when they flash by.

It is for these reasons that God chooses the Word as the basis for his relationships with people. It is another way in which his love for humanity expresses itself. Using the Word prevents people from being crushed. This is why it is so exceptional that a person such as Isaiah, Ezekiel, or Amos can say that they saw God. However, his placing himself on our level does not give us the right to make any image of him. Nevertheless, there is an image of God in the Bible, namely, Jesus Christ as a person who was weak and humble. It is Jesus who says that those who have seen him have seen the Father. This is the only image we are allowed to make of God. We must also remember that it is Jesus who is the Word.[6]

Having pointed out a first problem related to this text, namely, the opposition between seeing and hearing/speaking, we must now turn to a second one: the fact that Amos had visions. We are so permeated with pagan concepts that we have endlessly confused visions with mystical ecstasies. We have even carried out medical studies of what has been referred to as the ecstasy syndrome with all its manifestations, including exaltations, hallucinations, hypnoses, hysteria, double personalities, and more. Quite some time ago this interpretation was very fashionable, although it was strongly criticized by theologians. For example, they pointed out that a distinction had to be made between the form ecstatic experiences took and their content. Moreover, people who have widely been regarded as the most spiritual rarely experienced ecstasies. Paul speaks of two such experiences in his life, as did Pascal and Luther. Moreover, the great mystics do not appear to come away from these experiences with anything that is not already well known. They do not seem to add anything new. In any case, we have moved away from considering visions such as those of Amos as originating from hallucination-like processes coming from within a person. Seeing a swarm of locusts or a basket of fruit has nothing in common with ecstasies.

Why then do we find visions in the Bible? In our discussions, many of you have noted the close correspondence that exists between the five visions of Amos and the proclamations made by his words. The locusts were already spoken of in chapter 4, which also announced Amos's prayer. The same chapter spoke of the fire when a drought was felt all over the earth. The level or plumb line with the play on words referring to God himself reflects back to the text in which God tells his people "prepare yourselves to meet me." What is remarkable in Amos 8:1–3 is the silence that we had already encountered in Amos 6, where we read about the relative who came for the body to take it out of the house to be burned. Meeting someone in front of the house, he asks whether anyone else is left and is told "No." The relative responds by asking for silence.

Is there a significance to the placement of the five visions together near the end of this text? I believe one of the commentators on Amos (Neher)[7] has understood this perfectly well. Because seeing connects us to reality, these visions must be regarded as a prelude to – or a call for – action. Prior to these five visions, Amos had proclaimed the prophecies given to him. He had already made his political position very clear. He had condemned the dynasty of Jehu, whose descendants had all become heretical. During this time the people had become hypocritical with regard to their religion and had instead devoted themselves to their economic activities. After all this has been announced, the time has come to go further. The visions had a power with regard to reality as well as the power to confirm the proclamations. As such they helped prepare the way for a concrete intervention by means of action, whether of a spiritual or a political character. During the first two visions, Amos himself intervenes by means of prayer, something we had not encountered until then. By these visions, he was pushed towards this act of a spiritual kind.

The third vision took on a political character: the high places of Isaac will be made desolate, the sanctuaries of Israel will be destroyed, and God will rise against the house of Jeroboam with the sword. The sequence of visions is then interrupted by the quarrel between Amos and the high priest Amaziah, which we will examine in the next chapter. It is clear that this time the prophet Amos was asked to intervene on the political level.

The fourth vision engaged Amos in what might be called the dialectical movement between the covenant and the law on the one hand and the people on the other. He must act as a mediator between these two. As a prophet he must be the pivot in this movement: when the people of Israel believe they have taken hold of God, they actually seize their end; while when they think everything is lost, they will meet God. Amos was to take up the responsibility for this movement by becoming the turning point, as it were, between the law and the people.

In the fifth vision, the prophet Amos was called to confront and destroy the false representations. Doing so amounted to an intervention of a religious character.

To sum up: because of the five visions, the prophet Amos intervenes by every mode of action. He intervenes spiritually (by means of prayer), politically, socio-economically, dialectically (in the interplay between the law and the people), and religiously (by the destruction of false forms of worship). It is even clearer now how very different these visions are from mystical experiences. Such experiences are personal, made as it were for the individual, and that is as far as they go. The movement associated with visions in the Bible is the exact opposite. When a prophet receives a vision, he becomes engaged in an action. However, any such action must be preceded by an announcement of what will happen. Only then can a vision compel him to act and to intervene. I believe this is the reason why these five visions, corresponding exactly to the different phases of the preceding prophecies, were placed at the end: first, there is the proclamation of the truth accompanied by an announcement of what will happen, followed by a vision of a certain reality, and then the entry of the prophet into that reality in order to intervene.

This explanation of why the five visions follow the prophetic message is not intended to suggest that this is exactly how this unfolded in Amos's life and work. It does not imply that Amos first made all his proclamations and only later sprang into action. It is more likely that he closely integrated the prophecies and the visions. However, I believe that the deeper significance of the relationships between the prophecies and the visions is clarified by their separation in this account. There is first the proclamation of the truth, then the seeing of a certain reality, and finally an intervention in this reality on many different levels. All this may appear to be a little theoretical and abstract, but I believe it to be of fundamental significance.

It is also worth noting that in these visions God questions Amos. It reminds us of God asking Adam where he was, Cain what he had done, and so on. By being questioned they and all of us are obliged to engage ourselves by answering the question God addresses to us. Our text further underscores the fundamental importance of our being questioned by God.

In conclusion, I would like to say that these texts are difficult, but I like them very much. As we struggle with these or other texts, there is always something that goes beyond what we have understood up to that point. We have probably all had this experience: after reading a certain text dozens of times, we suddenly encounter something entirely different. It is impossible to exhaust the meaning of the revelation. I experienced that once again as I was preparing for these discussions and discovered things I had not seen before.

Chapter Eight

Confronting the Religious Establishment, and the Silence of God

Overview

During this study session, we will examine two passages that have little in common with one another, and yet each one is very important. The first is the account of the quarrel Amos had with Amaziah, as reported in chapter 7:10–17. Following this, we will study chapter 8:11–14.

The Quarrel with the High Priest of Bethel

The debate between Amaziah and Amos is both political and religious in character. Amos does not engage in politics in the usual sense of the word, and yet Amaziah accuses him of political meddling. Nevertheless, there is a connection between what we might call the religious prophecies (the sanctuaries of Israel will be destroyed) and the political ones (I will rise against the house of Jeroboam), because it was the fault of the king and his royal house that the religious life of the people had been perverted. He had claimed to be their religious leader. The result was a confusion between politics and religion that Amaziah utilizes to accuse Amos of political interference.

This account of the conflict between Amaziah and Amos follows after the first three visions Amos received from God (involving locusts, fire, and a level). During the first two visions, Amaziah remains silent, only to speak up after the third vision. This is understandable, because in the first two, Amos attacks the mores and the idolatrous religious orientation of the people. However, when Amos criticizes the king and announces the destruction of the royal house, Amaziah speaks out because he is in the service of the king. He interprets this third vision as a political judgment and an act of rebellion against the king. A very complex situation is thus created because of the conflict between the official religion, including its clergy, and the prophetic spirit in the form of the non-traditional personal religious experiences of the prophet. Every genuine prophet ran into this conflict with the official religious establishment. All this is but a first aspect of this complex situation.

There is an additional conflict between this priest, as an official of the king, and this free person, independent of the king, who declares himself to be a farmer who has herds of cattle. Their political conflict is made even sharper by the involuntary admission of Amaziah regarding the extent to which the religion practised at Bethel had been perverted. We have already discussed the fact that Jeroboam was a descendant of Jehu, who had sought to re-establish the true worship of God in Israel by eliminating all the Baals. One of the surprising results had been that everyone declared themselves for Jehu. He became the "father" of the people, who now regarded everything as having been set right. In theory, Jeroboam II and Amaziah represented the true "religion" of Israel. They were apparently convinced of this. Nevertheless, as Amos makes clear, their practices were the complete opposite of what the Torah demanded as the true faith. There had been a gradual and progressive perversion, and in the end, false gods were worshipped at Bethel. The high priest shows the depth of the problem when he declares that Bethel, which in Hebrew means house of God, is the sanctuary of the king. The sanctuary of God had become the sanctuary of the king, and royal power had been substituted for the power of God.

All this reveals an even more fundamental confusion, which we continue to make as well. The opposition between the house of God and the sanctuary of the king and between the priest of the king and the true prophet covers over a more fundamental opposition between the sacred and the holy. For many of us today, the sacred and the holy amount more or less to the same thing. For example, in our churches we speak of the consecration of pastors, which is completely unacceptable. It is we as human beings who attribute a sacred dimension to certain things, places, behaviour, or people. Doing so divides the world into the sacred and the profane.[1] It is a result of human decisions, which are driven by our need to provide ourselves with an orientation in the world. This orientation must be immutable and absolute, which can only be accomplished through sacralization. One of the best sociologists and philosophers of the sacred, Rudolph Otto, qualified the sacred as what makes us tremble, and what fascinates us.[2] Every human community has to create these points of reference and ways of organizing the world. The God of Israel, the biblical revelation, and everything that comes with it have no sacred content whatsoever. On the contrary, the entire biblical message desacralizes the world. We have seen that the opening chapters of Genesis have as one of their aims the desacralization of the world.[3] For example, there is nothing sacred about the stars; they simply are one of God's creations. Anything related to the God of Israel is holy. His temple contained the Holy of Holies, which had nothing in common with a sacred place. Something is holy when God sets it apart. A person to whom he reveals himself is holy. The seventh day, which was set apart, is holy. I know some translations state that this day was consecrated, but that is a very serious error. Holiness is a matter of separation: for example, separating a person from all the others in order to serve or separating something from everything else for a certain purpose before God.

The conflict between Amaziah and Amos represents the opposition between the sacred and what is holy. Amaziah represents the sacred as organized by the priesthood in the service of the king. Amos is called and set apart by God to bear and speak his revelation, and as such, he represents what is holy. In the same vein, when we speak of the holy universal church, we do not mean that what happens in churches is particularly saintly, but that this church is a people set apart to render a service to which they are called by God. We have turned this holiness into the doing of miracles, the mortification of the body, striving for perfection, the pursuit of morality, and much else that has nothing to do with it. We only need to take another look at the beginning of Paul's first letter to the Corinthians, in which he addressed those who were sanctified (called to be holy), following which, chapter after chapter, he had to deal with the ways in which these people lived their lives. Many of them were clearly no better than most other people, but having been set apart to render a service, they did not have the right to live in whatever way they pleased.

Keeping in mind this distinction between the sacred and what is holy, let us return to the conflict between Amaziah and Amos. Amaziah was the spokesperson for the priests, and the one who legitimated them as the descendants of Jehu. He denounced Amos to King Jeroboam II. The king was not particularly interested, and we know from other sources that he allowed things to run their course. In any case, the king took no action. Amaziah then began to attack Amos directly, claiming that the people could no longer tolerate what he had to say because they were all against him. Many commentators think that this conflict was very public. Amaziah launched his accusations in public, and Amos was also in the habit of speaking openly. From what we read in the book of Amos, it would appear that few, if any, people took the side of Amaziah, or the priests he represented. It is interesting to compare this story with a similar one found in Jeremiah 26. At first, the priests and the people rose up against Jeremiah, but once he spoke a revelation from God, the people changed completely, and they attacked the priests. In the case of Amos, the people did not behave the same way, but they certainly did not support the high priest.

It is in this text that we find some of the details regarding Amos as a prophet and a person, of which we spoke in the introduction. Amos denies being a prophet or the son of a prophet. Of the three Hebrew words to designate a prophet, Amaziah uses *hozeh,* which refers mostly to a professional prophet who, as a trained visionary, may have a somewhat strange or mad discourse, with the result that this word can have a connotation that is somewhat insulting. When Amos denies that he is a prophet, he means that no person can ever declare himself to be one, nor is it possible for any human being to point to someone else as being a prophet. Ultimately, the only question is, "Has the Word of God been proclaimed in a way that is exact and true?" It is perhaps instructive to read how a later prophet (Micah 3:5) announced what God had to say to the prophets who led his people astray: "They announce peace when they are given to eat, and they announce war when they are not fed. Because of this there will be night and you will have no more visions, and you will have darkness and no more prophecies."

Amos clearly wanted nothing to do with this kind of prophet, and by denying being the son of a prophet, he denounced the schools that trained them. The prophets that followed Amos, including Isaiah and Jeremiah, spoke of these prophets as dreamers and creators of illusions. Ezekiel called them artists because of their ability to craft beautiful speeches and songs, but their words had no prophetic content. Amos declares that his message is entirely from God, and that he is responsible to God alone. Israel is in a covenant with God, and nothing must stand in the way, including injustice or wealth. As we have seen, Amos is not a prophet of social justice and a just society. He is the prophet of the application of the will of God as set out in his covenant. It is as a consequence of this covenant that a greater justice and a better society may come, but that is not his primary concern. The second great commandment is like the first, and from it everything else flows. Everything outside of our love for the will of God is evil.

Neher[4] puts it well when he suggests that the function of a prophet is one of destitution and restitution. The prophet must forsake false and usurping values and restore true values in a manner that allows the most humble people to gain a level of true existence before God.

The Silence of God

We now turn to Amos 8:11–14. In Amos and a number of other prophets, the phrase "The time is surely coming" nearly always introduces an unhappy future. It is a time when God remains silent. The reason for his silence is that God has granted what everyone desired. The people no longer wanted to hear what the prophet had to say. As a result, they would no longer hear him. The punishment, as it were, is the silence of God they desired.

This silence of God must be understood in the context of what Amos had just declared in the preceding text. God had sent the locusts, and yet the people did not return to him. They had not understood what God was trying to tell them. Similarly, God sent them the plague, and they did not understand it any better. Moreover, Amaziah had declared that the king and the people could no longer stand what Amos had to say. They were granted what they wished for.

We may wonder if this was announced in the text we dealt with earlier, namely, chapter 4:12–13. The first of these two verses did not inform us what God was going to do with Israel. Also, the people had to prepare for their encounter with God, but nothing was said about how they were to do this, or what would happen. Must we understand these earlier texts in terms of the silence of God now announced in our text? In any case, when the true prophets were banished, the Word of God became excluded from people's lives. They will now discover how essential this Word is, because without it, they are going towards death. It does not mean that God is going to kill them. God did not cease to call them towards life, but it was their refusal to listen to his Word that led to God's silence and towards death. Until now, the people had not noticed how God's Word sustained their lives and their world, and indeed the whole creation. As soon as it is absent, they are going to feel its loss as much as they would notice the loss of food and drink. It reminds us of the text in Deuteronomy, and later spoken by Jesus, that we will not live by bread alone, but by the Word God speaks. It is as essential as bread and water. Most of the time we are not aware of this need; however, there are times when we hunger and thirst for the Truth that permits us to live. At that point, we start looking for the Word. As verse 12 puts it, "They will wander from sea to sea, and from north to east; they shall run to and fro to seek the word of the Lord, but they shall not find it."

This text is not trivial, and has a deep meaning. The people who worshipped the idols of Dan will wander in pilgrimage from Beersheba to

Bethel, which is a route that goes from the north to the south. They will then wander in a different direction, from the Mediterranean to the Dead Sea, which is from the west to the east. They will move thus from the north to the east, that is, from Beersheba via Bethel to go east. In both cases (from the Mediterranean to the Dead Sea, or from Beersheba via Bethel to the east), the people will be oriented towards Jerusalem, which gives this text its deep significance. However, they will not necessarily find God in Jerusalem, because they are wandering and are not sure of the right direction. The God who calls his people to live provides direction, but when the people refuse to listen and accept his forgiveness, they have no choice but to wander.

Is it really possible to die when God's Word is no longer proclaimed? Is this not an exaggeration? Faced with these questions, some commentators have concluded that these verses describe a vision or an image of a spiritual death. I do not believe this is true. During the silence of God, there is an absence of meaning in our lives because it is God who provides it when he speaks. We then wander everywhere and anywhere to find some meaning. I am tempted to say that this is exactly how we currently live in our civilization. I blame the churches for this. Until the nineteenth century, the churches in various ways at least did something to announce God's Word. That is no longer the case today. This Word has now been excluded from society, and we no longer know what it is. What we believed to be scientific, economic, political, and ideological truths have all more or less collapsed, and we have lost the sense of our lives. We cannot live this way. We need a point of reference. As the frequently quoted text puts it, "I place before you the good and the evil; choose the good that you may live." When God is silent, there is no other possibility than to create this good and evil by ourselves and for ourselves, which is what we have seen for a long time. It corresponds to the tree of the knowledge of good and evil.[5] All the truths that we have fabricated for ourselves, by ourselves, have collapsed one after the other. For some hundred and fifty years we have taken science to be true, but now more and more of it is called into question in one way or another. When taken together with the absence of meaning, value, and direction, it all leads towards death. If life no longer makes sense and no longer has any support, it has no value or price, which permits the proliferation of suicide and murder.

It reminds me of last night's television interviews with automobile drivers. A young man who seemed pleasant enough stated that he drove rather fast, and if this would lead to a child being killed, he would be very sorry, but if he would kill an old geezer, well ... Another driver said that whenever he saw a pedestrian, he was tempted to accelerate. All this simply means is that life no longer has any meaning. It is no longer a question of the commandment not to kill but of something much more fundamental.

To get back to our text: the people of Israel are not condemned by God. Rather, it is a question of the consequences that arise out of the silence of God. People literally die from this hunger and thirst for the Word of God, which they can no longer stand. As far as the thirst is concerned, it reminds us of Jesus telling the Samaritan woman that if she drinks of his water she will never thirst again. The text continues by showing that when life no longer has any meaning, people have no choice but to create some, and thus return to their idols. They swear by Ashimah, who was one of the Aramean gods: "May your god live, O Dan," and "Celebrate the way of Beersheba." When the Word of God has been rejected, God is silent, and the people have no other recourse than to go back to what leads to death.

The text tells us that the people will search for the Word, but they will not find it. This Word will not be found just because they have now decided to search for it. It is a Word that intervenes when God decides to come towards his people. All through the prophecy of Amos, we see this happening in his life and in the lives of the people. It is up to them to welcome that Word when God decides to reveal himself. At the same time, they must not feel excluded, like bystanders, so to speak. Throughout the Bible, God tells us to seek him so that we may live. We must seek him when he is there. It is a double movement. We cannot search for God as we see fit. We must search for him when he tells us to do so. It is at this point that we hear a new Word from him. We must not sit around for a ready-made revelation. We must seek him when we are invited to do so, and we hope that is the case in our churches. It is this invitation that should get us going, and that then will make us discover a Word prepared for us in advance. I believe this seeking is essential in the Christian life.

There is also a point of irony in the text. It speaks of the beautiful young women and men who will faint for thirst. It is the young who will faint. This corresponds to what Ecclesiastes tells us in chapter 12: it is in our youth that we should search for the Word and know the fear of God. It is during our youth that this ought to be done, when everything is possible and all possibilities are still open. It is also the time when we are most tempted to go our own ways according to our own faiths. Hence, this is the time when we must hear the Word without being diverted by everything else. This is what I hear from these verses.[6]

Chapter Nine

Reconciliation

Overview

We will now turn to the concluding verses found in Amos 9:5–15. As before, the first impression we get from this text is that it does not have a lot
to say. However, a careful consideration of the Hebrew text reveals something very different. Amos makes many references to other biblical texts
known during his time, which so increases the breadth of this passage
that I had to ask myself whether the commentators and I were reading
things into it. Having carefully considered this possibility, I have become
convinced that this is not the case. Together we will discover that a great
deal is reflected in this passage. I will begin by examining verses 5 to 10
before turning to verses 11 to 15.

Israel in History

The first two verses follow immediately after the fifth vision, that of the
destruction of the temples and places of Israel. They deal with God's
entry into human history, beginning with the proclamation of his name,
followed by the revelation of his unlimited power. About God's name,
the Hebrew words say, "my Lord, Eternal God Sabaoth," which is commonly translated as the Lord God of hosts. As we have noted, it means
the creator of the entire universe. "Sabaoth" refers to the hosts that make
up this universe. However, the Hebrew does not say *the* Lord but *my* Lord.
It is the way Amos refers to the One who inspires him.

This passage makes three references to the earth. However, the Hebrew
word *erets* refers to this earth in the sense of a people's native land.[1] The
first reference is in relation to the earth itself. The text tells us that when

God touches this earth, it melts. The next reference is in relation to heaven. He establishes part of his earth in heaven, referring to bringing this *erets* into heaven, as it were. The last occurrence is in relation to the waters. In other words, this passage reveals God as having full powers over everything in heaven, on earth, and in the waters – all of it is his *erets*. He only needs to touch it, and it changes its form and is no longer the same.

The usual translations to the effect that God builds his "upper chambers" or his "abode" in heaven are incorrect. What he establishes are his "heights." What the Hebrew refers to is God's establishment of his transcendence in heaven. It completes the description of this God who has power over everything, who does great things every time he acts or speaks; and now we learn that he is also transcendent. In Old Testament Hebrew, "heaven" always refers to God's abode, while "the heavens" refers to the stars and galaxies of the universe. It is in this heaven where God is the transcendent One, which does not mean that he does not have any relationships with our world and our earth. The text makes this very clear by emphasizing that it is on this earth that he establishes his vault. There can be no doubt of the meaning of this expression because it is used in the same way in other contexts. Genesis 9:12–17 refers to the rainbow as the sign of the covenant between God and his earth, given after the Flood. This distant God, of whom we perceive only his voice, has a relationship of peace with the earth because there will not be another such flood or catastrophe ever again. That this is the case is implied in the text that immediately follows (Amos 6): "he pours out the waters over the earth," which is a reference to the Flood – but it is not a complete destruction because his name is the Eternal One. This passage closely resembles a prophecy in Jeremiah pronounced much later.

Let us now turn our attention to verses 7 to 10. The Cushites were the black African people living in Ethiopia. They, along with the Philistines and the Syrians (the Hebrew text refers to them as Arameans), are referred to along with Israel. This represents another way of understanding Israel's relationships with other nations. These verses may be interpreted in three ways. They could mean that God will raise up every nation to Israel's level. They can also mean that Israel will be brought down to the level of all other nations because of her breaking the covenant, adopting a bad religion, and being idolatrous. This interpretation can be defended by assuming that the black Cushites were despised. The third explanation places these verses in the context of God's declaring that the Israelites belong to him. They are his, as are all the other people; and this does not change when Israel has behaved very badly and deserves to be punished. This notion of belonging becomes evident when we examine the different people named in the text.

On several occasions in the Old Testament, the Cushites represent "natural men and women," as it were. They are a people within nature. Several texts suggest that, just as the leopard cannot change its spots, so also the Cushites cannot the change the colour of their skin. We must be very careful not to interpret this in any negative way. These people are naturally black, and that is all there is to it. In other words, when God declares that before him the Israelites are like the Cushites, it means that, from the perspective of basic human nature associated with life within nature (without any prejudice or judgment), they belong to God.

The first step in the development of this text is thus that, as natural beings, they belong to God. A second step develops this argument further by declaring that all these people were brought out by God from somewhere. It is now also a question of belonging, as people living within history. "I (God) brought you (Israel) up from Egypt, and I will judge you in the course of your participation in your history." Having liberated Israel from slavery, God has launched it on a historical journey. Because of this first and decisive action by God, Israel no longer lives in a cyclical time, as do people living within nature, but in a linear time. This opposition between cyclical and linear time is essential in the Old Testament: people within nature live by the cycles of the seasons, in which everything that finishes begins again; while the entire Bible establishes a linear time that originated in Israel. This linear time has a past, a present, and a future, which do not repeat themselves. All this has been well explained by Cullman.[2] Even though Israel invented this kind of time, it is not the only people launched into history, because God brought the Philistines up from Caphtor and the Syrians from Kir.

This declaration poses some difficulties from a historical perspective. Caphtor is the island of Crete. However, the version recorded in Genesis, which goes back a long time, has the Philistines come up from Egypt. It is possible that the Philistines originated in Egypt, from where they moved to Crete, perhaps as captives, until they were set free by God and moved to what today is Palestine. The Arameans lived in the city called Damascus, in Syria. The Assyrians deported them as captives to Kir. They also were set free by God, just like the people of Israel, but with one important difference. Israel was the only people to be delivered from Egypt, whose Hebrew name means "the land of the double anguish" (of life and death). This deliverance set Israel apart as God's people. The Philistines and the Arameans thus also began their historical journeys, which brought them into constant conflict with the people of Israel over the possession of the Promised Land.

If Israel was set free like the other two peoples and they were set free as Israel was, what remains of its election? This question reveals a warning to Israel. If it regards its history as having a nationalistic character (Amos has already reproached it for this), if it regards its religion as patriotic or associated with the king, if it no longer knows the beginning of its history and the role God played in it, then Israel is no different from the Philistines and the Arameans. Israel has received a revelation, but if it does not refer its history to the God who delivered it, it is no different from the other peoples.

We have now seen the first two steps of the argument: that Israel belongs to God from both a natural and a historical perspective. The third step is developed in verses 10 to 12, which show the spiritual or religious dimension of this belonging. It is associated with an eschatological promise. Neher[3] observes that these three perspectives constitute the plan for the entire book of Amos. Chapters 1 to 4 examine the relationships between Israel and the other peoples from a natural perspective. Chapters 5 and 6 show Israel from a historical perspective, with its behaviour being judged in that history. Chapters 7 and 8 deal with the future of Israel from a "theological" and spiritual perspective. In sum, these verses are a kind of summary and recapitulation of the entire book.

Two issues remain. In verse 8 we read that the eyes of the Lord God are on the guilty kingdom. In Hebrew, this later phrase is preceded by an article that universalizes it, as it were. Either this means "the totality of the guilty kingdom" or "all guilty kingdoms." Luther and Calvin interpreted this as referring to any unjust government. For many contemporary commentators, the guilty kingdom is Israel, which is accused throughout this prophecy, whereas Judah is the kingdom that is not guilty. However, this kind of explanation ignores the early prophecy against Judah. In my view, Neher[4] hits the nail on the head when he recognizes that this verse distinguishes between "the guilty kingdom" and "the house of Jacob," which will not be entirely destroyed. This house of Jacob is constituted by people from Israel as well as from Judah. Both kingdoms have people who are just and who will be received into the house of Jacob. Hence, what this verse contests is not the one people or the other, or even both, but the kingdom. In the previous chapter, we saw that the temple of God in Bethel had become the house of the king. It is now the king who covers over what had been the truth from a spiritual or "theological" perspective. In other words, what is attacked is the royal and political character of the people who were supposed to be holy (set apart by God). The people are sorted according to the trust they place in political power. Hence, this is a reference to a time when this political power will be destroyed, which will most affect the people who have placed their trust in it. God will shake the house of Israel as with a sieve, but no grain will be lost.[5] All those who have placed their ultimate trust in political power believe that it can protect them.[6] Recall that this was a time during which political power was steadily growing in Israel and that this was accompanied by the subversion of the worship of God that we discussed earlier.[7]

The second issue is related to the image of God shaking the house of Israel as with a sieve aided by the wind. In the gospel of Luke, John the Baptist uses this same image. God will come with the wind and he will shake the wheat in a manner that will retain only the grain, but the chaff will disappear. It is one of the very few prophetic passages that involve the wind; hence it is probable that John the Baptist referred to this image from Amos. In Hebrew, John the Baptist is called *yo anan,* which means that God grants grace. We have encountered the same Hebrew word in chapter 5, verse 4, where Amos calls the people to repentance and says that perhaps God will grant grace. It is the name of John the Baptist with the addition of the word "perhaps." His name in Luke has no such "perhaps": God grants grace – it is done. I believe it is no accident that the name of John the Baptist is an exact reference to a text in Amos.

Israel from an Eschatological Perspective

We now turn to Amos 9:11–15. It is somewhat surprising that the text speaks of the fallen booth of David, even though during Amos's days the kingdoms of Israel and Judah were successful and growing. We have noted their economic and political successes, which created a wealthy elite endlessly criticized by Amos. Never had David's dynasty been so successful. However, this same text refers back to the past, when there was no schism between Judah and Israel, who are now enemies. For Amos, as for most of the prophets, this break-up of God's people was the greatest possible scandal and even a symbol of evil (in Isaiah). As Christians we ought to reflect on the significance of all the schisms in the Christian community today.

Already in verse 11, but continuing throughout this passage, we encounter a promise: the booth will be raised, its breaches repaired, and its ruins rebuilt. We are no longer dealing with a text that has a historical character; and the remainder of this passage further confirms its eschatological character. Until now Amos had harshly criticized the present in terms of what was happening in his society, to the point of proclaiming its destruction. He now speaks of a promise, and the final result as the kingdom of God. We are in the habit of interpreting an eschatological promise as something that will happen sometime in the future. However, this kingdom of God, which is eschatological, is present in the sense that it is a promise for today. In other words, it is today that this promise must be acted on, even though it will not happen until later. What is permanent or eschatological must be brought into the present, which is temporary. Although this promise is addressed to God's people, it will be for everyone through Jesus Christ. It is he who announces a general reconciliation.

The extension and generalization of this promise to the entire world is found in verse twelve. It is to reunite (and not to possess, as is sometimes translated) "the remnant of Edom and every nation in which my name will have been invoked." They will all be reunited to the house of David. Edom was constituted by the descendants of Esau, who was cursed because he and his descendants were not interested in the covenant with God. It all began with Esau's selling of his birthright, including the promise and blessing from God that came with it. Edom thus signifies those who have rejected God's promise.

The remnant of Edom will be reunited with God's chosen people in the house of Jacob. There will be remnants among all the pagan people who rejected God's promise. So will it be with all the nations in which God's name was invoked. In other words, the promise is completely opened up: wherever God's name has been invoked, there will be a remnant, and these will be added to the house of Jacob. It amounts to an announcement of a universal salvation.[8]

In verses 13 to 15, Amos restates a text from Leviticus, which is found immediately following what is referred to as "the code of holiness." This code spans some ten chapters that established a law that may be regarded as being socially and politically perfect. For example, it entitled the land to a rest every seventh year, when it was not being worked. It also ordered that every forty-ninth year was a year of jubilee, when all debts were to be forgiven and all slaves set free. This code even bound God's people to the spiritual obligation of buying back slaves in order to set them free. They were also bound to support the poor, to protect and support strangers, and to extend the right to anyone to repurchase his property if he had been compelled to sell it in a time of economic hardship. In the latter case, whoever had purchased the property was obliged to sell it back. These are but a few examples of the kinds of provisions that were included in this "code of holiness" to set God's people apart. The code ends with the same promises with which Amos concluded his prophecy. After all, he had accused the people of Israel of no longer respecting the provisions of this code.

Two mistakes must be avoided when we interpret this eschatological promise. The first would be to judge the Jewish people as being interested only in their material well-being, symbolized by an abundance of sweet wine, fruit, and new cities. After all, there is no mention of such matters as justice, paradise, or the kingdom of God. It is true that the Jewish people tend to be very pragmatic and down to earth, but this does not in any way diminish the spiritual value and importance of these verses, as we will see.

A second mistake would be to conclude that this eschatological promise is going to be realized by means of a society of abundance, happiness, and justice. This would imply that such a society must essentially be regarded as the establishment of the kingdom of God on this earth. If this is the case, why wait for God to establish his kingdom? We may as well get on with it right away. In fact, such an interpretation is not uncommon among the Jews who no longer believe in God. However, if they still believe in this promise, they will commit to undertaking whatever activities can establish such a society. In the Christian community, we have the exact equivalent in terms of a desire to create the good society for the millennium, following which the kingdom of God will be established. However, all this has nothing whatsoever to do with these verses.

The Hebrew text in verse 14 is quite remarkable. It is also found at the end of the book of Job, when God returns to him everything he had lost.[9] Translations to the effect that God restored Job to the situation he was in before all the calamities happened simply do not come close to rendering the Hebrew. I believe that only Chouraqui has provided the real meaning in his translation: the Eternal One brought to Job what has ceased to be.[10] The Hebrew verb is impossible to translate into French or English. God will do the same for Israel. Translations to the effect that God will restore the fortunes of Israel or that he will bring back the captives disregard what the Hebrew says. The people of Israel have ceased to be, and God may bring back what has ceased to be.

The promise includes the ability of the land once again, on its own, to produce wheat and grapes. This is the meaning of "the one who ploughs will overtake the one who reaps, and the one who treads the grapes the one who sows the seed." What this designates is the end of the curse of Adam, which decreed that the land would produce thorns and thistles.[11] The land will now again be fruitful.

The people are also promised that never again will they be driven from their place, being uprooted from the land. Since this promise is also eschatological in character, it is not simply a question of the Jewish people returning to the Promised Land, but of a return to Eden.[12] If Israel is tied to Edom and all other nations when this happens, this means that God includes all of humanity in the joy and peace of Eden. The fact that they will never again be uprooted from their places thus means that never again will humanity be chased from this new Eden, the kingdom of God. This is further confirmed by the last few words, to which the translations generally do not do justice: "says the Lord your God." The last two words derive from the Hebrew *elohekah*. It occurs rarely in the Bible, and it really means, "I am the God who gives himself to you." Such a meaning goes much farther and is much deeper than "I am the Lord your God." The latter means little more than that the God who has revealed himself dominates us. The Hebrew goes much further by telling us that God gives himself to us and thus belongs to us. It corresponds exactly to the proclamation that we are his people.

I have frequently warned against separating texts from the entirety of the biblical message. All along in our study of Amos we have experienced its harshness and severity. Yet it ends with the uniting of all people in Israel in Eden, where nature is again reconciled with humanity. Once again, we have encountered a text that ends with an eschatological promise, the opposite of all the threats and judgments that preceded it. We also observe this in the preaching of Jesus. Some historians have concluded that this contrast between most of the book of Amos and its ending makes it impossible that this could all have come from the same author. The hypothesis is then advanced that the last part must have been added later by someone else so that it would have a happy ending. I believe all this is nonsense because of the profound and deep unity of this text.

The concluding passage was developed in three stages. In verse 7 it refers to the children of Israel, in verse 9 to the house of Israel, and in verse 14 to Israel my people. There is a clear progression: from a natural perspective there are the children of Israel, from a historical perspective there is the house of Israel, and from a spiritual perspective (that of the personal relationship with God) there is Israel my people. Moreover, this text furnishes the key to understanding the underlying unity of the three covenants: one with Noah, one with Abraham, and one with Moses. Amos considers it to be the mission of the Jewish people to announce the covenant of God with Noah to all people. When they refuse to do so, God decides to shake them up until there is only a remnant. From a historical perspective, God offers to the house of Israel the choice of a historical existence either with or without him. If they decide on an existence without God, then the prophecies proclaimed by Amos will take place and Israel will be destroyed by its enemies. From the spiritual perspective, God will restore to his people what has ceased to be, and he will be their God. The full communion between God and his people will be restored, even if the people who are elected for a service refuse. We are reminded of the other prophecy that occurs in Amos (chapter 5:18–20) about the day of the Lord being like a person who comes home and when touching the wall is bitten by a snake, or one who flees a lion only to encounter a bear. From this spiritual perspective and according to this prophecy, God encircles Israel along with all the other people who were elected through it and welcomed within it – he lets no one escape.[13] Behind all this is Jesus Christ, the last and ultimate remnant of Israel. He is the affirmation of this concluding eschatological promise for every human being: wherever people may flee, be it in nature, history, politics, or ideology, they will entirely and once and for all be included in the One of whom it is written, "Here is the man" (John 19:5). Everyone is included in him. It is our very history. I believe that as Christians this is what we are called to announce to those around us, which was and is also Israel's calling. We have come a long way from our early impression that this text does not have a lot to contribute. It shows the extraordinary rigour and precision of the vocabulary and language of Amos the shepherd of Tekoa, the pruner of sycamore trees, and the prophet inspired by the Holy Spirit.

In answer to your questions: The problem for the Jews as well as the Christians has always been (and continues to be) to regard as their central mission to preserve from generation to generation the revelation received from God. To a large extent this is true, but it has led these communities to regard it as their property. In the case of the Jews, they saw little need to share it with others; and some have considered it as a merit that they did not proselytize. Although the Christians attempted to share the good news with all nations, the way they did it was usually a disaster because they also thought they owned the truth. This attitude does not lead to freely sharing what was freely given. This was often reflected in the means they employed, such as the strategy of telling everyone else that they were going to hell and would be damned. What everyone should have been told is that they are first and foremost loved by God. In this way the gospel was made into a message that terrorized people, which is exactly what most religions do. I am speaking generally and recognize that there have been minor exceptions.

Initially, there was always a faithful remnant among God's people.
Over time, the remnant derived from previous remnants diminished and
disappeared, to the point that Jesus Christ was the only remnant.

This brings us to our Bible reading. I believe it is essential to do this as
a church because, in each and every age, we must ask ourselves what the
gospel means for that time. There is no such thing as an eternal theology
– it must be formulated by each and every generation. It must also become a truth that we all live. We must constantly understand, in the context of our time, how Jesus was the pivot of history – it is only in him that
God is incarnated, and it is only through him that God becomes our God
and that we become his people. To use a traditional theological vocabulary, it is only in him that the two "natures," God and humanity, are united without one dominating the other.

There was a long period of God's silence between the completion of the
Old Testament (around 350 B.C.) and the early Gospels (around the year
30 A.D.). During this interval of approximately four hundred years there
were other writings, but I must confess that (speaking personally) I feel
that these do not seem to add much. Between the writings that have been
accepted into the canon and all the other writings there exists such an
enormous qualitative gap that for me it confirms the canon. In the same
vein, during the time of Paul's writing there were certainly other manu-
scripts, including the gospel of Thomas, but I have always come to the
same conclusion. There were essentially two canons in Israel: there was
the one established in Jerusalem, which is essentially what the Protestants
accept, and the other established by the community in Alexandria, which
is more commonly (but not generally) accepted by the Catholics.

There have been times when God was silent. Nothing was feared more
by some of the biblical authors than this silence, when God turned away
his face.

From our discussions, it is clear that the Hebrew text is very difficult to
translate. Not only are there plays on words, but there are many other
difficulties. The text must be explained. A translation such as the one by
Chouraqui is the most literal translation possible, but it is difficult if not
impossible to use in a service because it is hard to read out loud. However,
it is very useful for study purposes. The problem with most of the usual
translations is that they greatly weaken the meaning of the Hebrew text.
I recognize that some very strong language may shock some people, but
it is there nevertheless. Of course, there is also the problem of imposing
a theological position on any translation. This problem has been all too
common.

PART TWO

The Letter of James

Chapter Ten

Introduction to James

A quick reading of this epistle may create the impression that it is entirely made up of moral advice. Martin Luther wanted it removed from the canon of the New Testament, referring to it as the epistle of straw, because in his view there was nothing in it. Moreover, it was the epistle the Roman Catholic church used as a foundation for its theology regarding the role works play in salvation. Among those who defended it we find Kierkegaard, whom I regard as one of the greatest Protestant theologians. Although he did not write a complete commentary on this text, he has written what, in my opinion, are some of the most remarkable things about it.[1] I will not incorporate these writings in my remarks because this would require an extensive explanation of his thought, but it remains fundamental for the understanding of the epistle of James.[2]

There really are no good commentaries on this biblical book. The one written by Louis Simon, *Une ethique de la sagesse*,[3] has been described as "the epistle of Simon reviewed by James" because of its suggestive and fanciful nature. However, I believe that this commentary has the merit of realizing that the letter of James is not about morality but about wisdom, dealing as it does with a variety of issues that, from a spiritual perspective, are decisive and fundamental. Unfortunately, his exegetical approach to the text is among the worst. He begins by disassembling it into small elements, which are then reassembled into something entirely different.

The subtitles commonly found in our Bibles create the impression that there are no apparent links between the different parts of this text. For example, in the Louis Segond (French) translation we find subtitles such as "Trials and Temptations," "Putting the Word into Practice," "Discrimination and Favouritism," "Faith without Works," "Moderation in Speaking," "Wisdom," "Resisting our Passions," and "The Evil Rich." It

creates the impression of a long list of advice. Nevertheless, I believe that
a careful reading of the text reveals a kind of deeper logic, as it were,
which brings it all together.

What hints at this possibility is the widespread agreement among
Hellenist grammarians that, from the perspective of the Greek language,
this is one of the most literary and remarkable texts in the New Testament.
There are no breaks in style; and it is likely that it was written by a single
author with a deep understanding of the culture, as opposed to an edit-
ing together of elements from various sources. For example, Kierkegaard's
interpretation of the thrust of this epistle could briefly be summarized as
follows: Our being put to the test by daily-life events must be a subject of
joy. If you cannot experience daily life in this way, you lack wisdom. This
wisdom is not that of Greek thinking, nor does it entirely conform to the
Jewish notion. It is neither theoretical nor abstract, but of a highly practical character that permits us to live our lives as though being constantly
tested as to whether our faith holds. Hence, if we lack this wisdom we
must ask for it. Poverty and riches are among the most common tests of
our Christian faith.

It is highly unlikely, therefore, that the author of this letter was James
the brother of Jesus, who, according to the Gospels, initially did not believe Jesus' teachings, along with others of his family, and who, after the
Resurrection, became a convert and eventually the head of the church in
Jerusalem. This traditional explanation cannot account for the literary
quality of this letter, since Jesus and his family came from a modest background where Aramaic would have been spoken, and certainly not Greek.
Perhaps it was someone among Jesus' following. Some historians believe
that this James may have played a role in the churches in Greece because
of the quality of his Greek. At the same time, it is recognized that this text
reveals a thinking that is profoundly Jewish – in its view of the law, for
example. The text is generally dated thirty years after Jesus' death. If this
is correct, the letter of James would be one of the oldest texts in the New
Testament and older than the Gospels. Nevertheless, it was not accepted
into the canon until the fourth century, in part because it appeared to be
contrary to the dominant theology of Paul, which was seen as emphasizing faith over works, while James was seen as emphasizing works over
faith. I will later show that no such contradiction exists.

Chapter Eleven

Overview of the Christian Life

To All People

As the opening verse indicates, this letter is addressed to the twelve tribes who lived dispersed from each other. Because of its reference to the twelve tribes, I believe that we need to consider the possibility that it is addressed not only to the church but also to the Jews, and thus to all God's people, thereby giving a deeper meaning to the dispersion.

At one point, some historians interpreted this as being related to the destruction and dispersion of the church in Jerusalem, following which James (as its former head) wrote to its members who were now dispersed. Other historians, who believed that James was someone else, held that the dispersion refers to the results of the first persecution. Personally, I believe that all this misses the point, because the meaning of the text cannot be restricted to such a positivistic historical interpretation.

The twelve tribes represent the totality of the Jewish people. At the same time, this letter is addressed to fellow Christian brothers and sisters. I believe the text makes it increasingly clear, therefore, that the twelve tribes represent the totality of God's people, which is divided and dispersed. The significance of this clearly transcends any particular historical event. It refers to a kind of permanent character of God's people: Israel and the church are separated; the Jewish people are scattered in the diaspora; the church is divided into churches; and these churches are dispersed. This letter thus has a catholic (i.e., universal) character, and it is important to recognize that it always and permanently addresses God's people in their dispersion. In the verses that follow, we will see that, despite this dispersion, there is nevertheless a church. It exists because it is addressed by God's creative Word.

A second element in the opening verse of salutation is the qualifica-
tion of James as the servant of God and the Lord Jesus Christ. We do not
sufficiently plumb the depth of the meaning of the term "servant." A
servant is someone who is called by God, who renders a service on behalf
of God, and who, because of this fact, represents God and has a certain
authority from him. Even though servants are representatives of an absolute power, they may take no power or authority for themselves. Servants
within our churches, however, have become those who render a service
but also claim authority and power. They rarely assume the position and
orientation of a servant. In the Bible, however, servants assume the condition and orientation of non-authority and non-power by placing themselves entirely in God's hands. Representing God in any other way by
claiming any authority or power is to do the work of Satan, the great accuser. The radical opposition between the way Jesus lived and the way
Satan tried to tempt him makes this very clear. The role of Christians as
servants will be dealt with later in this letter of James.

James begins by telling his readers to be joyful, although this is commonly translated as "Greetings." However, such a translation does not do
justice to the Greek text. The second verse returns to this subject.

Life as a Test of Who We Are

James 1:2–8 deals with four themes: considering trials to be a complete
joy, committing oneself to perseverance, asking for wisdom, and never
doubting but asking in faith. I will begin with the first theme in verses
2 to 4.

The opening greeting (to be joyful) is immediately followed by what
appears to be a commandment from God to regard trials or testing as a
complete joy. Even though the persecutions probably had not begun at
the time of the writing of this letter, our being joyful when on trial appears absurd. No human being would react this way to a trial. It signals a
change in perspective, of not regarding our lives from our own vantage
points but from that of Jesus Christ. Faith implies putting Jesus at the
centre of our lives. It is not exactly what we do naturally, which drives
home the point that Christianity is not normal or natural. I recognize
that there was a time when we sought to convince ourselves that the observation of natural laws was the equivalent of Christian faith, but this is
entirely false. Living by faith is the opposite of doing what comes naturally. As a result, doing so requires a transformation of every aspect of
our daily lives.[1]

How can God command us to be joyful? This question touches on a common misunderstanding of what happens when God gives his commandments in the Old Testament. From the Hebrew it is clear that a commandment is never an order or an obligation. It is a permission, a promise, and the opening up of a new possibility. For example, the commandment not to kill also means that the day will surely come when the need for killing will have been eliminated and people will no longer kill each other. Hence, it is a promise with an eschatological dimension and an opening up of that possibility in the present. Similarly, the commandments to love God and our neighbour make no sense if they are only interpreted as orders. Love cannot be commanded. The first great commandment tells us that we have been granted permission to address this God of the entire universe, that it is possible to do so, and that one day we will fully love him. When God addresses us with a commandment, he is at the same time creating the very possibility for it to happen by his Word, which opens up a new beginning. It is the same Word with which he created the world, as we saw in Genesis, as well as Jesus Christ, its personification, as we saw in the opening verses of the gospel of John.[2] It remains that same Word when it is addressed to us in order to create a new situation and a new possibility. A commandment thus creates a newness of life. Understood in this way, the commandment to be joyful is a permission and a creation of that possibility. We are granted the freedom to be joyful even when that is not natural. What makes this joy possible is that, first and foremost, we become aware of God as having forgiven us through Jesus (as the Word having become human). When God speaks to us, he is with us. He grants us the ability to do what otherwise would be impossible, and we thus become his people. All this is implied in the commandment to be joyful.

The trials the text speaks of are those of faith. The Greek text involves a play on words. The Greek word usually translated as trial is also used to designate the crushing of metals in order to purify them by fire. This image of the purification of metals, well known to the people of that time, occurs frequently in the Bible and is essential for understanding this text. The testing of our faith transforms each and every moment of our lives into a test to see whether that faith holds and leads to purification. Will it hold for the good and for life? Kierkegaard asked what reply we would give to the question of whether or not it is important for me to be a child of God. If we say yes, then we ought to be less interested in all daily-life issues and problems because these will be overshadowed by our joy of belonging to God. The rest all becomes secondary. What we do in each and every daily-life situation is a reply to the question whether or not we are a child of God. Since everything in our lives is a trial of our faith, it is not simply a question of singling out those events involving suffering. Happiness and riches are included. These also will be a test of whether or not our faith holds.

Trials of faith have a second meaning related to our participation in the suffering of Jesus Christ. It is important to understand what the Bible means by this. Jesus suffered in order to encounter us where we are as people suffering from the "double anguish" of life and death. We encounter Jesus as the one who was crucified and killed. As long as humanity suffers, Jesus suffers. The book of Revelation clearly shows this when, for all of human history, Jesus is portrayed as the slain lamb. Pascal put it well when he said that Jesus is crucified until the end of the world. Even though he rose from the dead and ascended to be seated on God's right hand, he remains crucified and suffers because it is in that suffering where we meet him. The Bible also tells us that we participate in his suffering, which brings us the joy of meeting him there. Suffering has no value in itself and it cannot save us. Nor is there any point in deliberately seeking out suffering, as if that has merit. The only value and meaning in suffering is that there we meet Jesus Christ, are tested, and are purified. We certainly do not accumulate rewards in heaven for suffering on earth.

The trials of our faith produce perseverance. The Greek word translated here as "perseverance" or "endurance" is sometimes translated as "patience." However, this is far too weak, implying as it does a certain passivity. It is not at all a question of resigning ourselves. Any church teaching that those who suffer must resign themselves is completely false. It cannot be drawn from a text that speaks about joy; moreover, an orientation of passivity and resignation in the face of suffering is foreign to this letter and the Bible. We see this clearly in Job, who struggles and fights and is hardly resigned to his suffering. Job dismissed the intellectual arguments of his friends because he was suffering, and that is what concerned him. He thus shifted the focus from the intellectual to the practical and existential.

Perseverance implies resisting, persisting, and enduring. Depending on their background, translators and commentators have emphasized three orientations. The first is the perseverance of faith because the work of Christ within us is gradual and does not occur all at once. There is a common and mistaken notion that a conversion marks a complete change, but it is simply the beginning of a long process through which our faith grows. It never ends. We are mistaken when we say that we have faith. We cannot possess it. Instead it is faith that has us. As Paul points out, our faith may be very small or it may it have grown a lot, but nevertheless, it is faith and we must respect it as such and expect it to grow indefinitely. Hence, there is a process that requires a perseverance in and a continuity of faith. All this happens by means of trials that steadily purify our lives so that a new life emerges. To use a contemporary French vocabulary that reflects a strong Hegelian and Marxist influence, a trial would be the equivalent of a crisis, just as in earlier cultures a trial was the equivalent of the crushing of metals before they were passed through fire for purification. There is a convergence between these two concepts: a crisis causes a situation to evolve, and the fire tests the metal to make it pure.

The second orientation of perseverance comes from the Greek word being used in the second century to specifically designate the perseverance of martyrs. It referred to their boldness and unwillingness to compromise when they were placed before a specific question – whether, yes or no, they would do or say something particular – in the full knowledge that, depending on their answer, they would live or die. This implies an intransigence but also a dissidence, causing a break with what is normal in an established order.

A third orientation in perseverance is that of non-violence in our being tested. As we will see in the text that follows, the victory in any trial is that of God. We do not need to bring about this victory by means of force, violence, or efficient means in order to dominate and overcome these trials. God will give the victory by creating the possibility for us to move beyond them. Hence, perseverance means that we put the means for achieving the victory back in God's hands. What we keep for ourselves is the certainty of the victory through faith. In other words, we must adopt the way of a servant who does not use authority, domination, or power, thus leaving the glory to God.

Perseverance with its three orientations must accomplish its work in us. It is the work of the continuation and the development of our faith, the work of the martyr's resistance, and the work of non-violence, of refusing to use any means of oppression. It will produce a development of faith and of our Christian being. It works within us to make us mature and perfect. However, this is not a goal we can achieve but something that happens within us.

Our text now turns to the subject of wisdom and doubt. I noted earlier that Simon entitles his commentary on James as *Une éthique de la sagesse (An Ethics of Wisdom)*.[3] Wisdom in the Bible has nothing in common with what philosophers speak about. It is not intellectual and abstract but utterly

practical.[4] Biblical wisdom deals with the way the pardon and grace given
in Christ relate to our daily lives. The pardon we have received, the life we
have been given, and the promise of which we are certain suggest a different engagement in our lives from the usual daily-life routines. We cannot
wait for God to come and solve our problems. We must persevere, and this
is possible through wisdom. We must ask God for this wisdom, which will
permit us to make the necessary decisions ourselves. God does not replace
us. In our daily-life difficulties, he grants us the possibility through this
wisdom to do what is right by making good decisions. This is not a human
wisdom that comes from a certain intellectual and cultural development.
Instead, it is a gift from God. We must ask for it whenever we find ourselves
lacking in wisdom, that is, whenever we do not have the ability to understand what is happening and to decide what ought to be done. God will
freely give it to everyone who asks for it. We cannot conquer it by whatever
means it takes. It is a gift that God is at liberty to grant or not, without any
obligation, but we are given the promise of this gift. In the Gospels, we are
advised to ask for the Holy Spirit, which is the same thing. In each case, we
confront the difficulties of daily life in the knowledge that, above all, God
is the One who gives. Another way of saying this is that God is love. We
know this because Jesus Christ is the greatest and most perfect gift of them
all and the guarantee of everything God gives.

Our text informs us that God gives to everyone. No distinction is made
between the just and the unjust. This is exactly what Jesus tells us when he
declares that God makes the sun shine and the rain fall on both good and
evil people. Everyone can ask God for the gifts of the Holy Spirit or the
gift of wisdom. The text also tells us that God gives generously and un-
grudgingly, but the meaning of the Greek text is "without conditions and
without second thoughts." God does not have a specific objective or intention, as it were. There are no reasons for giving or for withholding, because he is the One who grants grace. There are no conditions attached
and no reproaches made. Nor is there any expectation of gratitude.

The gift of wisdom must be asked in faith without doubting. There is a
recognition of the possibility of the existence of doubt in our prayers. For
example, we may wonder whether God is really there and willing to listen
to us, or whether he really has the power to grant us what we ask. The
Greek verb usually translated as doubting means hesitating between two
things that cannot coexist together. This is a good definition of what constitutes doubting. It results from the contradiction between what we observe as being real and what the Word of God asks us to believe as being

true.[5] We cannot have both at the same time. For example, we may feel that God has not heard our prayer. We may confront death, while the Word of God speaks of the triumph of life over death. We may observe that nothing much has changed in our lives, even though the Word of God may tell us that we are saved. We simply cannot live as if what we experience and what the Word of God tells us are both true. Despite a common theological interpretation, doubt is not a contradiction of faith, as if the former excludes the latter. When we read the pronouncements of the Bible on this subject, I believe we can summarize them as follows: faith permits me to discern the reality of my doubt. In other words, there is doubt only where there is faith. For too long, certain theologians have declared that where there is doubt there no longer is faith, or that faith excludes the possibility of doubt. This is impossible. There can be doubt only where there is faith. If I did not live in faith, I could not possibly doubt. It is only when I believe in God's Word that I can face this contradiction.[6]

Faith makes me pray to God for the exclusion of doubt: Lord, I believe, rescue me from my unbelief. Doubt is a trial of faith. It purifies that faith and makes it grow by overcoming doubt. Faith will produce perseverance through these trials of doubt.

Finally, the granting of our prayer for wisdom is not a matter of making life easier. The text makes this clear when it says that doubters are double-minded and unstable in their ways. They are torn between what they experience and what they more or less believe, and between the reality of daily life and what in faith they know to be true. God grants wisdom in the face of the difficulties of the world, but he does not eliminate them. He grants joy through trials, but he does not remove them. We would rather that these trials be done away with, but instead God grants the means to overcome and transcend them. We pray for peace, and war comes, but even in war I know that God is our Father. We pray for health, and we find ourselves faced with death, but we know that via this death comes eternal life. As a result, those who doubt will not understand what is happening. They will be divided because they cannot conduct their lives or have their prayers heard because these prayers make almost no sense. They do not ask for the wisdom that would allow them to deal with and overcome the situation in which they find themselves. This reveals their predicament and the relationship between faith and doubt.

This is the first example of how the text integrates a diversity of issues. It is hardly a question of some simple moral advice. The text is much richer and deeper.

Money as a Test

In this text (James 1:9–15) we encounter the issue of money, with both riches and poverty being considered as trials, as well as the questions of temptation and coveting. It is a continuation of the teachings about trials, yet it introduces something new.

In order to understand the first two verses dealing with money, it is essential to recall the three fundamental biblical teachings on this matter.[7] First, in the Bible money is always a power in the world that we sacralize by behaving towards it as to a divinity. In other words, money is more than just an economic instrument: it is a power that we sacralize. Although Jesus occasionally mentions a demon or power, he almost never names one. Second, money is a sign of buying and selling as well as of alienation. The reason so much attention is paid to this issue in the Bible is that it represents the opposite of things being gratis, and thus the opposite of grace. Everything has a price and therefore nothing is free, while the sign of all God's actions is that everything is free and for nothing. In other words, the law of God is that of grace, while the law of money is that of buying and selling. Third, throughout the Bible we are told that money belongs to God, with the result that we do not own it. Although we believe ourselves to be the masters of this economic instrument that we have created, it is neither ours nor Mammon's but God's. There is only one way to destroy the power of money and that is to submit it to God's law of grace by giving it away.

In verses 9 to 11, all this is regarded from the perspective of money as a trial. There is a temptation in being poor as well as in being wealthy. The essential text is that of Proverbs 30:8–9, which cites the prayer of one of its authors: Grant me neither poverty nor wealth, but give me my necessary bread, so that in abundance I will not deny you by saying: Who is the Lord?; or that in poverty I do not steal and defile the name of my God. The temptations of poverty or wealth are in some ways the same. The rich believe that they no longer need God because they regard themselves as self-sufficient, while the poor may steal and "attack the name of my God" (literally translated). The common explanation that this deals with the protection of private property is perfectly stupid. The text must be understood in the context of a subsistence economy in which people had barely enough to survive, with the result that when you stole something from someone else, you were attacking his or her life. What you would steal in a society like the one found in the eighth century before Christ in Palestine would be the absolute bare minimum to live on, thus

making theft a decisive and fundamental act. As a result, defiling the
name of your God has a double element. Theft is an act against your
neighbour, and when your neighbour becomes poor, he or she is tempted to curse God and die, as explained throughout the Old Testament. In
other words, poverty and wealth represent a double temptation.

Our text explains that the poor can glorify themselves in their being
raised up. It goes directly against what we and most other people have
always believed, namely that the poor will do everything to improve their
lot and cease being poor, and that this is perfectly normal. So what is this
business of being raised up? In the Bible, poverty is multidimensional
and can involve not only a lack of money but also of social support or
social acceptance. It is really not a matter of the poor being raised up but
of Jesus lowering himself. Philippians 2 tells us that Jesus gave up being
God, became a human being, took on the role of a servant, and allowed
himself to be condemned and crucified. As one who gave up everything,
he is the model of what it is to be poor. It is on this level, as it were, where
he encounters the poor, which is why they are raised up to his level. In
other words, the poor are not being raised by providing them with money and the good things of the earth. Jesus encounters them, and that is
the relationship he has with them. Jesus says that it is to the poor that the
Kingdom of Heaven belongs, and this is what their glorification is all
about. Recall that in the Bible glorification has nothing whatsoever to do
with taking pride in being a good human being. To glorify yourself means
to reveal who you are. To glorify God means revealing God to someone.
When the Bible says that Jesus glorifies God, it means that Jesus reveals
who God is. In the same vein, in the Bible the woman is the glory of the
man, which means that she reveals who the man is. Since Jesus encounters us where we are, it is he who reveals who we are. Also, he reveals who
we are before God. In doing so he saves us in his role as our advocate who
puts himself in our place. Consequently, when the Bible speaks of the
poor being raised up it does not mean that they are better than anyone
else but that they have a unique relationship with Jesus Christ. When they
cease to be poor, this relationship changes. All this has nothing in common with our ideas that we can glorify God by singing hymns and engaging in worship.

When we are told that the poor glorify themselves in their being raised
up, this means that they reveal who they are by recognizing that they are
raised up instead of being humiliated because Jesus Christ is the one who
was poor. The teaching regarding the rich is the inverse. In verses 10 and
11, we read that the rich glorify themselves in their humiliation because

they will disappear like the flowers in the field, and what follows parallels the well-known text in Isaiah. In other words, in the letter of James, the rich cannot thank God for their wealth. This is a rather important difference with the Old Testament, where riches are taken as a kind of benediction from God. This was later turned into an entirely erroneous foundation of Protestant Puritanism, where riches became a kind of proof of God's benediction on the lives of the rich. They read the Old Testament and completely forgot about the New Testament.

What is meant by the humiliation of the rich? I do not agree with those who believe that this text calls on the rich to give up their wealth and to humble themselves in the same way as Jesus asked the rich young man to do in Mark 10. The text does not speak of the rich humbling themselves in this way but of their being humiliated because they will fade away in their pursuits. In other words, the rich will fail in their endeavours and face the probable loss of their wealth. Most of us react to this text with considerable scepticism. We have all heard of families who remain wealthy for generations. However, the text is addressed to fellow Christians, both rich and poor. Consequently, the heart of matter is whether Christians can remain wealthy and be believers at the same time. According to the text, the course of events will deprive the rich of their wealth, much as the sun withers the flowers in the field. I would almost say – and I know I am pushing the text in doing so – that God will in the end take away their wealth. I take this to be the case as well for those who have a great deal of political power in high office: they also cannot exercise that power and remain faithful.

There is more. The humiliation of the wealthy also includes words from God, perhaps not of condemnation, but certainly of warning. The rich are not close to God. They must face a very long journey before they reach Jesus Christ. I believe that the Christmas story is highly significant in this respect. The shepherds who represented the poor were present soon after the birth, but the wise men came from the east, having to travel a very long road. When they finally arrived, they presented the three gifts representing the three forms of wealth: power, money, and science. In the end, after a very long journey, they finally gave them up.

Nevertheless, the rich must also glorify themselves in their humiliation. How is it possible to do so when you know you are going to lose your wealth if you manage it in a way befitting a Christian? As an aside, the question is equally valid for many of our professions. In 1944 and 1945 we organized groups of professionals (including professors, lawyers, doctors, bankers, insurers, and business people) to carefully study the implications of the Bible for their work. The people who seriously tried to practise what they had learned quickly ran into impossible situations. This was not so much the case for professors, but for lawyers it was already more difficult because you may not defend a cause that is clearly unjust. It called us all into question. It was next to impossible to live our Christianity in our work.

However, I believe it is possible to glorify ourselves in what God has done for us because it means that God has turned himself towards us. God has turned himself towards the rich to address them despite their wealth. In this the rich can glorify themselves in their humiliation, even though they are faced with failure and with a word of condemnation if not outright rejection. It is a matter of revealing who they really are under these circumstances. When God calls them into question, announces their failure, and practically condemns them, is it still a Word of God when it is impossible to hear and to bear it? We can only make sense of this when we remember that the most terrible thing that can happen is when God no longer speaks to us. Such a situation is far worse than to face a God who is angry with us or even condemns us. Again and again in the Old Testament, people plead with God above all not to turn his face away from them because this would be absolutely unbearable. Hence, texts of this kind, in which God speaks a word of condemnation, mean that God is turned towards these people who in this case are rich. God has not turned away from them. He reaches out his hand towards them and helps them by his Word in order to warn them of the trap and temptation of wealth.

This matter of wealthy Christians who must glorify themselves in their humiliation reminds me of the story of Cain and Abel.[8] After God's refusal to accept Cain's sacrifice, he did not turn away. He addressed Cain by asking him why he looked so sad. Cain should have taken courage, since although God had refused his sacrifice, he continued to be with him. But this was exactly what Cain was unable to hear. After Cain murdered his brother Abel, God turned to him and pronounced that terrible condemnation. Cain pleaded with God, saying that this was too hard to bear and would be unendurable. God responded by telling Cain that he would not be killed because he would place his sign on him. In other words, Cain this condemned criminal was nevertheless under the protection of God. He was condemned, but God granted him grace. It is exactly the same for wealthy Christians.

I am also reminded of how Jesus felt about the young man who approached him to find out what he lacked. When Jesus told him to sell everything he had and give the money away, he was very sad and turned away. Even though he disobeyed, we are told quite explicitly that Jesus loved him. Although the young man could not get himself to give his wealth away, he was clearly not lost. In other words, when the rich are humiliated in this manner, they can nevertheless glorify themselves because God continues to be with them. Throughout their being tested by wealth, God reaches out to the rich in order that they not be possessed by their wealth. If they glorified themselves because of their wealth and status instead of their humiliation, then indeed they would be lost because they would no longer have any use for God. The text from Proverbs that I cited above is very clear on this point. If they confide in a power (the power of wealth), they no longer have any use for God.

In this text James cites Isaiah 40:6–8. Isaiah does not address the rich, but all human beings (all flesh is grass, which soon withers). Consequently, I believe that, by citing this text, James implies that in one way or another every human being is rich. We all have some kind of riches, which we must take into account before we look at our poverty. It puts us on guard to avoid our getting carried away when we feel particularly unhappy or deprived.

I would like to make three remarks regarding the use of these texts to keep the poor in their place. First, this kind of thinking did not come from the wealthy echelons within the Roman Empire. It represents a kind of thinking that emerged among the poor and the slaves. This kind of argument began in the seventeenth and eighteenth centuries when wealthy churches used it to control the poor, much as it is commonly used today. However, at the time this text was written, this kind of critique would have been absolutely false.

Second, the text we have been explaining is addressed to fellow Christians. It simply does not address the socio-economic issue of wealth. It deals with both rich and poor fellow Christians, and that is all. It is a teaching for Christians engaged in their faith and cannot be extrapolated to a social movement because that would be the opposite of biblical thinking.

Third, if we as Christians think that these texts can justify wealth and serve as an opium of the people, does that not reveal us as considering the material conditions of life to be by far the most important? Does that not show that we think that social and political questions are much more important than spiritual truth or ethical behaviour? If we interpret and judge these texts in this way, we obey an unconscious and materialistic presupposition that makes everyone today not only think this way but also accept it as self-evident. We take the position that human life is all about having or not having money, and that this determines everything else. The biblical text tells us the exact opposite – that this is not what counts most in life.

The last comment I would like to make regarding these three verses is that their message was exceedingly timely. It corresponds to a truth that, during the time that this letter was written, was becoming the doctrine of incarnation. It held that Jesus Christ, who was equal with God, and wealthy in the absolute sense, gave all that up. That is what incarnation meant: he gave up his riches, power, status, and eventually his life. Once again, it is exactly as described in the second chapter in Paul's letter to the Philippians. Jesus Christ gave up his power in becoming a human being; as a human being he gave up all power in order to become a servant; and as a servant he gave up all he had left, namely his life, in accepting being condemned to death. This process of the stripping away of all power is exactly what we find in our text. It in turn corresponds to the affirmation in the Old Testament that the powerful and the rich have no need for any assistance whatsoever. They have no need for God to sustain them in any way, with the result that God is not among them. As a result, the God who revealed himself to Abraham is always and only with the poor. He is with those people where this is absolutely indispensable because of weakness, vulnerability, poverty, or sickness. He is nowhere else. Consequently, these three verses of our text have enormous ethical and also social implications for the church. They are founded on both the Old Testament and the theological interpretation of who Jesus was in the New Testament.

In response to your questions, the fundamental importance of money in the Bible stems from its being the opposite of grace. It is also the exemplar and symbol of all forms of power, all forms of domination, and all forms of superiority. Moreover, what the text reveals about the rich is not limited to those who are rich in monetary terms. It applies equally to those who are rich in intelligence, political power, beauty, physical strength, and so on. All these riches of one kind or another are included when the Bible speaks of monetary riches. From a biblical perspective, I believe this is extremely important. For example, Solomon had every imaginable form of wealth and power. Things went so badly during his reign that God warned him that although he could hold on to them during his life, the situation would not continue with his children.

Similarly, in Israel the exercise of political power by the kings usually turned out very badly.[9] Generally speaking, when Christians took hold of political power, they did no better. They also did not hesitate to impose their moral values on everyone, including non-Christians. In France this pattern goes back to Charlemagne, who massacred the Saxons and converted Germany by threats of the exercise of power. Even St Louis, who is perhaps less guilty than most, was still the one who persecuted the Cathars. Jeanne d'Arc for me remains a tragic problem. I believe she was a saintly person, and she said some very remarkable things about faith, but everything turned out very badly. If she indeed heard voices, then I cannot understand God's politics in this affair. I believe that, had the French kingdom passed into the hands of the English, the course of events would have changed for the better. Since I cannot believe that God made a mistake here, there must have been a short-circuit somewhere. Since the Second World War, France has had two statesmen (one Catholic and one Protestant) who were unquestionably sincere, but they did a lot of stupid things.[10]

When Christians manipulate the powers, it always seems to turn out badly. The Bible tells us that the only counter-power, as it were, is the way of non-power. God chooses this approach when he accompanies humanity throughout its history. All our powers belong to him, that is, to his non-power. It may be helpful to read in the first chapter of the letter to the Corinthians, "Where are the wise, the learned, and the debaters of this age? Has God not made foolish the wisdom of the world, because the world with its wisdom has not known God through the wisdom of God? It has pleased God to save the believers by the folly of preaching. Jews demand miracles, Greeks search for wisdom, but we preach the crucified Christ (religious scandal for the Jews, foolishness for the unbelievers, but the power of God and the wisdom of God)." In other words, what is irreligious, what is sacrilege in the eyes of the Jews – that is the power of God. What is foolishness in terms of people's intelligence – that is the wisdom of God, because the foolishness of God is wiser than people. The choice of the non-power of God is what is destructive of the powers of humanity. It is not the "more" of power, but the "less" of power that will destroy the powers of humanity. We also need to remember that in the thirteenth chapter of the first letter to the Corinthians, we are told that if we gave away everything we owned without love, it would serve no purpose.

Following the way of non-power is to put ourselves entirely in God's hands and rely on his decision to grant grace. We find this extremely difficult if not unbearable. As a result, we constantly attempt to get around this by finding ways of placing our money, political influence, eloquence, or whatever power we have, at God's disposal; but this is exactly what

God constantly rejects. We are always looking for ways and means of not having to depend on God's grace in order to remain self-reliant, but we are warned of this danger. We are back to what we said earlier about our roles as servants, in the study of the opening chapters of Genesis and in the parables of the Kingdom of Heaven.[11]

When we are mindful that in the Bible riches represent any form of power and status, the possibility of having money may be eclipsed by being socially isolated, by traversing a period of mourning alone, by being shunned and despised by others, and so on. I would say that the real question is where we place our trust. With regard to riches, it is thus a question of our ultimately putting our trust in a power and status destined for destruction during the final judgment. Jesus points this out when he declares that where your heart is, there will be your life.

I have never understood how Protestantism could help pave the way for capitalism. Of course, I understand very well how, humanly and historically, this came about. By living modestly, humbly, and soberly and not spending any money on luxuries, people began to accumulate money and, in some cases, a great deal of capital. The Protestants were unique in not spending that money on anything, including church buildings. Such behaviour was at the root of the development of the capitalist system, which completely obliterated any notions of grace and the possibility of at least certain things being free and gratis. Everything had to be privatized and monetized. It was the demonic twisting of the process of reformation. However, God's grace makes us rich in the revelation and the hope it brings. It does so relative to those who do not share this hope, which in turn brings us back to the importance of this text and the need to live humbly.

In verses 12 to 15, we encounter three principal themes. They begin with the relationship between trials and our love for Jesus Christ. Next, the question is posed as to whether God tempts us. Finally, there is the business of coveting, which is absolutely fundamental. Beginning with the first theme, some of this overlaps with what we have already learned about trials and temptations, but there is something new as well. It is the relation between our love for Jesus Christ and the ability to endure temptations. "Blessed are those who patiently endure temptations, because after having been tested, they will receive the crown of life that the Lord has promised to those who love him." It is not energy, courage, virtue, attitude, education, or anything else that permits us to withstand a temptation or trial. It is by the love of Jesus Christ that we can do so. Why is this the case? It is a matter of loving Jesus Christ more than what may tempt us, which permits us to resist a temptation. In other words, the problem with regard to money, or any other object of power, is ultimately a question of love. Those who can resist the temptation of having money or the temptation of not having it are those who love Jesus Christ.

By implication, our love binds us to what we love. If we love the Lord (it is significant that this title is not used everywhere in this letter), we attach ourselves to the one who has passed through death, is resurrected, and has overcome all temptations, including death. He is victorious and gives the crown of life. Hence, if we love him, and are attached to him, then he will help us overcome all temptations. In other words, to love money or to love the Lord has absolutely nothing to do with morality, nor with any moral legalisms. The law is replaced by love, around which everything turns and by which we can understand and overcome temptations. The reason for this is that all temptations force us to face the question of whom or what we love. For whom or for what do we really live our lives? Do I live for my money? Do I live for my power and influence? Or do I live for love of Jesus Christ? Trials force us, one way or another, to decide what are the fundamental values of our lives.

To love God and Jesus Christ is not at all about following a stream of moral and spiritual sentiments. Nor is it an intellectual construction by a distinguished theologian. Instead, it has to do with the difficulties of our daily lives and patiently persevering while being tested. It is the outcome of these tests that will show who or what we really love.

The second question raised by this text is whether God wills or permits temptations. James first eliminates the usual excuse that God, in tempting us, is responsible for the consequences. The first instance of this is found in the book of Genesis, when Adam answers God that he was tempted and seduced by the woman he was given. He thus tries to shift the blame to God. James brushes all these kinds of excuses aside by saying that no one should claim that God tempted them.

However, in the preamble to the book of Job, we are told that God permitted Job to be tempted. Satan (the accuser) appears before God and questions Job's faithfulness and piety by suggesting that these are simply the result of God having made him very rich and granting him every possible blessing. God responds that Satan can take all this away, but that he cannot touch his life. Hence, God permits Job to be exposed to a number of temptations.

The letter of James completely eliminates all these demonic and satanic dimensions, leaving temptations as a completely human phenomenon. This creates some difficult theological problems, but we are nevertheless clearly told that God does not tempt us.[12] James makes it very clear that temptations are the result of our coveting. We are tempted when we covet something, which gives rise to sin, and this sin produces death. This teaching regarding the role of coveting in human life is a fundamental and central theme in the Bible.

Coveting is a perversion of desiring. Adam was created with desires; and in and of themselves, these desires were not evil. They represented the wish to enjoy everything around him that God had created. As such, desires were an element of the freedom God wished him to have. It is this desire that turned Adam towards other animals and towards the woman, and turned her towards him and also towards God. In a sense, these desires were the equivalent of God's desire to create. God wanted to create, and he acted on it.

After the relationship between God and Adam was severed, these desires became something entirely different. They were no longer integral to a universe that was one with God. Desires became something else, as described in the covenant with Noah, namely, they became an expression of the spirit of power. Covetousness is the desire to possess more and more things, to dominate others, and to be master of one's own life. The latter includes relying on your own strengths, and yourself bringing about what is good. The understanding that this will to power and this will to dominate are the exact opposite of love and freedom goes to the very heart of what is at stake. This is why coveting is the last of the ten Words of the Decalogue: You will not covet. Everything else depends on it. People create other gods, steal, or kill because they covet something else. This tenth Word is the motive of the other nine, as it were. Throughout the Bible, coveting is revealed as the very depth of our being human. It monetizes itself; it leads to selfishness; it leads to pride and many other secondary expressions of it. These in turn trigger the temptations because we really love something else above Jesus Christ. We may then attempt to explain this by claiming that God tempted us in the first place by placing us in the situation that gave rise to these temptations. However, if we say that God tempts us we accuse him, thus showing that we do not love and trust him. We are back to whom or what we ultimately love. It cannot be our power and wealth as well as Jesus Christ. If I covet I do not love Jesus Christ. Loving him can never be a question of attempting to control him – a theological coveting. Loving Jesus Christ and being attached to him rules out coveting, dominating others, accumulating riches, and so on.

To give free rein to coveting leads to behaviour that produces evil and harms God and our neighbour. All the harm we do to those around us

always comes from a spirit of power and domination, that is, from coveting as the will to possess others. As our text explains, evil produces death.
In other words, covetousness reveals where I am, namely, separated from
God. If God is the living one, this means that where I am is death. James
uses this argument to uncover our personal responsibility. Whether temptation comes from others or from myself, it remains on the level of inter-
personal relationships and thus is a human phenomenon. We cannot
blame God, society, our family, or heredity for the evil we do. It all grows
out of covetousness. We may be able to use psychoanalytic approaches to
discover some of its elements, or even to reveal that coveting appears to
be at the centre of our being, but that would only confirm the processes
described in James. As a final note, we may now interpret Satan's accusation of Job as an act of covetousness, of Job's attitude to God, and the
possibility of a person being just.

The fundamental importance of coveting is encountered throughout
the Bible. I will give several examples. It can be the will always to possess
more than we have. It dominates the wealthy, who never have enough.
The desires of the kings always involved dominating everyone. Another
expression of coveting is the claim of conducting our life by our own
strengths without any need for God, without any truth other than ourselves, or without acknowledging any good outside of ourselves. Such coveting commonly leads to a desire to judge God, which presupposes a
greater good than he is. For example, when we claim that God is not just,
we are inferring that there is a justice superior to his by which we can
judge him. We encounter this as far back as Eve, who desired to judge for
herself what was good and what was evil.[13] All these situations are manifestations of coveting. Its role and place in human life are so fundamental
that it is dealt with in the last of the Ten Commandments. It is not a matter
of its being least important but of its concluding and summing up all the
others, which thus may be understood as forms of coveting. As our text
puts it, coveting gives birth (literally in the manner of an animal bringing
down its young behind it) to sin, and sin engenders death. The words
used in the Greek text are unusual and rarely used. The death referred to
is probably not a physical but a spiritual death, in the sense of life becoming absurd because of anomie – a complete absence of meaning.

Our text describes the process as human, in the sense that it does not
come from God. We are fully responsible, although there is no implication that we are able to master it. I believe this is very important in a society like ours where what people do tends to be attributed to family,
heredity, education, poverty, unhappiness, and the list goes on and on.

There is always a social explanation, as it were. I must say that judging from my personal experience, having worked with troubled youth for twenty years in the Club de Prévention,[14] all human attitudes are able to engender evil. It simply is not true that these kids come from "bad" families. I am almost tempted to say that it is the opposite. They often come from perfectly normal families and have received a good upbringing.[15] Of course, there are contributing factors, but that does not take away from the fact that it ultimately is a matter of the heart and the process explained in the text.

Beginning a New Life

The first fifteen verses of this letter of James have what may be called an existential character. They deal with the daily lives of Christians as they are being tested while in the grip of covetousness. From this perspective, these verses are a preamble to what follows. Given the existential situation of our daily lives, what kind of Christian life is possible? The letter now turns to dealing with this ethical question.

I believe this text (James 1:16–21) deals with five themes: an introduction to morality and the Christian life, the new birth through the Word, the creative Word, hearing the Word, and putting the Word into practice. The theme throughout is the Word. The first three themes are covered in chapter 1:16–18 and the last two in chapter 1:19–21.

Everything good done by human beings (every excellent grace and perfect gift, according to the Greek) comes from God. In the first phrase, James deliberately introduces a play on words. The word "grace" refers at the same time to the grace we receive and to every expression in our lives of what is happy. The Greek word contains both elements. The excellence of this grace, which God grants us, roughly corresponds to saving us in this moment. A similar play on words occurs in "every perfect gift." It refers to the gifts we have in our person as well as to those moments in our life when we have received something. All this comes from God. What this implies is that God is not testing us and that he cannot be held responsible for our being tempted by what we covet. Instead, he is responsible for everything good in our lives, which means that we can never glorify ourselves by our works. It also means that the entire Christian ethic that follows can be lived only by grace. The Christian life is a gift.

I believe that it is here that we have the answer to an endless debate that has gone on for centuries, seeking to resolve the tension between the emphasis of James on works and the emphasis of Paul on grace.

James begins his discussion of the Christian life by pointing to the fundamental importance of grace. Following this, he turns to other aspects of
this life, but they must always be interpreted as beginning with God's
grace. James warns us not to have any illusions that we invent the good
we do. This perspective is the diametrical opposite of saving ourselves by
our works.

All excellent grace and all perfect gifts come from the "Father of lights,"
with whom there is no change or a shadow of variation. The "Father of
lights" brings back the question of light, especially in the prologue to the
gospel of John, reminding us that there is no light without the night. We
might say that light creates the difference between the two. This is fundamental in the letter of James because the Christian life exists only because
of the world. It is in relation to this world separated from God that the
light has meaning. In the same way, the Christian life also creates a difference and a distance between it and the world. In other words, there is
nothing extraordinary about Christians other than their being placed in
and relating to the world.

The text adds that with God there is neither change nor a shadow of
variation. It is directly related to what we were told in the sixth verse,
where those who doubt are compared to the waves of the sea blown by
the wind. They are unresolved, they lack constancy in their ways, and as
Paul puts it, are swept along by every new doctrine. Here we find the
same idea in verses 14 and 15 applied to coveting, characterized by in-
consistency and constant change. In contrast, the "Father of lights" is
described as the one in whom there is no change or shadow of variation,
that is, he remains the same Father.

In traditional church theology, this teaching was transposed into the
language of philosophy as an attribute of God, namely, his immutability.
Eternity became a kind of solid block that could not be changed or varied by anything. This immutability of God became a fundamental theological concept. For example, it can be found in the work of Calvin and,
to a lesser extent, in Luther's writings. It placed people in the presence
of a God who could not be moved.

As tempting as it may have been to imagine God in this way, it is completely unbiblical. The God of the Bible is not immovable at all. It was
the result of projecting on God the characterology of the gods of Greek
philosophy. In contrast, the God of the Bible not only exists in history
but also participates in the history of humanity and follows his people.
The Bible tells us that he repents, decides, comes, or goes, and does a
great deal else. I am not suggesting that this does not raise other difficult

theological issues. The experience of the Jewish people and of Jesus confirms a God intermingled, as it were, with history and people's lives. He changes his pedagogy. He tries something, and when it fails, he may even reverse his decision. All this makes him hardly immutable. In any case, we cannot know whether this is what God is like in his entirety, or whether it is the face he reveals as the One who is with us, who follows our individual and collective lives and who constantly remakes his relationships with the Jewish people and the church, but also with us individually. We cannot know whether all of God is present in his revelation, or whether there is something more and other beyond what we call God. There have been two interpretations of this issue. For some, all of God is in history. He is integrally revealed in the Bible to the people of Israel and in Jesus Christ, and we may not think there is another dimension. The risk of such an interpretation is that it can easily slide into the kind of theology exemplified by "God is dead," which means that in the twentieth century the God envisaged in the eighteenth and nineteenth centuries was indeed no more. According to it, we only know Jesus, hence the only thing that should interest us is the historical Jesus, and the rest is not worth bothering with.

Others, including myself, take a position that is very close to those of the nominalists of the Middle Ages, who held that what God wishes to reveal of himself is in the Bible, but this does not mean that there is nothing more. Without question, God is entirely in Jesus Christ, but I can certainly not fully grasp the union of the two natures (to use the classical expression), nor what we mean when we say that God is fully in Jesus. It is certainly something else than Jesus the man in his human nature resolving all the issues of the divine. For myself, there is certainly more and beyond this, as it were, but this is not my business, because everything that concerns me has been revealed.

If we adopt this perspective, what are the implications for our text, which, in opposition to human beings who drift with every current, reveals that with the "Father of lights" there is neither change nor a shadow of variation? It is essentially a question of God's being a faithful and dependable Father. When he says something, he keeps his Word, and when he promises something, he will do it. It is this that is invariable with God: his promise lasts forever, and his Word is forever. If we take this revelation seriously, we cannot claim that there are contradictions from one revelation to another, nor can there be any changes in God's commandments. Jesus is very clear on this point when he says that he keeps the commandments to the letter and does not abolish a single one of them.

He does not cancel anything that has been revealed. It is this faithfulness of God with respect to his Word that for us represents God's permanence. Even though the way God is present in our history varies, what he says and promises endures.

Some commentators have observed that in Greek the phrase "Father of Lights" came from the astronomy of those days. It evoked the movement of the sun, the solstice, what was referred to as the balancing of the stars, and their shadows. It means that God is not subject to the forces of the stars, which in the astrology of those days was regarded as determining people's lives. If God is not affected by these powers because he dominates them, then he is able to grant freedom to people. For the Greeks, it also meant a liberation from stoicism, which was dominated by astronomy.

In sum, God is the Living One. He has revealed that he chose to accompany us on our historical journey. In doing so he uses various approaches and pedagogies to deal with our rebellion against him and to bring about reconciliation. However, what never changes are his grace, promises, and love. The book of Jonah provides us with an excellent example.[16]

Verse 18 links what we have learned thus far to the importance of the Word. We learn two new things. First, the Christian life begins with a new birth. This life is neither an intellectual adhesion to a doctrine nor another morality. Instead, it is a renewal of people in their very being. Jesus speaks about how they are rooted: a good tree cannot produce bad fruit and a bad tree cannot produce good fruit. It is not the fruit but the tree itself that matters most. It is the same with this renewal of our whole being, which is compared to a new birth. It is as radical as our first birth: a new existence comes into being that was not there before. Prior to this second birth, we did not exist in God, as it were. After it, we come to life in God. There is a complete break. Moreover, the comparison to our first birth reminds us that in our second birth, just as in the first, we did not actively participate as wanting to be born. It happens unexpectedly. Verse 18 says clearly that God makes this happen according to his will; and verse 21 complements this by telling us that the Word has been planted within us. Once again, this is an intervention of grace, which is free. We did not desire it, buy it, or earn it in any way. Paul says the same thing: it does not depend on those who want it or run for it. It is an intervention of God.

Verse 18 also tells us that God chose to give us birth so that we may become the first fruits of everything he created. The Old Testament has explained the importance of the first fruits: a portion of the harvest was dedicated to God in recognition that the entire harvest came from him. This portion was an image or symbol of giving everything. At the same

time, the first fruits were also what God gave as a promise of what would
follow, as in the case of the first born. In other words, there are two reciprocal dimensions to the first fruits. There is a harvest, of which a first
portion is given to God in recognition that, in the end, everything comes
from him. Reciprocally, this first fruit bears the promise of a new Creation
to come.

Our text must be understood in this way. In this world of separation
from God, there must be people who do not follow their destiny because
they are born anew. The transformation of this world into a new Creation
does not come all at once, because that would mean the end of this world
and the beginning of the kingdom of God. In other words, God chooses
a part to represent the whole. The people of Israel were chosen to represent all the nations, and those who were chosen within it were to represent all of Israel. As we will see, this pattern continued with the Christians.

After the first newborn, who was Jesus Christ, God continues to engender newborns so that we may be the first fruits of all he created. Those
who receive this new birth by grace and the intervention of the Word do
so not for their own benefit and their own salvation. The text does not
say that God gives us a new birth in order to save us. The text says something else. We are given a new birth so that we can play a certain role in
the Creation. We are given a place, a function, or a mission. So often
Christians have turned God's grace or their knowledge of the revelation
into a privilege when, in the Bible, this is never a matter of privilege.
When God reveals himself, it is always to charge us with a mission; and
this mission, according to our text, is to be the first fruits of a new world.
It is this teaching that characterizes everything that follows in the letter
of James. Who must we be and how should we behave as the first fruits
who bear God's promise in the midst of this world? It is not a question of
how we must behave to please God or to be saved. We have been placed
in this world in order to assure it that its future is not a catastrophe or a
death but the Resurrection and the kingdom of God. This must now be
addressed in the most concrete terms.

God grants a new birth by the Word. There is but one Word, which
means that this Word is always the same as the Word that creates. In
Genesis, God created everything by his Word, and it is by this same Word
that he created Jesus in the Virgin Mary. It has been traditionally described as the virgin birth, or the birth by the Holy Spirit. It reminds me
of the statues of the Virgin I have seen in Frankfurt, where a tiny angel
enters her ear. This is exactly what is happening. It is God's creative Word
that enters into the Virgin and creates a new being. It is at the heart of

the meaning of Christmas. God's Word continues to be the same when it is addressed to each one of us. It engenders something new in us.

We must accept this Word of God in all its dimensions. It is the Word that we read in the Bible, hear being preached, and so on. It is a power capable of re-creating human beings. This Word continues to be creative, and in the end will bring forth the new Creation.

I believe this to be a fundamental theme in the Bible. From the beginning, the Jewish people designated the creative power as the Word. In the same vein, what was regarded as making us human was our ability to speak. One of the interpretations of humanity as being in the image of God is that, like God, human beings speak. In Jewish theology, God creates relationships by means of the Word. In the New Testament, this Word is incarnated in Jesus, who is the fullness of the Word according to the prologue to the gospel of John.[17] What this means is that he is the totality of God's act of reconciliation on earth. The Creation was a reconciliation of everything that formed a whole. The new Creation is also a reconciliation. The dual nature of Jesus Christ means the reconciliation of God and humanity.

Next, let us take a look at verses 19 to 21. As people who are born by the Word, our first act is to listen. This listening is more important than the actions we take because these actions depend on what we hear. When we ask ourselves what we should do ourselves or what the church should be doing, we must begin by listening. Many commentators believe that what James has in mind here is the church service, where we should listen and be slow to speak – a kind of order for the service so that we do not all speak at once, and so on. Ecclesiastes 5:2 confirms this. Other commentators think that this text refers to the preaching of the Word during the service, which reproduces the miracle of our new birth. Understood in this manner, an enormous importance is given to the Mass or the worship service, making the Christian life deeply dependent on it. From this perspective, it is not difficult to understand why, after a few centuries, attending Mass became an obligation. By hearing the Word, the members of the church were recreated. It is hard to believe that, almost automatically, when we hear a sermon preached we hear the Word of God, and that again and again we are made new. The Bible appears to indicate the opposite, since the Word of God is always surprising and is often heard when and where people least expect it. God decides when to speak, and that is all. Hence, we must be patient in our listening, and when we do listen it must fully engage us. Careful listening is an active rather than a passive activity.

We must guard against speaking whenever and however we feel like it. This is not only the case for what we say in general, but also for what we say in prayer. Jesus warns us to be plain and sober with our words. When we listen to the Bible, we should do our utmost not to read our ideas and interpretations into it. To use the traditional Protestant expression: we must read the Bible having made a silence within ourselves. All this has further implications, as, for example, when we bear witness. This must never be done carelessly and with a flood of words, because we will run the risk of converting the other to our view of things. We must, as much as possible, allow the Word to speak for itself and substitute our words as little as possible. Among other things, this precept is clearly aimed at the danger of substituting the words of theologians for the Word of God. At this point, the denomination becomes much more important than the truth. This happens when the church speaks in the place of God or when the institution comes before everything else. All this has enormous implications.

In this exhortation, to listen and to be slow to speak, we encounter the problem of anger. The relationship is concrete and practical. I believe that words spoken in anger in the church are almost always false words when people use God's Word in this way. We must never use the Word to find means within it by which others can be judged. As the text explains, human anger does not accomplish God's justice. We must not use God's Word to fuel our anger. We must strongly mistrust any attempt to base our arguments on biblical texts in order to condemn a particular group of people, a certain political orientation, a moral choice, and so on. When we do this, we put our anger in the place of God's Word. We must always remember that when the prophets pronounce a Word of God, it is never simply a question of warnings, judgments, punishments, and so on. These are always integral to a Word that creates. It is never a curse on people. It moves beyond the warnings and condemnations in order to create something new.

In other words, our most passionate defence of God is a bad thing. So is our most spirited defence of the truth of the Bible. So is any attempt to take God's cause in hand. Even what is sometimes referred to as a holy anger can never accomplish God's justice, because his justice is for salvation, while our anger is unto death. Jesus puts it very succinctly in the Sermon on the Mount in the gospel of Matthew, when he says that when you are angry at someone and you treat that person as a dog, you have killed him or her. It all fits together. We must not listen to God's Word in order to speak for ourselves or use it to kill someone. Anything done in anger always kills. It reveals our orientation with regard to the Word of God.

The justice of God to which our text refers may be interpreted in three ways. First, it refers to what is just in the eyes of God. Second, in the Old Testament, this justice is the rights God has with regard to his Creation, which are expressed in his covenant with it. When this covenant is obeyed, justice reigns. Finally, as Paul puts it, justice is the power of justification, which refers to the power God has in Jesus Christ to make us just. Our anger clearly has no place in this whatsoever because it puts us in God's place in order to judge. The result will certainly not be the justice of God.

How does the anger of the prophets fit into all of this? To answer this question, we must confront the possibility that, generally speaking, we interpret the prophets rather poorly. As I explained in the study of Amos, the prophet has an intimate knowledge of the historical situation in which he finds himself. Based on this understanding, he announces what is going to happen if people continue as they are. He does not say that God will punish them but that they must interpret what will happen as coming from God: a call to repent and to change direction. What the prophet announces is certainly not a curse for eternity.

The text invites us to receive the Word of God, which has been planted in us. Once again, we encounter this dialectical "play" of ideas so common in the Bible. It is always related to the freedom of human beings within the freedom of God. In other words, when you hear the Word of God, it has been planted in you whether you like it or not. At the same time, we must receive this Word now that it is there. Logically, this makes no sense. If the Word has been planted, I do not need to receive it, and if I receive it, it has not already been planted. However, in the dialectics of the Bible, these two aspects affect one another in a reciprocal fashion. We need to do it in a responsible and voluntary way, much like a baby at birth seems to manifest the will to live.

The text introduces what I believe to be our role in all of this. Even though the Word has already been implanted in us, it requires a deliberate act on our part to receive it. Doing so is our responsibility. Our new birth cannot take place unless we accept it. It is for this very reason that Mary's response to the announcement of her pregnancy by the angel is so exemplary. God's Word will create a child in her, but she accepts this. Our attitude may never be one of indifference – that is, arguing that if God does something, it is done and I do not need to do anything. God works with us, and we must act because he is with us. God does everything, but if we do nothing, nothing will happen. This is how Jesus acted when he fed the crowd. He had the disciples gather up what there was to eat: some loaves of bread and a few fish. He then multiplied these to feed everyone. In other words, if the disciples had not done their part, there would have been nothing to eat. What little we can do we must bring to God, and he will multiply it beyond anything we could have imagined or hoped for. God always takes what we do into account.

A more delicate problem is posed when the text declares that we must receive the Word and reject defilement and all excess of malice. We have the same dialectics in rejecting defilement: the Word purifies us, and at the same time we must purify ourselves. What are we to make of defilement? We can immediately rule out considering anything sexual as the "sin of sins." In the Bible, sexuality is never equated with defilement. We are dealing with something much more fundamental. Must we interpret this text as a theology or a code of the sacred, of which we find a number of aspects in the Old Testament? Some commentators have argued that certain texts forbid the touching or eating of certain things because they are defiled. They suggest that all such texts are elements of a code of the sacred because defilement can occur only as a result of the presence of a sacred. When the people of that time asked their rabbi how they could identify the sacred objects, they might have been told that these were the ones which, when touched, required the washing of their hands. The sacred is defined as our being defiled by it, thus requiring purification. All this relates to the sacred, religious rites, and magic in the religions of that time. However, does this mean that it meant the same thing for the Jews? Here we touch on one of the reasons that the letter of James is the most Jewish in character of all the New Testament writings.

I very much doubt that our text in James has much to do with the sacred and defilement by it. A little further on, the text speaks of preserving ourselves from the defilement of the world. This world, which is harshly judged in the letter of James, is not a matter of defilement by the sacred. Instead, this letter presents us with a remarkable instance of how Christian thinking takes the Jewish concept of defilement and interprets it further into something new. This evolution in meaning will become apparent when we examine the block of text following the one we are dealing with now. It is impossible to speak of defilement in relation to a code of the sacred, when verse 25 refers to those who intently look into the perfect law, the law of freedom. Furthermore, verse 27 tells us that the religion that is pure and faultless consists of visiting the orphans and widows in their distress. In other words, we have here a shift in meaning, as it were, because the new purity no longer results from ritual self-purification by magical and religious means. Instead, we encounter something entirely different, namely an entry into a domain of freedom, and a new law of

that freedom. It is exactly the same as in Peter's dream recorded in the
Acts of the Apostles. When he sees the descent from heaven of a cloth full
of food and hears an angel commanding him to eat, Peter refuses by answering that he may not eat animals that are unclean. The vision reap-
pears three times, and each time he is told that there is nothing impure
in it. There is thus a new freedom with regard to what until then had
been classified as unclean.

Henceforth, no human act or thing can be impure. Jesus says the same
thing when he declares that what makes us unclean is not what we eat
but what comes from our hearts in what we say. No longer is anything
impure in and of itself. Paul echoes this when he tells people that everything they eat or drink they must do for the glory of God. Everything may
be done for his glory, and nothing is excluded any longer.

In the light of these texts, what is defilement? I believe that it is ultimately a question of the heart, the words coming from the depths of our
being, and thus of not receiving the Word. To put it slightly differently:
the defilement that separates us from God is neither things, nor even our
sins, but our unwillingness to hear the Word of forgiveness. Our defilement is our unwillingness to allow God to forgive us. It turns everything
into defilement. In contrast, the moment I receive the Word and understand that I have been forgiven, I become free, and nothing is defiled any
longer. This is the correspondence between receiving the Word and rejecting defilement.

That leaves us with making sense of the phrase "an excess of malice."
The original Greek text is somewhat perplexing because it speaks of malice in the positive sense, as related to intelligence. I believe the translators were confused, thinking that this could not be possible. Hence, they
translated the meaning of the Greek term in a negative sense. However,
it speaks of an excess of intellectual refinement because God's Word can
be received in all simplicity, as was the case with Mary's obedience. Hence,
the Greek phrase designates an excess of intellectual refinement when
it comes to understanding God's Word. It is obviously aimed at theologians! However, James is not an anti-intellectual. If a person has a high
level of intellectual development, that is part of who he or she is, and the
text certainly does not imply that you must give this up. We are simply
warned against the excess, so that we do not get carried away with our
own explanations, but receive the Word with the greatest simplicity.
Failure to do so means that the Word is no longer planted within us, and
that it can no longer transform our lives. It poses the same question we
encountered when we studied the parables of the kingdom of heaven

regarding those who had been invited to the wedding banquet but did not put on their festive garments. They were rejected because they had not done what little was within their own power, namely, to change their garments. In the same way, we must make the effort to receive the Word with simplicity even when we are intellectuals. We must remember that in the true wisdom of the church, the doctor (the equivalent of the modern theologian) is the last (least) in the list of the ministries because he or she runs the risk of having the greatest authority and power.

The Word and the New Life

In these verses (James 1:22–5 and 2:12–13), we encounter two main themes: putting the Word into practice, and freedom. The former is the third step in the development of what, in a highly condensed form, may be thought of as the Christian life. The first step was the new birth (1:18). The second was listening to the Word (1:19). The next step is putting this Word into practice (1:22). These three steps belong together because the life in Christ is one. Because we are born anew, we are called to live, and thus to act. Doing so involves putting things into practice. In the same vein, those who do not act do not live; and we will encounter this several times in the letter of James. Because we have heard the Word, we must put it into practice. Conversely, we can neither act nor put it into practice other than by listening to the Word and having been born anew. The three elements of the Christian life are so closely interrelated that you cannot have one without the other two.

Next, let us take a closer look at verses 22–4. The Word of God does not lead us to the kind of knowledge that is purely intellectual. To transform it into an objective, formal, and theological system would lead to our condemnation. For example, in chapter 2:19 (to which we shall return), we are told that if you believe in the one true God, that is good, but the devils believe it as well, and they tremble. In other words, faith alone is not sufficient, nor is the knowledge that there is only one true God. Hence, intellectualizing our knowledge of the Word of God is not a good thing. Remember the following three things. First, this is exactly the position in which Adam puts himself when he appropriates the tree of the knowledge of good and evil for his own benefit. His ability to discern good and evil is of a purely intellectual character because he acquires it through disobedience and by substituting himself for God's decision regarding good and evil. As a result, Adam now ultimately knows only one thing; that he is separated from God. This knowledge is what the devils possess, and they tremble because they are separated from and outside of God.

The second element that we need to keep in mind is that the knowledge of the Word of God needs to be put into practice. The decisive text
is the parable about the building of a house (found in Matthew 7, beginning with verse 24). The people who hear the words of Jesus and put
them into practice are like a wise person who builds a house on a rock.
It can withstand the elements because of this foundation. However, those
who hear his words but do not put them into practice are like a foolish
person who builds a house on the sand, and this house does not withstand the elements. The traditional explanation as to why the first house
stands up to the elements is because the rock is Jesus Christ. However,
this is not what the text says. The rock is the putting into practice. There
are two persons each building a house, and the difference is that in the
one case what is heard is put into practice and in the other case it is not.
The person who did not do it is ruined because he built exclusively on
the basis of his intellectual knowledge of the Word of God, and it is safe
to say that this is even worse than not building at all. Once again, the
knowledge of the Word cannot remain purely intellectual. In the Bible,
there is an ongoing movement: the putting into practice, which makes
us discover the Word of God; and the Word of God, which induces and
results in the putting into practice. For those who know the thought of
Karl Marx, this may resonate with his dialectic between theory and prax-
is. I do not believe that I am forcing the text in saying this, or that Marx
drew his theory from this text (certainly not consciously).

Returning to the text, it tells us that it is possible to stop hearing the
Word, either by forgetting (forgetting your face that you saw in the mirror) or by making a mistake as a consequence of false reasoning. In the
latter case, this false reasoning is an intellectual process that avoids putting the Word into practice because of the mistaken conviction that we do
not need to do so. Such a mistaken conviction can be one of the unfortunate consequences of having a good theology. (I did not say a bad theology!) There is no better theology than that the Word of God acting
powerfully within us is sufficient to save us. It is the doctrine that we are
saved by grace through faith, and yet this doctrine can be catastrophic in
its consequences. It turns into a self-justification: I do not need to do anything because God saves me by grace. It is the false reasoning of our text
that, because God does everything, I do not need to do anything. It is one
of the risks of Luther's theology, for example. In all such cases of false
reasoning, we deceive our person and our heart with all its desires, anxiet-
ies, repentances, and much more, and we mistakenly reassure ourselves.

There is a third element in our text. It compares people who listen to the Word but who do not do what it says to people who look at their face in the mirror and after doing so go away and immediately forget what they look like. The mirror symbolizes the Word of God. In other words, we have heard the Word, which leaves us no illusions about who we really are, and also how distant we are from him in our sins. We also discover that we are within his love, having been pardoned. Those who claim that they do not need to put this Word into practice forget what that revelation has told them regarding themselves. The text warns us that there is the possibility that we hear the Word only as a revelation regarding God, a revelation from God about himself, and that as a consequence, we do nothing. We go on living as if we had never learned who we are truly are before God. In contrast, if the Word has revealed who we really are, our works putting it into practice will follow out of conviction. It is what we will want to do. Once more, we encounter the risks of a theology of grace and a theology of transcendence. An excellent theology regarding God alone forgets humanity. Such theologies essentially speak only of God. Doing so is good, but we cannot forget that the God of the Bible is the one who speaks to humanity about humanity. In a sense, we try to make ourselves better theologians than the Bible itself by focusing only on God's approach to us.

This teaching must be understood in the context of the Christian life, which has as its point of departure God's pardon and the possibility of a new birth and a new life. A new life cannot come from the world but only by putting God's Word into practice. Salvation is the very beginning of all of this and not something that happens at the end of that new life. There is no possible dilemma between a way that leads to salvation by faith and another by works, because both are intertwined in one new life. Grace is granted, and this is followed by putting the Word into practice. There can be no faith without works. We will encounter this later when James asks his readers to show him a faith that exists without works. Paul declares that we are saved by grace through faith, therefore work out your salvation with fear and trembling. It is another one of these logical contradictions: everything in our lives begins with the knowledge that we are saved from the very outset, and now we must get to work. Salvation does not come at the end of a long life of faith and works. It was granted at the very beginning.

We now reach a second main theme in the text, namely, freedom. After telling us about the importance of putting the Word into practice, the text examines what this is all about. Is it obedience to a law, a morality, or a religion? We are told that it is nothing else but the law of freedom. Verse 25 tells us that those who look in depth into the perfect law, the law of freedom, and who do not forget it but persevere in applying it will be happy in what they do. This verse should be read as a beatitude, namely, a Jewish form of expression that Jesus also used in the Sermon on the Mount. The translation of the opening phrase is rather poor. The Greek verb in this phrase is rarely used in classical Greek and only occurs twice in the New Testament. It is used in the gospel of Luke in 24:12, which describes the disciples of Jesus approaching the tomb after the Resurrection. Peter bends down and sees nothing but the strips of linen on the ground. The Greek verb translated as bending down is the same. Our text literally speaks of bending down to see the law of freedom. In other words, this law of freedom is not in the sky so that you must look up in order to see it. In contrast, the attitude with which God asks us to hear his Word involves bending down. In the other text, bending down was required to see how low Christ had stooped. In the same vein, following the law of freedom presupposes following the way of Christ – that of being the least by lowering yourself.

The Greek verb is followed by a rather remarkable phrase translated as "the perfect law, the law of freedom." The freedom referred to is first of all the freedom of God, which is obedient to nothing. The implication is that God saves us by pure grace, which obeys nothing and thus is not tied to the good or to the evil that we do. God is entirely free, and the salvation he grants us comes out of pure grace.

This freedom of God implies and leads to the freedom of humanity. The perfect law, the law of freedom, is not a law of morality or a law of imperatives. What God desires for humanity is its freedom. As a result, everything that is contrary to freedom is contrary to God. It also means that humanity is not free because of its own nature. If God is the one who liberates, it is obvious that he will not set us free from sin, evil, and oppression only to subject us to another form of slavery. All this is implied in this remarkable phrase: the perfect law, the law of freedom. The only relationship that can exist between God and his creatures is one of love. There can be no question of fear, servile obedience, or anything of the kind. The only definition we know of God is that he is love. The only expectation God has is to be loved because he loves; and there can be no such love without freedom. Relationships of love are freedom itself in every respect. There can be no other law and no other morality than the law and morality of freedom. Of course, this has absolutely nothing in common with the freedom of the French Revolution or that of Jean-Paul Sartre. This freedom is a work of God, which he creates in us.

As a result, listening to the Word of God sets us free. This is why this text follows verses 22, 23, and 24 regarding the Word and putting it into practice. This may appear self-evident, but it gets us into a rather difficult theological problem. The traditional argument goes roughly as follows: What happens when God speaks to us? If we are entirely enslaved to sin, and thus separated from God, we are incapable of hearing the Word of God as such, that is, the way people understand the words they speak to each other. For us to hear God's Word, it must be endowed with his power, in which case that Word imposes itself on us by means of that power. It would break our sins and any possible resistance we may have, thereby turning us into toys in God's hands, as it were. To oversimplify greatly: humanity is totally sinful, God's Word is totally powerful, and humanity is transformed by it. Although this is a caricature, it is essentially the Protestant interpretation.

The opposite interpretation is essentially that of the Roman Catholic tradition. We are not toys in God's hands, and therefore humanity cannot be entirely enslaved to sin. There is something left in humanity to which God's Word can appeal. In the Middle Ages, this was referred to as the third ear, which was the only good one capable of hearing the Word. There was thus an organ, as it were, which was adapted to receiving God's Word, and remained intact following the break with God.

I must confess, I find these kinds of arguments entirely foreign to the Bible. They represent logical mechanisms that all boil down to who or what has the greatest power. Is it God, his Word, or sin? This is not to be found in the Bible. In contrast, James tells us that when the Word of God is addressed to us, it places us in a position of freedom. Its intervention in our lives has no other consequences than our liberation.

We must take seriously what the Bible tells us, and avoid getting lost in logical arguments. What we find is that throughout the Bible, God is engaged in setting humanity free. Because his Word liberates us when it is spoken, we are free when we hear it. It seems to me that the way classical theology poses the problem of freedom is entirely false. The only demand God places on us is to conduct ourselves as free people. I would put it even more strongly by saying that our only obligation is to be free. The only law of our Christian life is Christian freedom. Hence, the putting into practice of God's Word is this freedom. Of course, this is different from what we call freedom from a philosophical or political perspective. Nevertheless, they do contain elements that derive from that freedom.

Our text tells us that those who lower themselves to find the perfect law, the law of freedom, and who get to work and persevere in that work, will be full of happiness in their actions. They live, are free, and are happy. This is an essential element when we speak of a Christian ethic or the Christian life.

I will now turn to the consequences of all of this by paying particular attention to verses 12 and 13 from chapter 2. What we find here is an orientation for life that is rather astonishing. We are told that we must speak and act as those who will be judged by a law of freedom because the law of judgment is without mercy. The first act of this law of freedom is to accept being judged. This acceptance however, does not turn us into condemned persons before a judge. It makes us accountable for ourselves and for others. I believe this is rather important, given our typical rebellion against having our lives judged.

Another important detail in these two verses is our having to choose our words and actions not in relation to a pre-determined morality or a set of commandments but as an expression of our freedom. If we have understood the relationship between freedom and love, namely, that love can express itself only in freedom, and that this freedom has no other form than love, then we are constantly confronted with a choice in whatever we do: which word or deed will best express the freedom God grants through his Word. How can we best manifest the love that is the very form of freedom? These are the kinds of questions we must constantly ask ourselves. There are no other moral issues because we will be judged by a law of freedom. What this means is that there can be no question whatsoever of the kind of judgment we habitually think of: an enumeration of all the good and the bad we have done, followed by a calculation of the balance between the two. If the balance is negative, we are in trouble, and if it is positive, we will be all right. With the law of freedom, there can be no such calculation, even of its necessity. In other words, in everything we do, we have to place ourselves within God's freedom, which meets our freedom. This is how it plays out, as it were. I freely choose without constraint, law, or imperative, the word or deed that appears to me as best expressing the freedom of God that he gives, and the love he extends. In doing so, I cannot expect a reward or a salvation of any kind. In the end, I will encounter God's freedom. It will assess my actions according to his sovereign and independent freedom, which meets my own freedom. I choose in all freedom, and God assesses in all freedom as well. This is the judgment that awaits us.

On a number of occasions I have spoken of love, but it must be noted that this word is not in our text. However, in verse 13 we find something akin and comparable to it, namely mercy. On the one hand, the text tells us that the judgment will be without mercy for those who show no mercy, and that, on the other hand, mercy triumphs over judgment. Where there is no love and no mercy, what will remain? There will be nothing left but a calculation. In other words, the text speaks of a relationship between two beings, which means that either there is a relationship of freedom and love or there is one of domination, constraint, and force – which necessarily ends up with a calculation. The text says that the judgment is without mercy for those who are not merciful. This means that there are two possibilities. Either we accept this judgment of the freedom of God, knowing that God is love and that this moves us towards a judgment that is free in his love, or we accept a judgment where we must give an account. It takes us back to what we learned from the parables of the kingdom of heaven. I would almost say that God does what we expected or wanted him to do all along, as we see in the parable of the talents. The third servant returns his one talent by saying that he knew his master to be hard and without mercy, even harvesting where he had not sown. God replies that because the servant thought of him in this way, he will be that way and behave accordingly. I believe this to be absolutely fundamental. If we completely place our faith and trust in the God of love and freedom, we will encounter this God of love and freedom. That is the role faith plays here. Verse 2:13 does not express a condition: either you show mercy or you will be condemned. Nor does this text threaten us; it simply describes how things will develop when there is no freedom because then there is necessarily a judgment without mercy and love. Where there is love, there is the love of God, and there will be no judgment. Mercy triumphs over judgment.

This teaching regarding freedom implies that there is a world without freedom. The freedom that God grants by his Word refers to something that the world cannot know or understand. We all experience this very strongly. When we talk to the people around us, we all understand our obligations, our moral duties, and our legal responsibilities integral to that ensemble of constraints within which we live. However, this is neither freedom nor love. The moment you try to live out freedom and love you are immediately lost. It is no longer possible to know what will happen in advance, because if we did, there is no freedom but only the constraint of what awaits us. To live in freedom and love requires a constant and active

imagination, and this the world cannot understand. This is why the putting into practice is so important. From the perspective of the Bible, we
cannot simply internalize this freedom in our hearts or limit it to something spiritual. It involves a complete and total change of our lives, and
that implies an intervention of some kind in our behaviour and in the
structures of our society. This is the reason why the first act of God's Word
in our lives involves a liberation that requires the exhortation that we must
put it into practice. There is a relationship between this putting into practice and the freedom we were given. Once again, it shows how rich and
finely structured this letter of James is, because this Word of God, which
liberates me, frees me also from the constraint of that Word itself. It is not
a Word of compulsion but one I choose myself as it sets me free. As we
know, God does not liberate us from one kind of slavery in order to impose another. A good that enslaves me is really an evil. A god who turns me
into his slave is an evil god and not the God of the Bible. In other words,
there can only be an exhortation to put things into practice. The moment
we are set free by God's Word, we are not obligated and can turn away
from it or forget it. When we know God's Word, the decision to be made is
ours. This decision cannot be determined in advance, nor can anyone
make it for me as I put into practice the freedom I have been granted. God
will certainly not do it for me, and no one else can do it either.

Given the freedom we have been granted, what are we to make of the
Ten Commandments? They are not imperatives but a new future of what
we may do. For example, the sixth commandment does not say that you
must not kill. Instead, it says you *will* not kill, which means that the future
before you is one in which your freedom is such that killing your neighbour is no longer necessary. If we kill we enter into the law of killing,
where murder leads to revenge, revenge to more murder, and so on. In
other words, this commandment, like all the others, marks the boundary
between life and death. The Jewish people were alive when they lived
within this law, and when they transgressed against it they entered into
the domain of death. It is not that God would punish them if they transgressed. God told his people how, in the exercise of their new freedom,
things worked in life and how they could avoid death. Their freedom was
a matter of being able to make choices – of being able to choose what appeared best to them – and their freedom in making these choices could
have only one measure, namely, love. God granted freedom to his people
in order to make love possible. Love is impossible under duress or necessity. It is worth noting that the Hebrew does not speak of *obeying* this
law but of *doing* it. The former expression implies being subjected to an

external law outside of us. The Hebrew expression implies something very different. The law exists only because we are there to do it, as it were. This Hebrew orientation is taken up in the Greek text in the expression of putting the Word into practice. The Greek literally says that we must become the people who realize the Word, in the sense of incorporating it into our daily lives. As a result, the Ten Commandments turn every moral obligation upside down by transforming every constraint into a promise.

In response to your questions, let us put Paul's saying that all things are permitted but not all things are useful into the context of a prostitute whom you do not love and may even detest. To have a relationship with her on that basis is to lose your own freedom. What the text shows is that the only thing you are not permitted to do is exactly that. God's law is one of liberty, seeking to set us free from everything that enslaves us.

The church forgets this all the time. The moment an appropriate response to a situation is found, it turns it into a rule, a doctrine, or a theology. It is then added to the stock of existing rules, dogmas, and theologies, which are then endlessly repeated, learned, and organized. The result is that all freedom is lost.

Ultimately, the difference between Christians and non-Christians is not a question of salvation for the former and damnation for the latter. The fundamental difference is that Christians know that they are loved by God and the others do not. Hence, when we speak to non-Christians regarding the Word, it must not be for the purpose of converting them and bringing them to our church. It is simply to pass on the joy of being loved by God, being accompanied by him in our lives, and knowing that our lives are not moving towards death but to the Resurrection. That is the good news and none other.

Chapter Twelve

The Other

Life without Religion?

A first reading of our texts (James 1:26–7 and 2:1–11) could leave us with the impression that they are rather superficial and morally a little simplistic. However, with further study, we quickly find that this is not the case.

I will begin with the last two verses of chapter 1. They describe the Christian life in three main themes, each of which will be worked out in the subsequent chapters, albeit in a slightly different order. The first theme deals with the importance of language and particularly the need to keep our tongues under control when speaking. The second theme deals with the importance of charity (in the broad sense of the term) as the only religion acceptable to God. This love for our neighbour is represented by caring for orphans and widows in their vulnerability. The third theme deals with the importance of a person's having been set apart and avoiding being defiled by the world. If you look at the rest of James's letter from this perspective, you will see that all of chapter 2 deals with our behaviour towards and support of others and our love for our neighbour. The third chapter up to the eleventh verse deals with the word, our use of language, and learning to keep our tongues on a tight reign. The remainder of the third chapter, all of the fourth chapter, and the beginning of chapter five deal with being defiled by the world. We now have a good idea of how this letter is put together. It begins with a general introduction, which we have been studying up to this point. We learn that the Christian life is constantly being tested, that wisdom is required for its conduct, that it entirely depends on listening to the Word, and that it follows the law of freedom. Next comes the body of the letter, which is divided into the above three parts related to putting the Word into practice. The conclusion deals with patience and prayer. The whole is very well put together, and even the plan is well integrated into the text. In addressing what the Christian life is, this letter is somewhat different from those of Paul, which may be characterized as being more theological in character.

The Christian life is one entity, so that the above three components are intertwined. For example, in the Christian life, visiting orphans and widows is not merely a question of rendering a social service. In order to truly visit them, we must ourselves be free from the defilement of the world, and that is not an easy task. To put it differently: the inner being of the person doing the visiting contributes fundamentally to the relationship. Moreover, this service of love involves speaking to the other, which requires knowing exactly what you are saying by keeping your tongue under control. Everything we do must be an integral part of the Christian life.

Our text also raises the problem of religion. As a result of the sociological and historical studies of religion, it has become generally accepted that the religious phenomenon corresponds to a need in the hearts of all people. We are seen as religious animals, and religion itself has become something natural. Everyone needs a religion. This interpretation poses some obvious questions for Christians. For example, in France following the Second World War, there was a long discussion about whether Judaism was any different from the religions of the surrounding Semitic peoples. It was pointed out that the ziggurats were a clear expression of a desire to ascend towards God, and for some, Judaism was no different. Others were not so sure. They pointed out that the Bible speaks only of the opposite movement, that of God descending towards his people. We already find this throughout the book of Genesis when, for example, God descends to communicate with Adam or to see the building of the Tower of Babel. In Jesus Christ, God fully descends to his people. Such differences led to the making of a distinction beween the revelation of God and all religions. I believe Karl Barth pushed this radical distinction between Christianity and all religions to its limits.[1] The revelation coming from God and received by humanity is the opposite of the religious acts of humanity. In the case of the former, God descends, while in the case of the latter, humanity ascends.

Only God can reveal himself to us, and he came among us in the person of Jesus Christ. However, this revelation never satisfies our religious needs and aspirations. The Bible makes this very clear. For example, when God is speaking with Moses on Mount Sinai, the Hebrew people immediately set out to create a god in the form of a golden calf to satisfy their religious needs. These clearly had not been met by the God who had liberated them from Egypt and was leading them towards the Promised Land. The people would now have a little god whom they could see and touch and who would always be available to them. The God revealéd to them had been experienced as the complete opposite.

Despite this opposition, it appears as if our text consecrates religion. It tells us that when people believe themselves to be religious but do not keep a tight rein on their tongues, their religion is in vain. The religion that is pure and faultless before God consists of visiting orphans and widows and preserving oneself from the defilement of the world. In reading this, we may well get the impression that James thoroughly confuses religion with Christianity because he appears to be talking about the latter. I believe that the text is a great deal more subtle than it may appear. Remember that it is addressed to a Greek audience and draws on the high level of its culture. These people would know very well that what they regarded as religion had nothing in common with what is described here. In their world, religion involved the sacred, sacrifices, rituals, services, piety, and mysteries. The text does not deal with any of these. Hence, it implicitly says that all these forms of religious expression have no meaning or value whatsoever. All these manifestations of a religion are simply worthless. In other words, the sacred and all its religious trappings must be replaced by the revelation, the descent of God towards humanity. The only form of religion (James does not speak of Christianity or of faith) that God accepts is not the religious services and the rituals but the love for your neighbour and preserving yourself from the defilement of the world.

This text corresponds to the one we find in Matthew 25 dealing with the judgment of the nations. It is a matter of feeding the hungry, providing clothing, nursing the ill, taking care of strangers, and visiting prisoners. The nations that did so question Jesus as to when they did these things for him. Jesus answers that every time they did these things for the least of their fellow human beings, they did it for him. The nations who failed to do so are cursed because of what they did to Jesus. It is important to be clear: the text does not speak of those who have received the revelation. It only speaks of the nations and their judgment. The Greek term translated as nations refers to those who do not know the revelation. If God accepts aiding those who are poor or in need as religion and religious acts from those who know nothing of it, he will surely not expect any less from those who have received that revelation. Our text thus turns the argument back to us as Christians. Because we have received the revelation, we are exempted from sacrifices, rituals, services, mysteries, and all the other religious trappings, but what about our love and responsibility for our neighbour? James has now set the stage for a long and detailed discussion of Christian works. It begins, in the opening verses of the second chapter, by invoking Jesus Christ and showing that our religion, as it were, is the same as the one expected of the nations. We have received the revelation, and that is good, but we also have religious needs as human beings, and these needs must be expressed in the same way: by keeping our language in check, by aid to the poor, and by acts of holiness that preserve our purity by avoiding defilement.

The opening verses of chapter 2 show that in Jesus Christ our religion, so to speak, is the same as it is for others. We receive the revelation from God, and that is good, but we must express our religious needs in the same way as everyone else. We cannot expect to touch God by the traditional religious trappings but by doing what was expected in the judgment of the nations in terms of what they did or did not do for Jesus (Matthew 25:31–46). We find ourselves in the same situation as everyone else. In other words, to know God's Word gives us no dispensation from this orientation, which is good for everyone. All this must have been extremely disturbing for the Greeks to whom this epistle was addressed, especially because it was perfectly interwoven with all the other texts in this letter of James. It is also a warning to us as Christians.

Throughout its history, Christianity has frequently been transformed into a religion. The tendency had already shown itself during Paul's ministry. He acknowledged that one of the gifts of the Spirit was the speaking in tongues: a language that was unknown and incomprehensible. Paul warned that this has no significance or value unless there is someone to interpret what has been said. It is another instance of keeping our tongues under control. Paul thus barred the way to the usual religious experiences with which everyone of that time was familiar: the mysteries, ecstasies, being seized by a god, and a general and complete lack of control over what was said. What Paul did with regard to the speaking in tongues, we must continue for every religious manifestation in our churches. We cannot escape the fact that wherever there is a church, there is an institution and services with a liturgy. We are constantly transforming all this into a religion. Our lives demonstrate that we have religious needs like everyone else, but Christians are called upon to live differently. We must begin by holding our tongues while we listen to what God has to say, and then we may speak. We must show the love of Jesus Christ for our neighbour and allow the Holy Spirit to purify us from the defilement of the world. I do not believe that I am forcing the text when I say that it is the work of the Trinity: God speaks, Jesus Christ expresses his love through us, and the

Holy Spirit purifies us. These are the three fundamental themes of this letter of James.

In response to your questions, the purification from the defilement of the world will be dealt with later in this letter. It refers to what in the Hebrew Bible was regarded as the code of holiness. It is not simply a matter of sins against the commandments but of conformity with the powers of evil at work in the world. As an example, Satan is the power of accusation in the Bible and is present whenever someone is accused. This teaching presents a very difficult problem for a Christian working for the attorney general's office or its equivalent, which is in the business of accusation. Remember what Jesus did when confronted with the woman caught in adultery. She was guilty, but instead of accusing her, he forgave her and told her to go and not sin again. Obviously, a society cannot do this, and this is why Christians may find these kinds of situations extremely difficult. To believe that the only way out is the creation of a Christian society is perfectly illusory. There can never be a Christian way of accusing, any more than there can be a Christian society, politics, or state, as the book of Revelation makes very clear. We are called to live in a world dominated by powers, including those of money, the economy, and the state. This is why we need to be purified over and over again.

Ever since humanity was separated from God as described in Genesis, we have harboured evil impulses of all kinds. For example, when Jesus accused the Pharisees of hypocrisy, we must remember who they were. If all Christians were to do as much as the Pharisees did, the churches would undoubtedly be transformed. However, Jesus reveals that, ultimately, much or all of this rested on evil impulses, which led them to justify themselves before God, to consider themselves good and pure, and much else. They were ultimately motivated by something that was evil before God. However, we do not discover the depth of the evil within us other than before the cross of Jesus Christ. God saw no other way than to die on a cross in the person of his son to remove this evil from humanity in order to save it. Nothing else can show us the depth of our evil – the knowledge that we have been forgiven by that crucifixion.

It is in this world, where evil powers are at work, that we have received God's Word. It was brought into this world of lies. It is for this reason that Christians must not surrender the Word of truth to the powers of the lie.

Of the first seven verses of the second chapter, the first is more complex than it appears at first sight. It begins with "my brothers and sisters," as if we are all one, and then asks why we make distinctions and divisions among ourselves. We cannot be one and divided at the same time. Once more, James shows his ability to take complex issues and cut right to the heart of them. He establishes a relationship between our faith in Jesus Christ and the divisions and separations that we bring about. Not to do so is an expression of love, as the text will explain a little later. In other words, love for others appears as a consequence or even a condition of faith in Jesus Christ. The text has now moved beyond the good that can be done by anyone to something more specific to Christians. Faith brings with it a kind of love that can overcome all distinctions. I believe that this is perhaps one of the particularities of Christian love that cannot be demanded of non-Christians, namely, not to treat anyone differently. Non-Christians have no choice but to judge people with the criteria of the world. However, Christians cannot distinguish between people by placing some above or below others. There is therefore nothing "natural" about this love, as it can only derive from faith.

Our text refers to Jesus Christ as our glorious lord. He is glorious in that he has been revealed as the Lord. This would be somewhat astonishing, were it not for the fact that this lordship makes it possible not to differentiate between people. Jesus is lord of everyone without any difference whatsoever. He is lord of the rich and the poor, free people and slaves, Greeks and Jews, men and women, Christians and non-Christians, and so on. As Paul tells us, in Christ there is absolutely no difference between us. It is based on his lordship, and not on his being a saviour. If by faith we are attached to him, we are thus also attached to everyone else of whom he is lord. He exercises this lordship not by his authority, domination, and will but through his love for us. In other words, fraternity among all people is not natural, nor is it the result of the Creation. I believe the letter of James adds this to our traditional theological understanding. We have become accustomed to thinking that because we are all created by the same Creator, we are all brothers and sisters. However, the result has hardly been a fraternity of humanity. The Bible tells us that it is the lordship of Jesus Christ that transforms us into brothers and sisters to others. He is the intermediary that allows us all to be brothers and sisters. It is not because we have a common Creator but because we have a common Father. Jesus taught us that God is our Father and that he himself is the first-born. Believing that Jesus Christ is lord implies that we stop judging others in order to separate, classify, and hierarchize them according to the values of the world.

The lordship of Jesus Christ itself is very different from that of the rulers and powerbrokers of the world. It is based on his humiliation and sacrifice, and thus has nothing in common with power. We must look at others

in the same way and stop judging them by the criteria and hierarchies of
the world. There may be no exceptions of any kind: moral, political, intellectual, religious, racial, or anything else. The acceptance of everyone –
the refusal of no one – means opening ourselves to everyone without any
differentiation. We are all brothers and sisters because we are equally
loved by God. That is what the first verse of this second chapter tells us.

Having dealt with the first verse, we find that the next six are straightforward and illustrative. They speak of churches (assemblies) with divisions
between rich and poor. Their honouring of the rich implies a judgment
based on the criteria and values of this society, and this is condemned.
Honouring those whom a society regards as honourable is inspired by evil
thought. It is not a question of a mere conformity to our society but of a
real evil. It is in conflict with the true judgment of God, who chose those
who are poor in the eyes of the world (as we saw in chapter 1) so that they
will be rich in faith. This does not mean, however, that they are the only
ones to have faith. Moreover, they will inherit the kingdom of heaven,
which must be distinguished from the kingdom of God at the end of
time.[2] In other words, in this world, it is the poor who bear the royalty of
Jesus Christ. It is their vocation, and the role they are called to fulfil.

It is important to emphasize that this choice of the poor by God for this
role does not mean that they are better than others or that they love God
more, or anything of the kind. They are certainly not the bearers of history,
as Marx believed. The poor are chosen simply because they have no power
of their own, no resources of their own, and nothing the world would be
proud of. As a result, there can be no confusion whatsoever between what
God does via the intermediary of people and what people do themselves. I
am reminded of Paul saying to the Corinthians that it was fortunate they
did not have many intellectuals among them because, when the latter
spoke of the Word of God, the congregation risked confusing the Word of
God with their brilliant arguments and oratory. This is why the ministry of
the learned doctor was the least and most humble of the ministries in the
churches. We encounter the same kinds of choices throughout the Bible.
For example, this is the "logic" behind the choice of people such as David
and Samuel, and even the choice of the Jewish people themselves. Israel
was chosen because it was the smallest of all peoples.

Does all this mean that the rich are excluded? We will see, near the
end of this epistle, that they are judged extremely harshly. Does this not
imply a certain discrimination and even a rejection rather than an acceptance of people? Is it simply a question of reversing the usual hierar-
chy by now placing the poor at the top? I believe the Bible tells us that

what is important is not to treat the rich and the poor differently. It is
not a replacement of discrimination against the poor with discrimination against the rich. Once again, at the birth of Jesus Christ, the rich
wise men are also present along with the poor, with the difference that
the wise men had to travel a very long route to get there. It is symbolic
of how the rich come to the revelation regardless of the kinds of riches
they possess. In any case, in the churches no distinction must be made
between the rich and the poor, and the rich can certainly not be excluded. However, the rich are not chosen to be rich in faith and to bear
the royalty of Jesus Christ on the earth. That is not their role.

Verses 6 and 7 add an additional detail of historical interest. They ask
whether it is not the rich who oppress you, drag you before the courts,
and blaspheme the name you bear. This implies that the Christians of
that time were deeply honoured when rich people came to their churches, and that the majority of the members were poor. It may also imply that
this letter of James is older than we usually think, because from the middle of the second century on, there were many converts from the higher
strata of society. This is the point in time when Christianity began to
spread through these higher social strata. It was only during the first two
generations after Jesus' death that Christianity primarily spread among
the poor and the slaves. The text would appear to indicate that, at the
time of its writing, these churches were made up of a majority of poor
people and that the rich were mostly hostile to them – with a few exceptions, of course. James simply refers to this situation in order to ask the
churches why they honoured the rich.

James warns his fellow Christians that not only are they following the
ways in which the world judges people, they are also honouring the very
people who drag them before the courts. Since it was forbidden to be a
follower of Christ, they risked having the courts take away what little they
had, which was an incentive for others to accuse them. Moreover, the rich
blasphemed the good name of him to whom they belonged because of
the radical contradiction between the declaration of their faith and the
way they behaved, which was another reason for not honouring them.

If we should not honour those who are rich, we should not do the opposite either by honouring the poor to the point of despising the rich.
Doing so would simply replace one kind of discrimination with another.
The book of Deuteronomy instructs us not to change our judgment of
others according to their being rich or poor. The rich and powerful must
be treated like anyone else, but we must know that they are not the bearers of the kingdom of heaven among us.

In response to your questions, I believe these texts have vast implications. For example, following the liberation at the end of the Second World War, many collaborators with the Germans were very badly treated. We did not have the right to take advantage of the victory at their expense. People were often accused of crimes they had not committed, and we had no choice but to help and support them. In the same vein, I strongly believe that we must not combat extremists with their own kinds of weapons and tactics. As Christians, we must follow our Lord and deal with power the way he did. We must certainly not believe that we can crush opposing religious or political movements by destroying them through the police and the army. If Christians behaved the way Jesus did, I am convinced that this would have a profound influence on the social fabric in which we find ourselves. Tolerance is not a matter of accepting what people do or teach but of not judging them. I know full well that an anarchist society or a Christian one is an impossibility. Any society requires a variety of laws and rules in order to operate. No community can function without them, but this does not mean that we can love a particular kind of social or political form of society. This is very important in our time, when the state always wants to be adored and loved. We must obey the state, but we can never love anything or anyone other than our Lord.

We cannot avoid making the kinds of legal judgments our societies make, but we must remember that the law intervenes when something has already gone wrong. For example, when a marriage between two people works well, the law is not necessary. It intervenes when there is a crisis. As Christians we follow a different route, namely, to defend and aid those who are poor, oppressed, or profoundly unhappy, a route that often includes interpreting economic, social, or political issues differently in order to seek reconciliation. Doing so means, in some cases, that we must be very firm. For example, we must protect a secular society and not permit the state to meddle in religious matters if there is to be tolerance. In some cases this may be extremely difficult when, as in the case of some or most Muslims, the law and the Koran are the same thing, and so are the state and religion. This makes it next to impossible to play by the rules that govern our society. In the same vein, we must resist all claims that God is on the side of our nation in times of war. Doing so has created the absurd situation where God was on everyone's side. In the same way, I do not believe we are ever going to be able to resolve the problem of terrorism as long as the enormous gap in wealth continues to exist between the North and the South. It will never be resolved by the police or by security agencies. In a world of power, we must always show that there is another way, that of non-power. When God is with us this non-power will have its effects, although they may not be what we or the world expects. I also recognize that following the way of non-power often makes us a target for violence. The clear example is that of Martin Luther King, who always sought non-violent means, and who as a result had a much deeper effect than the Black Panthers or black Muslim groups had with their violence. I believe that non-violence disarms violence in the end. I myself have seen it several times, when a single person interposing himself between the police and a violent group has had this effect.

Turning to verses 8 to 11, we encounter two principal themes: the royal law, and the unity of this law. The law of love (to love your neighbour as yourself) is referred to as the royal law because it comes from the king. It is the law the king imposes on all who receive his revelation, and he imposes it as Lord. However, because this Lord is also our saviour, that law is completely different from any law that exists in the world. It is a law based on love and freedom. Living in this way changes the very concept of what a law is. It is legally impossible to make someone love someone else, just as it is legally impossible to practise freedom. In the world, there is a complete contradiction between the law on the one side and freedom and love on the other. Once again, the Word of God reveals a promise and not an obligation. When you hear it, the way of love and freedom is opened for you, and you can love your neighbour. In the same vein, you are set free when this Word penetrates your heart.

This law of love and the previously discussed law of freedom are different from physical laws or juridical laws. They are a Word addressed to us that we must observe as laws unto life. Our lives are made for love and freedom. It is the very law of being alive. If we stop living by love and freedom we stop living altogether.

When James speaks of the law he is thinking about the Hebrew Torah with all its details. Jesus declared that whoever suppresses even the smallest commandment and who teaches people to do the same will be called the smallest in the kingdom of heaven, but whoever does all of them and teaches this to others will be called great in the kingdom of heaven. In other words, there are no great and small commandments. This brings us to the unity of the law, because the violation of a single one amounts to the violation of the entire law. James makes it very clear that the law is not what we usually think: a long series of commandments. God's law is the will of God expressed in a way that aims to protect our entire life. It is very easy to talk about loving your neighbour as yourself in general terms, but this love expressed itself in detail through more than

800 commandments in the Torah. The love of God unites all of them in one love, just as his will is one. Neither his love nor his will can be divided into small pieces. As all these commandments show, there is not a single aspect of our lives that is foreign to the love of God. I recognize that this poses a difficult theological problem because we have traditionally argued that on one end of the spectrum we define what is good and on the other end what is bad, with a kind of middle neutral ground of indifference where you can do anything. For example, it is in this middle ground where technique was developed. It is indifferent to what is good or bad, as if it were morally neutral. The multiplicity of commands teaches us that there is no such neutral territory in human life. God sees everything and judges everything. Hence, all the commandments are expressions of love that jointly constitute our whole life, as it were. Moreover, even if we accomplished the entire law, we would still not have exhausted this love because it transcends these commandments. Jesus tells us this very clearly at the beginning of the Sermon on the Mount, when he teaches that "your ancestors were told not to commit adultery, but I tell you that anyone who looks at a woman with desire has already committed adultery in his heart." In other words, the law gives us an example of what love implies, but God's love goes much further than that. The Christians have all too easily dismissed the Torah in favour of this love, and in doing so have ended up doing much less than the law. For example, when the Torah tells us to give away one tenth of what we earn, we think we can safely ignore this. The contrary is the case. Love requires that we do more than the law, not less. All the commandments are but examples of a much greater love. Moreover, this is not a legalistic law but a law of freedom.

If we accept all this, it is likely to make us rather discouraged. For centuries, the Jews struggled to discover everything that was implied in the Torah, and every aspect of their lives became framed by it. If Christians are asked to do even more, we may well feel defeated before we start. Here we do well to recall what Paul says when he teaches that the law is a pedagogy to lead us to understand how deeply we depend on grace. We must do everything the Jews did and more, and in recognizing that this is impossible we have no other recourse but to ask God for pardon. In other words, the law as such refers us back to God's love. This is why our text finishes with the two verses we have already discussed, which declare that mercy triumphs over judgment. It is all we have in our inability to follow the law, let alone to do better.

Our text also shows that when we differentiate and classify others, we do not recognize their freedom, and in effect eliminate it. Nevertheless, they are set free just as I am. If I judge them, I claim that they must do the same thing as I do and behave according to a certain code, as opposed to acting according to the freedom they have been granted.

The second consequence of this judging of others is that I am judged myself. When we do not accept someone, we bring upon ourselves the judgment of God. As Jesus puts it, you will be measured with the yardstick you use to measure others.

Finally, the differentiation, classification, and non-acceptance of others remind me of a long passage in Solzhenitsyn in which he deals with a just judgment and an unjust judgment. He concludes that the unjust judgment is the most terrible thing we can possibly experience on this earth. The reason he gives is that every person expects a just judgment. Hence, when you receive an unjust judgment, it is a dreadful disillusionment. When we begin to judge others, we enter into a situation that is the exact opposite of love and contrary to God's will. Again, I believe this is one of the great merits of this epistle: to lead us through complex theological principles by extremely practical situations.

When James speaks of the love for your neighbour, it must be understood in its totality, knowing full well that any action that goes against this love, whatever it may be, destroys the totality of the love for your neighbour. This brings us back to our discussion of verses 12 and 13 regarding a morality that becomes more and more legalistic. The great temptation is to go down that road. Recall the argument. The love for your neighbour is something whole. The smallest transgression of this love destroys this whole, and if we engage in what churches have done from time to time, namely the ever more detailed and fine-tuned analysis of what the love for our neighbour might be, in order to formulate thousands of little commandments in an attempt to anticipate every possible situation, then we have completely missed the point. The epistle of James clearly says that this is not what it is all about, and this is why the epistle is not in the least moralistic. We are placed within a law of freedom; hence, we must speak and act like those who will be judged by the law of freedom.

Once again, I find myself marvelling at the structure of this text. It begins by saying that you must love your neighbour as yourself. Doing so is extremely complex because the smallest and finest detail can destroy everything. The law is one. Whatever you do, do not enter into an analysis and an accumulation of endless rules and obligations. Because you know that the law is a whole, speak and act like a person having to be judged by the law of freedom. Do not judge others, in the knowledge that you will never be able to accomplish the entire royal law but that mercy will triumph over judgment. All along our journeys with love and freedom, there will be grace because without it we would not survive. Again, mercy triumphs over judgment: we have been involved in judging others, but we have received grace and hence no longer judge others. In a nutshell, this is the argument of our text.

Life as the Practice of Faith

It is essential to read James 2:14–26 as a continuation of everything that has gone before. It is also important to remember that for a very long time, theologians have focused the entire biblical message on the question of salvation, especially individual salvation. This emphasis had already started before the Reformation, but the Reformation aggravated the situation by creating tensions between salvation by faith and salvation by works. Clearly, the theme of salvation is important in the Bible. It is often spoken of from two sides, as it were. The negative side has to do with our reaction of fear with regard to salvation versus damnation by God's wrath, salvation versus death, salvation versus Satan, and much more. This reaction of fear tends to be associated with a religious orientation, as it were, and is accompanied by a consolation that is also rooted in that fear (an idea that we encounter in Feuerbach).[3] I believe that what this side represents is not an important element of the biblical message.

The positive side of salvation is far more important, having to do with the reconciliation between God and humanity and the re-establishment of our relationship with him. I would say that all the other things are never much more than of secondary importance compared to the reconciliation with God. It is much more a question of a salvation given to God's people rather than to individuals. Moreover, this salvation has more to do with the establishment of the kingdom of God than with separating out the saved from the damned. In my view, putting the emphasis on this separation is a serious misinterpretation. Everything about salvation must be situated within the establishment of the kingdom of God, including the debates between the theology of Paul and the theology of James. This latter debate is over salvation by faith or salvation by works. What makes all this even worse is that this debate appears to be based on a misinterpretation of our text. It is the common error of isolating a portion of the text from the rest. In this case, the question as to whether faith without works can save people, as it is posed in verse 14, is taken out of context to demonstrate that James supposedly thinks that faith cannot save anyone, while Paul asserts that faith suffices.

It is essential to keep this question in context. If we examine verses 15 and 16, we immediately encounter two important elements. If a brother or sister lacks clothing or food, what is the use of telling them to go in peace, to keep warm, and to eat well without providing them with what is necessary? Once again, notice how this text is structured. The first eleven verses deal with the love for our neighbour, its relationship to the application of the law, the issue of works, followed by a particular instance of this love for our neighbour. If you address someone as a fellow Christian in faith, and you wish him or her peace, to keep warm, and to eat well, you must provide what they need. The Salvation Army puts it well: soup, soap, and salvation. The prayer to give us our daily bread (referring to a collective us) now includes a commitment to provide this bread for others. In other words, we cannot say something without doing the equivalent. Doing so does not imply that this giving means works of charity. Moreover, it is useless to bring the gospel if we do not provide food. We are not in the habit of automatically linking the two together. According to the text, our words must be accompanied by whatever allows them to be carried out. Doing so is compared to faith, which is empty without works. Words by themselves mean nothing if we cannot turn them into actions.

I believe this is very important because we must remember that our words are not like the Word of God, even when we use the words of the Bible. The essential difference between the two is that the Word of God not only includes an act but an act that is also creative in kind. When God addresses someone, the reality of which he speaks exists. For us, that is clearly not the case. We can now understand the essential point of this text: when we speak, we have to accompany these words with the deeds that accomplish them, because together they become the expression of the Word of God. He speaks, and it is; but for us, we need to speak and act at the same time. In other words, faith requires the doing of that faith. It is what verses 15 to 17 are all about, namely, to remind us of the distance that exists between our words and God's words.

Another aspect of this text is that faith must be alive and that this faith consists of believing. However, believing by faith is different from what we usually understand because it cannot remain on the level of believing – or on the level of knowledge or sentiment, for that matter. Our faith must be existential in the sense that it must engage our entire existence, in the present and for eternity. Although it is not possible to fully develop it here, I would like to provide a sense of the existential dimension of faith by referring to two theologians.

For Moltmann,[4] faith involves three elements. First, it is a new understanding of our existence as a consequence of our faith in Jesus Christ. Second, it is our liberation from the social and religious rules and constraints of our society and the need to conform to our time. Finally, faith is dissidence: a break with what is normal and expected, and an opposition to it. Next, let us take a look at Karl Barth. I will summarize his understanding of faith by means of the following ten elements.[5] In faith we recognize that we have exhausted all our means and can go no further. In faith we may call God our Father and thus live as people who expect everything from him in the knowledge that we may ask. In faith, we face any testing as coming from God before turning to our own means for dealing with it. This reminds us of James, who tells us to regard the testing of our lives as a subject of joy. This element is closely related to the next one. In faith we know that God is always just towards us, and we must resist the temptation to blame him for our troubles. In faith we must live before God as those whom he has judged and made his own, and this judgment has nothing to do with condemnation. In faith we can resist our unfaithfulness by recalling God's faithfulness. In other words, when we think that we have lost our faith, God remains faithful, and because of that we can confront such situations. To live in faith is to take the place in life that comes to those to whom God has granted grace. Faith implies that we live in freedom because God has acquitted us. In judging us God has taken us as his own, and in doing so he sets us free. The one is indissociably linked to the other. In faith we must abandon the opinions we have of ourselves in order to become what God creates in us. This implies giving up all the judgments we make about ourselves and others in order to move forward in humility. It liberates me from everything that works deep within me in the knowledge that I am being re-created. Finally, we must move away from our disobedience – from doing the works we have decided to do according to our own will towards doing the kinds of works accomplished in obedience to and love for God. Even when these works turn out to be identical in each case, their driving force will not be the same at all. Recall the beautiful text of Paul regarding love. If I distribute all I have to the poor but it is done without love, it serves no purpose. However, if it is done in love it is full of meaning. The same act is very different depending on whether or not it is done in faith, love, and obedience.

This discussion of faith brings us back to our text and the question as to whether it is possible to live and not show your faith. James puts it succinctly when he asks "show me your faith without works, and I will show you my faith by what I do" (2:18). How is it possible to show your faith, which is necessary for any witness, if there are no tangible works? If faith remains completely inside us, it cannot be shown, and hence there cannot be any witness. Taking this a step farther brings us to the problem of incarnation. Faith must be incarnated in order to show the kind of existential character we spoke of earlier. Our faith must be incarnated because Jesus Christ is the incarnated one: it is a question of giving a body to that faith, which means that our entire being must be inspired by faith. We are told to love the Lord with all our heart, all our soul, all our mind, and all our strength. These are the four elements which, from a biblical perspective, constitute a human being; and all four are engaged in this love. Once again, it is not merely something intellectual or sentimental. There can be no divisions within our person, or within our areas of interest. For example, there cannot be a division between faith and the church on the one hand and daily life and politics on the other. It is always astounding to me that it is possible to think that in the churches we should especially not speak about politics, as if politics were not integral to people's lives. Faith has no meaning unless it enters into every area of human life.

When faith does not have this existential incarnation, when it is not expressed in works, it is useless and dead, according to our text. It goes even farther. A faith that is dead shows that grace has not played a real role in our lives. As a result, a faith that is not incarnated, that is not expressed in our lives, and that therefore remains within our individual selves and within the boundaries of our churches, is an accusation against us. The reason is that faith derives from the grace we have received, and this is so even when we are entirely mistaken or when our faith is dead for lack of works. A dead faith is not at all the same thing as an absence of faith, which occurs as a result of never having received grace or the Holy Spirit. This is made very clear in the beginning of the book of Revelation, where we encounter churches that have received grace, who know it, but who do not live it. Under these conditions, their faith turns against them. I believe we can say that it is the only danger that we run. It is part of what in the Gospels is referred to as the sin against the Holy Spirit. As I understand it, this relationship between faith and works is extremely important.

Our text clearly shows this by asking, "So you believe that there is one God? That is good, but the demons believe it as well and they tremble" (2:19). In other words, you have received a revelation of the one true God, you now know it, but it does not suffice because there are others apart from Christians who know it as well. (I cannot help smiling when I recall the debate over polytheism and monotheism, as if the latter was superior to the former.) We might say that even the devils are monotheistic, but they do not act in accordance with this knowledge, and they do not love God. They have knowledge without the love that leads to accomplishing God's will. It is this that makes them the demons they are. We have spoken of the prologue of the book of Job, where Satan clearly has knowledge of God because he is in a world that encounters him.[6] We find the same thing in the fifth chapter of the gospel of Mark in the account of the healing of the man possessed by demons in the country of the Gadarenes. He prostrates himself before Jesus, recognizing him for who he is. Jesus tells the spirit to come out, and the spirit begs Jesus not to torment him. When asked for his name, the man replies that it is Legion, for we are many. In other words, the *diabolos* who was in this man was the only one there who knew who Jesus was. Moreover, the demon makes his request in the name of God. When Jesus was tempted, the Devil also used the Word of God. In other words, he knows it, but he does not live in love and reconciliation. That is why he is the *Diabolos*, the separator who separates God from humanity and people from one another. It reminds me of Dostoevsky's book *The Brothers Karamazov,* in which Ivan in particular knows who God is but declares himself against him, which means he declares himself to be demonic. To place oneself in this position is the most dreadful of all because you will know God only as judge and nothing else. To know him without love is to know him only as judge. When we study the first chapters of the book of Genesis,[7] we encounter the same issue. In order to avoid the above situation, God removed Adam from paradise. Otherwise he would have remained in the position the demons are in: they know God in their independence, autonomy, and revolt. From a practical perspective, this means that we must avoid becoming immobilized by a good theology. We can have the best theology in the world and be demons. As we have seen, demons make good theologians. Of course, a good theology is useful, but we cannot rely on it.

Are we to conclude that James claims that works can save us, or that they can justify us before God? I believe that if we think this is what he says, we have not 'read the text carefully enough. In 2:24 we read that people are saved by works, and not by faith alone. He is still referring to a faith that is empty or dead and isolated from life. That kind of faith does nothing. In other words, the text says that faith must express itself. Can we take this argument of James a step farther and say that in order to be saved you need faith *and* works? It would be the most straightforward interpretation, but it is still not what the text says. What it does say is that there is no faith at all where there are no works. There can be knowledge, there can be belief, but there can be no faith unless it is incarnated. Otherwise it does not exist. However, it is not simply a question of adding works arising out of a development of learning to express faith. It is the same kind of problem we find among linguists who constantly debate whether we speak because we think or we think because we speak. One does not grow out of the other because the two are indissociably connected. I believe we have the same kind of relationship between faith and works.

Clearly, this kind of (dead) faith is not the faith Paul speaks about. I believe it is incomprehensible that we have made Paul the theologian of salvation by faith, never mind that this interpretation is itself theologically incorrect. How often do we have to say that we are not saved by faith because, as Paul says, we are saved by grace. We are saved by grace through the means of faith. It is impossible, therefore, to make Paul the theologian of faith independent from works. We have all read the letters of Paul, whose concluding chapters deal with works as expressions of faith. The whole business is truly unbelievable.

In order to further confirm the unbreakable connection between faith and works, James uses two examples that have become classics. The first comes from Genesis 15:6, affirming that Abraham's entire life was a life of faith. The letter to the Romans puts it this way in chapter 4: "What then shall we say about Abraham, our forefather according to the flesh? If Abraham was justified by works, he has something to boast about, but not before God. What does the scripture say? 'Abraham believed God and it was reckoned to him as righteousness.' Now to one who works, his wages are not reckoned as a gift, but as his due. And to one who does not work but trusts him who justifies the ungodly, his faith is reckoned as righteousness" (RSV, Romans 4:1–5). In other words, the argument is as follows. If Abraham was justified by works, then there is no grace because if he received payment for it, no grace has been granted to him. If there is no grace, there is no promise either. A little further in this text (verse 13), we read that Abraham was not saved by the law either. "The promise to Abraham and his descendants, that they should inherit the world, did not come through the law, but through the righteousness of faith. If it is the adherents of the law who are to be the heirs, faith is null, and the promise is void. For the law brings wrath, but where there is no law, there is no transgression. That is why it depends on faith, in order that the promise may rest on grace and be guaranteed to all his descendants – not only to the adherents to the law, but also to those who share the faith of Abraham, for he is the father of us all, as it is written, 'I have made you the father of many nations' – in the presence of the God in whom he believed, who gives life to the dead, and calls into existence the things that do not exist" (RSV, Romans 4:13–17).

In other words, Paul declares that in the journey of Abraham's life, there was faith all along. It also confirms once again that where there is no grace, there is no promise. In the same vein, there are several texts regarding Rahab, who was justified by faith.

Was this faith, as pietism would have us believe, something within us? When we look at how the Old Testament speaks of the faith of Abraham and Rahab, no philosophical or metaphysical terms are used. It only speaks about what they did. For example, it speaks of Abraham's departure from Ur of Chaldea, his sacrifice of Isaac, how he dealt with Lot, and so on. In the case of Rahab, we are told that she welcomed the spies by telling them that she believed they belonged to the people of the God in whom she believed. We know nothing about the theological knowledge or religious beliefs of these people. It is in the context of their works that we are told that their faith saved them. These accounts permit us to further clarify the relationship between faith and works. Paul speaks of the works of the law, and hence there is no fundamental difference between Paul and James. I do not understand how we got ourselves into believing the contrary. Paul speaks of the works of the law in Romans 3:28: "For we hold that a person is justified by faith apart from the works of the law." In other words, when Paul explains that Abraham was not saved by works, he is referring to the works of the law. It is not a matter of Abraham beginning with these works, after having done them becoming a believer, and once a believer, having God speak to him, and so on. Paul rules out the works of the law, and James only speaks of the works of faith because, for him, the law is the royal law of freedom. Hence, the works of this law, of freedom, are not the works of the Torah. James is talking about those works that are the very expression of the existence of faith. It is not a question of two different positions on the same issue.

In James 2:22, we are told that Abraham's faith and actions were working together, and that this made his faith complete. It is not that first there is faith, and then faith produces works. The relationship is much more existential, in the sense that faith is never perfect in itself as a kind of inner encounter with God, but it is through the living of the reality of our lives that our faith is strengthened. There is a reciprocity between faith and works – an ongoing movement of faith expressing itself in works (incarnation), and these works in turn demanding that this faith express itself as such. Our text insists on their inseparability when it denies that one person can have faith and another works. Many commentators believe that this argument of the text addresses a situation commonly found in the churches of that time. It amounted to a kind of division of labour: there were those who were pious, spending their time in contemplation and prayer, while others engaged in action and service. Paul recognizes a similar distinction between the ministry of the word and the ministry of service. The former includes theologians, preachers, evangelists, and apostles. The latter includes the deacons and all those providing services to those in need. If this is simply a question of a division of labour, that is one thing, but if this is justified by a kind of theological distinction between those who have faith and others who have works, it is completely unacceptable. In each and every person, the unity between faith and works must be maintained. I should point out that these texts must not be read from an individualistic perspective but from a communal one with a diversity of gifts and services. James made this very clear when he introduced himself as a servant to the twelve tribes in the dispersion. In other words, the unity between faith and works must be manifested in both churches and individual lives.

Finally, when the text speaks about works, it is not referring to traditional good works – acts of charity or the doing of what is good. The text makes this clear when it recalls that Abraham our father was justified by works when he offered his son Isaac on the altar. Surely this is as far away from the traditional ideas of good works and charity as we can get. Already in the Old Testament, people's works designated their entire lives. No distinctions are made of any kind. Work, family, politics, and art are all integral to our works. Nothing in a person's life is neutral or outside God's reign. In a sense, everything is either for or against the reconciliation. When we are warned that we will be judged according to our works, it is not a question of totalling up our good and bad works but of being judged according to our lives. We are asked to live and construct a life in all its diversity within the love of God so that our faith in Jesus Christ inspires our entire life. In such a case, this faith is alive, and in any other, it is dead. A faith that is alive becomes a force of justice in our lives. In the Bible, this justice is likened to an arrow which exactly completes a trajectory towards its target. It is we who are this arrow, following a trajectory that involves our entire lives. It has nothing to do with the fact that one of our actions may be just and another unjust, because our lives are never regarded as collections of separate acts. Our lives are a totality before God. Once again, this implies a unity between faith and works. In the letter of James, there is no theology that is any different from that of the Bible as a whole. It is (especially) deeply rooted in the Jewish thought of the Old Testament.

In response to your questions, the way early Christian theologians used the term "redemption" was derived from Roman law. If Roman citizens were captured in war, they became the slaves of their captors. If other Roman citizens set these slaves free, they would have to purchase them like any other slaves, thus effectively becoming their masters. To free a slave, the master would have to make a declaration before a magistrate that renounced his or her rights to be that master. This was the price paid to set that person free – an act of redemption.

When we live our lives before God, we should think of it as being analogous to small children playing in the presence of their parents. They experience this presence as reassuring, and potentially helpful at any point. They derive a certain pleasure from this and do not experience it as a threat to their freedom and enjoyment of life. They take their playing very seriously, but at the same time they know that it is only play. In the same vein, being children of our heavenly Father, we must take our lives seriously, knowing at the same time that ultimately nothing depends on us.

Chapter Thirteen

The Word

Our Words

In chapter 1:26–7, three central elements of the Christian life were introduced: visiting the orphans and widows, keeping a tight rein on our tongues, and preserving ourselves from being defiled from the world. James 3:1–12 deals with the second element, which is language, its use and its significance. I would like to deal with three themes: the power of language, a kind of theology of language, and some ethical implications.

Beginning with the power of language, it may strike us that the text exaggerates a little when in verses 3 to 8 it compares the tongue to a bit in the mouth of a horse or a rudder on a ship, as something that directs and ensures obedience. It is also compared to a spark that can set an entire forest ablaze. It is a fire able to enflame an entire life. Everything can be tamed except our words and our discussions about what we say. Once spoken, language cannot be tamed or controlled. James explains all this through the use of commonplace examples. With the use of language we can explain what is going on, enflame people's passions, poison situations (that is literally what he says), and more. Today, the power of language is greatly enhanced by the research into communication and semiotics, the role of language in psychotherapy, and the many forms of integration propaganda in mass societies.[1] The text reveals a kind of duality in our language. It can reveal what is in our hearts, veil who we are by hiding behind our words, or help craft an image of how we wish to be portrayed. Of all the areas of human life, it is the one in which we most intensely seek to be our own master, and this reveals who we are. I believe that is the significance of our simultaneously blessing and cursing with our language. We cannot curb the damage we do with it.

Why does language have this power? It is because language is the highest gift God gave to humanity at the time of Creation, as is made clear in the opening chapters of Genesis. Following the break between God and humanity, his gift continues to be powerful even though it has been completely turned away from what it ought to be. For this reason, the text refers to language as an absolute evil and a world of iniquity. We may think this an exaggeration, but you have to place all this in the context of a multiplicity of languages – that is, in the context of Babel. Its significance is not primarily related to its being a city, and even less a tower (it certainly is not anything like the Greek myth of mounting towards heaven). In Genesis 11 we are told that the people wanted to build a city, a tower with its top reaching the heavens, and to make a name for themselves so they would not be dispersed all over the earth. Their most decisive act in all of this is to make a name, that is, for them to name themselves. In the Bible, this means designating their spiritual being. Until then, the people had received their names from God, with the implication that God remained the master of their destiny. By naming themselves, they completely separated themselves from God. What had until then been the element that most directly represented God in his relationship with humanity would become the property of humanity and, by this act, language became an evil.[2] The Jewish rabbis generally agreed that this was much more than different people no longer understanding each other because of different languages. It also refers to individuals speaking the same language. Nevertheless, our words and language maintain their power because of their origin, and this poses a difficult theological problem regarding language.

We must avoid giving a moralistic interpretation to the text's assertion that language is an absolute evil, a world of iniquity, and a power that can defile the entire body. A moralistic interpretation would turn these claims into unbelievable exaggerations. As I have emphasized before, the letter of James has nothing to do with morality. This is not a question of enumerating all the sins that can be committed with the aid of language, such as we find in Calvin's writings, for example. There are clearly much greater sins than all of these. Such moralistic approaches completely miss the point of the text.

The characterization of language as an absolute evil, a world of iniquity, and full of deadly poison derives from the relationship between our word and the Word of God. By means of his Word, God speaks, acts, creates, and reveals; and Jesus Christ is himself that incarnated Word. The meaning of the word given to humanity is that it is a continuation or a prolongation of the Word of God. In other words, our word should speak the Word of God. In Genesis, we read that the word was given to Adam, and the very first application of that word was to name the animals. It signifies that humanity has a mastery over the world that conforms to the one that God has – a mastery via the medium of the Word.[3] Before the break with God there was no other mastery than by the word. It is the mastery of spiritually designating or naming something; and in this context, humanity has a certain power, and that is all. In addition, this word allows humanity to engage in a dialogue with God through listening, praying, and worshipping. By listening to the Word of God, humanity can speak that word, and in this way become a partner of sorts. In sum, this word makes humanity unique with respect to God in all Creation. Human beings speak because God speaks. I recognize that all this is difficult to understand because of our technique-inspired theories of language.[4] When the Bible claims that God speaks, we must not take this as a simplistic anthropocentrism. Human beings speak to say something, but that does not mean that we can conclude that, when God says something, he actually speaks. We must think of it in the opposite sense. When God reveals himself to us, the Word is the only means for communicating the truth to us. There are no other possibilities. By this, I do not mean that God literally pronounces words belonging to our language. It goes much deeper. A good friend of mine who is a Hebrew scholar puts it this way: "If God chose the people of Israel, it is because of their language – it being the only one capable of expressing the mystery of the revelation of God." There is a kind of parallel between God's Word and theirs, and it is by this Word that he makes his truth understood. It also means that we in turn are able to transmit this truth of God, with the result that our word becomes the only means for doing so.

All of this has two important consequences. The first is not directly found in our text, but it cannot be avoided. If God reveals himself only by the Word, he does not do so by means of images. From a biblical perspective, there can be no theophany. In the Bible there is a radical opposition between the image and the word.[5] Any representation of God is strictly forbidden. We cannot take hold of God or his truth by visual means. As I have examined elsewhere in detail, sight gives us access to reality but never the truth.[6] Whenever human beings make an image as a spiritual point of reference, they are always condemned in the Bible. God is invisible: he speaks but he never shows himself. Judaeo-Christianity is centred on the Word and is opposed to the image. This is another element that distinguishes it completely from all other religions: there simply is no common denominator of an intellectual, cultural, or spiritual kind between them. I recognize that, despite this, Christianity has often been distorted by a slew of images. Moreover, a revelation by the Word is progressive, much like our languages, in the sense that one word follows another until the sentence is completed, only to be followed by more sentences, and so on. In contrast, an image claims to give an instantaneous and comprehensive representation of an ensemble of things. This distinction is essential for understanding the relationship between God and humanity.

The second consequence is directly present in the text because, although the word is the bearer of the truth, it is susceptible to the lie. We cannot lie with our eyes the way we can do with our words. I am not suggesting that visually we are unable to show things in ways that are inexact because of a lack of conformity to reality, but this has nothing in common with the truth. It is only on the level of language that we encounter the matter of truth and lies, in the deeper sense of what lying means.[7] Lies take on their deepest significance in relation to God's revelation. It is the lie with regard to Jesus Christ as the truth. Generally speaking, lies are bad enough, but ultimately not decisive. In the Bible, the lie is to say what God did not say. It is reporting God's revelation as something else or even its opposite. All this is especially true with respect to Jesus Christ. What Satan ultimately seeks to accomplish is that human beings lie about Jesus Christ. It is for this reason that Satan is referred to as the father of lies. He seeks to ensure that Jesus Christ is not recognized for who he is. A text that clearly speaks to this is found in Matthew 12 beginning with verse 31, which tells us that "every sin and blasphemy will be forgiven, but the blasphemy against the Spirit will not be forgiven. Whoever speaks against the son of humanity will be forgiven, but whoever speaks against the Holy Spirit will not be forgiven, not in this age nor in the age to come. Say either this tree is good and its fruit is good, or say this tree is bad and its fruit is bad. Race of vipers! How can you say good things, evil as you are? It is from the abundance of the heart that the mouth speaks. Good people draw good things from their good treasure, and bad people draw bad things from their bad treasure. I tell you that in the day of judgment, everyone will give an account of every vain word they utter, because by your words you will be justified, and by your words you will be condemned."[8]

We see that this text from Matthew is carefully constructed. Everything we say can be forgiven except what is spoken against the Holy Spirit. The reason for this is that the Holy Spirit is the one who reveals the truth of God – it is the very discourse of God, so to speak, as opposed to the Word incarnated in Jesus Christ. It is the Holy Spirit who teaches us who the son of humanity is. Hence, speaking against the son of humanity is not necessarily to deny him. The seriousness of the sin against the Holy Spirit is the denial that Jesus Christ is both the son of God and of humanity. This denial may not be spoken, because the only way to forgiveness that God has chosen is Jesus Christ. It is ultimately what we say regarding Jesus Christ and whether or not this is inspired by the Holy Spirit. This is why, in the judgment, everyone will have to account for every vain word, which means every lie: "By your words you will be justified, and by your words you will be condemned". Will we have given a true discourse regarding Jesus Christ, or will we have lied with regard to him? The construction in verse 33 of the above text of Matthew has the same construction as our text from the letter of James: either this or that. I believe the text from the letter of James is directly inspired by the text from the gospel of Matthew. All this teaches us why our words and their usage are so decisive and fundamental.

Everything that we know about God has come to us via the Word. That Word is transmitted by our words. These words are true only if the Holy Spirit makes them so. We must not imagine that our knowledge and explanations of the Bible are words of truth. It is the Holy Spirit who transforms our attempts at speaking and hearing the truth. In the letter to the Romans, Paul explains that we are incapable of knowing what to ask God in our prayers. It is the Holy Spirit who transforms our prayers into ones that are true. This is the case for all our communications. They all depend on the intervention of the Holy Spirit, without which our communications would be blocked and life would be unliveable.

When language is in the service of other things than truth, thereby becoming the instrument of the lie, it becomes everything the letter of James describes: a fire, a world of evil, and more. It is set on fire by Gehenna. This is one of the two valleys between which Jerusalem is situated. It was considered a cursed place because, in earlier times, the Canaanites made human sacrifices there, with the result that the Jews used it as a garbage dump for the city. Even the bodies of executed criminals were thrown there. When the stench became unbearable it was set ablaze. In other words, it was the place where the Jews threw everything for which there was no longer any use and which would be burned along with all the rest of the garbage. Our text tells us that our language is inflamed by what people want to get rid of. It is an image of hell. The text also tells us that this language sets the course of people's lives, or the course of the entire Creation, on fire. The Greek is difficult to translate.

It literally means the wheel, or circle, of genesis. Hence, the usual translations (the course of our lives, or the course of Creation) are rather abstract, and a bit of a stretch. It has also been translated as the universe of
Creation, which I believe goes too far. Still others have translated this
phrase as the wheel of birth, which is also problematic, because I would
not translate "genesis" as "birth." I believe that the wheel of genesis implies that the discourse of lies also places itself within the beginning. We
must read this phrase in the context of the book of Genesis, which tells
us that in the beginning, God spoke. The first act of God was to speak.[9]
Instead of placing God's Word in the beginning, the lie places the flame
of hell, as it were, in the beginning. In other words: in the beginning, the
Word of God created; but with the break between God and humanity, the
desire arose for a new genesis, but one that was infernal and destructive
instead of creative. It is in this context, I believe, that translation of this
phrase as the course of our lives, or the Creation, takes on a much deeper
meaning. These verses thus acquire a dimension that is not only theological but also cosmogonic and metaphysical, as it were. In any case, all this
is very far removed from a simple matter of morality, which is not to deny
that there could be a moral dimension.

The text has four ethical implications (James 3:1–2 and 9–12). First,
we must face an impossibility. With the same tongue, we praise God our
Father and curse others made in his likeness; and this should not be so,
just as fresh and salt water cannot come from the same spring. It is not
possible to use language in a diabolical fashion and at the same time to
use it to bear witness or to praise God. We cannot serve two masters: if
language recovers its true place, it can never again tell a lie on any level.
If we are not mistaken about Jesus Christ, we can no longer be mistaken
about others either, not even in a single detail. We had better face ourselves, because if we lie to others or we curse them in any way, our language can no longer be a witness to God's truth. This is being radical,
not in a moral sense, but in an ontological sense: our language cannot
serve two purposes at the same time.

A second ethical implication is that no one can tame the tongue (3:8).
No human ability or quality such as self-mastery or any creation (including a morality) can change this situation. A radical change can come
about only as a consequence of a conversion, that is, if we cease being
rooted in our own human nature. The text explicitly says that, although
animals can be tamed by human beings, no human being can tame language. It is only by leaving our human nature, by receiving a new life, that
we can return to the centre of the truth: the relationship between the

Word of God and the word. Only then can human language be tamed; or, more accurately, it no longer needs to be tamed.

All this was already recognized in the Hebrew Bible. In Psalm 62 we read that he blesses with the mouth but with the depth of his heart he curses. Jesus tells us that the mouth speaks of what is in the depth of the heart. As a result, what we say expresses the very depth of our being. We either speak of the glory of God and his love and address him in prayer, or we remain the people of the lie, of anger, and of curses. Only a conversion of the heart can change our words. It is not a question of a kind of moral perfection but of being filled with the Holy Spirit.

The third implication derives from the second verse, which tells us that we all err in many ways. James has no illusions about the holiness of the Christians he is addressing. If someone does not stumble in the use of language, he or she is perfect. Some commentators have regarded this text as merely ironic, since obviously no one can accomplish this. However, not to stumble in our use of language is a question of knowing whether our words are used in conformity with God's truth, in which case the perfection referred to is not of people but of the Word of God, and nothing else. It is not at all a question of human beings reaching a moral or saintly perfection. When people speak the Word of God, they are clothed with its perfection. When this occurs, it is a tangible proof that God's spirit acts in us.

The fourth ethical implication brings us back to the opening of our text (James 3:1), which counsels us that not too many of us should become teachers because those who do will be judged more strictly. When the Word of God becomes the very centre of the attestation of our conversion, and of our obedience to the Holy Spirit, a warning must be provided to all those who use our words in the church. To recover the true relationship between the Word of God and our word is extremely difficult and must not be taken lightly. To witness to the truth is far more difficult than to live in a manner that is correct, as it were. The text informs us that if we do not stumble in our words, we are able to keep our entire body in check. In other words, it is easier to keep in check various passions than to put ourselves in the centre of the relationship between the Word of God and our human word. Only a small number of people are able to do this; hence it is better that only a few people talk. These certainly should not be limited to those who have studied theology but to those who have established a truth for their language; and it is they who should speak in the churches. It is better for all the others to be silent. In addition, those who do speak should do so with a great deal of moderation and discretion because of the difficulties involved. I would

even go so far as to say that words that are objectively exact can veil
rather than unveil the revelation. This is the reason that there is a big
difference between the preaching of the gospel and the making of theological constructions, because the former is the Word of God expressed
by human beings on the level of the truth here and now, as it were. When
intellect begins to play a role, and theological constructions become important, it is all too easy to obscure the truth of God. It is the danger
faced by every theology. This is yet another reason for being extremely
careful with our words. We had better leave the speaking to those who
are able because we will all be judged by our words, as our text says very
clearly. It brings us back to our discussion of the text in Matthew, that we
will be judged more severely according to our words.

Those who explain the Word of God to the churches must know that
they will be the first to be judged because, if they make a mistake, it may
mislead others as well. On a personal note, I have given many lectures in
my life, but I always find that preaching tires me out a lot more. It is because, in delivering a sermon, I must do everything possible to avoid making mistakes. To the very best of my ability, I must ensure that what I say is
true. It is a very heavy responsibility knowing that we will be judged by our
words and that those who speak in the name of God will be judged first.

It is clear that the advice given by the letter of James to the churches is
extremely well founded from a theological perspective. It leads us to a
series of consequences of an ethical character, much as we see in the
thinking of Paul.

Wisdom, Intelligence, Words, and Lies

Once again, a first reading of James 3:13–18 is likely to leave us with the
impression that this text lacks substance and depth. Furthermore, it appears to jump from topic to topic without there being any clear structure.
It successively speaks of wisdom, good conduct, bitter zeal and the spirit
of quarrelling, lies, and two opposing kinds of wisdom; and the closing
verse speaks of the fruits of justice sown in peace, which appears to be
tacked on. However, as we begin to examine this text more closely, it will
become apparent that once again there is a clear underlying structure.

It is important to remind ourselves that this text is located between the
second and third parts of the letter of James. The former dealt with the
word, and the latter with the conduct of our lives with regard to the world.
We will gradually discover that this text constitutes a remarkable transi-
tion from the one to the other.

The opening verse (3:13) is addressed to everyone. James takes the same approach that he did with regard to faith: who is wise and intelligent among you, let them show it by their works. We must be intelligent and wise, as both are integral to the Christian life. Intelligence must inspire our language, and our words must express wisdom. Intelligence and wisdom are not the same thing. The Greek word translated as "intelligence" has a precise meaning that is related not to a kind of overall quality but to a particular kind of intelligence. It represents the application of our intelligence to a kind of scientific research in search of universal knowledge as invented by the Greeks. It seeks a rigorous kind of knowledge. In the same vein, Greek wisdom derived from human thought and reflection and was regarded as humanity's highest calling. Given that this letter is addressed to the twelve tribes of Israel and the church, I believe that the text is not speaking of the intelligence found in philosophy or in any science, but of the intelligence found in the revelation of God. I would almost say the intelligence of theology, in the sense of applying our intelligence to the understanding of the Bible. Every possible effort of this kind must be made. The Bible never tells us to simply and uncritically accept any text as we read it. Instead, we must struggle with these texts as thoroughly as we are able. Our text makes it clear that this is not the work of specialists, because it asks who among its readers is intelligent and wise. The question is addressed to everyone.

In the letters of the New Testament, intelligence refers to an understanding of the revelation of God. Paul uses this very phrase in his letter to the Philippians, where he tells his readers that they must have this intelligence. Such intelligence does not simply come from listening to this revelation but from reflecting on it in an attempt to gain knowledge. Once again, faith by itself is insufficient. It must be worked out in this intelligence related to living in the world. In other words, there is no question of this being a theology, dogma, or doctrine developed once and for all. We change, our lives change, and the world evolves. We already find references to this intelligence in the Old Testament where, in the book of Deuteronomy, Joshua is told to take with him men who have intelligence and wisdom to help lead the people. This intelligence and wisdom came from the observation of the Commandments so that the Jewish people would live God's revelation. It is therefore a question of an existential intelligence, as it were, as opposed to an intellectual one. We constantly forget that the making of theology must contribute to the Christian life as a consequence of doing and living it. As a result, each generation must start anew. We must therefore bridge the gap between the conservatives who carefully study the biblical texts and the liberals who concentrate on thinking about what these texts mean, and thus re-integrate faith and works when it comes to intelligence. It is a task that each and every one of us must undertake.

In the Bible, wisdom is entirely different from intelligence. Throughout the Old Testament, we find references to this wisdom; and in the New Testament, Paul also tells us that Jesus Christ is the wisdom of God. To put it as simply as possible, wisdom is a way of governing. The wisdom of God is the way he governs and directs the world. We are asked to participate in God's wisdom through our works. The difference between intelligence and wisdom is now evident. The former is intellectual in character while the latter is existential, having to do with actively living our lives in the world. There can be no Christian life without wisdom depending on intelligence. If we are to do what is good and unto life, which is God's will, then we must know his revelation. From time to time, God may also intervene and directly tell us his will. It is important not to confuse God's wisdom with his providence (referring to his foreseeing everything that will happen). This is an entirely different matter. In any case, God permits people to get on with their lives and communities and to make their history, but he intervenes from time to time, as we see throughout the Bible.

Wisdom is thus the way God directs the world; and we must live our lives with the same kind of wisdom. Doing so involves our intelligence with regard to the Word as well as this wisdom. This text therefore is a bridge from the previous ones regarding the word to the ones that follow in chapters 4 and 5 dealing with the wisdom related to governing our lives.

Governing our lives in the world involves a discerning of what we must do in every sphere: our professions, families, politics, and more. At the same time (and this is where the letter of James builds on the entire Old Testament), this wisdom presupposes that humanity's role is to direct the world on God's behalf. It presupposes that humanity utilizes the world for God. According to the Old Testament, with God's covenant it is possible for humanity to have this wisdom. It brings the light of God into the world by the work of wisdom. This furnishes us with the two elements around which the Christian life is organized. One is intelligence with regard to the Word in order to know what it is to live. The other is the knowledge of how this life is to be lived and the decisions to be taken. None of this is theoretical since it concerns our works, which are the result of good conduct paired with a gentle wisdom.

What is here translated as "gentle" is not as vague as it may appear. The Greek word is not the same as *agape*, but it does mean our love for others, shown by accepting and supporting them. Hence, the term "gentle wisdom" refers to governing our lives by love. It is at the very heart of the Christian life.

In verses 14 and 15, we encounter situations in which the interdependence between intelligence and wisdom has not been maintained, with the result that one of them dominates the other. If your heart is full of bitter zeal and the spirit of quarrelling, do not glorify yourself and do not lie against the truth. James is addressing not people who have simply misunderstood the teachings of the Bible but those who do not live according to their understanding. It is possible for them to have an excellent theology, as it were, but their conduct contradicts their understanding. In other words, their intelligence is in contradiction with their wisdom, and the result is a "bitter zeal" and quarrelling. The former refers to the greatest possible engagement people can have, as was exhibited during that time by the zealots in politics. Paul holds them up as an example of how engaged Christians ought to be. However, it may result in quarrelling and infighting in churches.

There are a number of ways in which an improper relationship between intelligence and wisdom can produce these kinds of situations. First, when people are absolutely convinced that they have the truth, everyone else cannot have it. They can no longer listen to others, which only leaves room for accusations. At this point there is no way out, because under no circumstances may Christians accuse each other. Unfortunately, we have all encountered these kinds of situations. Some people know that they have understood a number of things in the Bible, and this becomes the whole truth. It makes others into heretics, fundamentalists, liberals, and so on. As the accusations are flying, there will also be attempts to put pressure on others by any means including an intellectual, theological, or philosophical superiority or a moral fanaticism. All this happens in the name of truth.

Second, bitter zeal and disputes may also occur when some people are very sure of how Christians ought to behave under certain circumstances. It leads to the kinds of situations that we have already discussed in relation to the discrimination that results from people judging each other, to the point of making moral judgments on every person who behaves differently than they do. Often it is done with a great deal of engagement and zeal, but it is a bitter spirit leading to the kind of conduct that Christians are not supposed to engage in.

Third, an engagement full of zeal can also give rise to a Christian activism, which is just as dangerous as any other kind. It is characterized by a spirit of competition, criticism, and exclusion, and a judging and denouncing of those who do not belong to it. The above kinds of situations are all too common among God's people. James may well be referring to the many struggles over leadership and power in the churches of his time. This reference to bitter zeal and the spirit of quarrelling as being common in churches reminds us that many things can be done in the name of the Lord that are not inspired by him. We are reminded of Jesus' warning that he will be approached by people calling him Lord, claiming to have done all kinds of things in his name. Nevertheless, he has to send them away because he does not know them.

What these verses talk about is situations characterized by a spirit of division and domination creating disorder. It is now possible to begin to see how everything comes together. We are called to thoroughly understand God's Word and to make decisions about how best to conduct our lives; but there is an ever-present risk of quarrelling when engaging in theology and of a bitter zeal when we fully engage ourselves in a church.

It is at this point that the lie appears. The people who are animated by this bitter zeal and claim a right to dominate and impose their truth are also the ones who claim to act in the name of Jesus Christ. They thus introduce the lie. Our text refers to the lie against the truth. When we get all wrapped up in this quarrelling, let neither side ever claim that this comes from Jesus Christ. If under these circumstances, anyone claims to speak in the name of Jesus Christ, it is a lie. We now see how the diverse elements of the text fit together.

The text tells us that the wisdom we have just discussed does not come from above. It is of this world, carnal, and diabolical (verse 15). After the break between God and humanity and between God and his creation, the Bible refers to what has been separated from him in the former as the flesh, and in the latter as the world. A clear opposition is thus established between two ways of governing the world. There is the way of God, and the way of the one Jesus calls the prince of this world. There is the wisdom of God for directing the world, and the wisdom of the Devil. In each case, wisdom implies an approach to governing the world. Since God never chooses the use of means of power, he does not destroy the Devil.

What ought to trouble us today is that most Christians live like everybody else. Our text has just informed us that there are two very different ways of conducting our lives. We either serve God or the one Jesus refers to as the prince of this world. At one point, the Devil shows Jesus all the kingdoms of the world and tells Jesus that all will be his if he only prostrates himself before him. Jesus does not contest that all these kingdoms

belong to him. He replies by saying, "you will only prostrate yourself
before the Lord your God." Earlier on, Jesus had declared that he saw
Satan fall from heaven, which means that he is now in the world. In other
words, he no longer accuses us before God but brings divisions and accusations among humanity. Our witness before the world is to adopt as
our approach to life the way Jesus approached the world by never using
his power and instead relying on love. Paul illustrates this very well when
he tells Christians that they can eat any kind of meat, even what has been
offered to pagan gods, because these have no existence or significance.
Although they are free to eat this meat, they should occasionally refrain
out of love for a brother or sister who may take offence. In other words,
we must live our freedom not by means of principles but in accordance
with a love for those around us. Doing so is the wisdom of Jesus Christ. It
does not mean that we may not be firm or harsh if necessary, but it must
be done out of love, as Jesus shows over and over again.

The contrary wisdom is that of Satan, which is based on violence, power, injustice, fanaticism, and disorder caused by useless agitation. It must
not be imagined that this wisdom of the world is ineffective or inefficient.
It often appears extremely effective and efficient in comparison to God's
wisdom, which often seems weak and even a failure. Just look around in
our modern world. Much of science, technique, the economy, politics,
morality, and a great deal else belongs to this earthly wisdom, which is of
the flesh and diabolical in character.[10] I am not saying that these spheres
of human activities are exclusively evil, but our current technical means
unquestionably serve a wisdom that is diabolical.

Since there are but two kinds of wisdom, there can be no such thing as
human wisdom. We depend either on God or on the prince of this world.
It is one or the other, but we often want to have it both ways, as the letters
to the seven churches in the book of Revelation point out.

Recall the important affirmation that Jesus Christ is the wisdom of God.
It is worth rereading the first letter to the Corinthians, verses 19 to 30,
where we read, on the one hand, that Jesus Christ is the wisdom of God
and on the other that for us he was made wisdom. I believe the first teaching means two things. The full meaning of God's actions since the beginning is revealed in Jesus Christ. He is the one who makes it possible for us
to understand what God intended to do from the very beginning. In his
giving up all power and accomplishing a complete love, Jesus Christ is the
model of all God's actions. The second teaching, that for us he was made
wisdom, means that in Jesus Christ, and only in him, are we able to discover our own wisdom. It is a human wisdom that comes from above, and

is that of Jesus Christ. The revelation that Jesus Christ is God's wisdom, and that he is the only witness of that wisdom, shows us that God directs the world by his love and not by his power. The wisdom of God is to love the world, even to the point of giving his life. Consequently, there can be no competition between the wisdom of God and the wisdom of the Devil.

In verse 17, we learn the characteristics of the wisdom that may be granted to Christians from above. First and foremost, we are told that this wisdom is pure. The Greek word can also be translated as "holy." In the Bible this has no moral significance whatsoever. It means that someone or something is set apart from all the rest for a particular task. The resulting purity has to do with not being contaminated by what is separated from God (the flesh, the carnal, and the world). As a result, a wisdom that is holy represents a complete break with the world and the impossibility of any compromise with it.

Although holiness comes first, it is followed by four additional qualities: it is peace loving, considerate, conciliatory, and merciful. The first one requires no explanation. Consideration is a term that frequently occurs in the writings of Paul, where the Greek word is sometimes translated as "moderation." It must not be understood in moral terms as the need to avoid doing anything to excess. What the Greek word refers to is judging everything in a balanced manner so as to be able to conduct life in a way that is the opposite of the delirium characterized by frenzy and incoherence (in Greek mythology, Minerva was the goddess of moderation while Bacchus was the god of delirium). In a world like ours this is rather important, given that much of what we do economically, financially, and militarily borders on delirium. Careful consideration can help us avoid this. Being conciliatory also contributes to order and peace among people. It seeks to establish relationships that are merciful and that actively abstain from duplicity and hypocrisy. Finally, to be merciful is to be with others the way God is with us.

Together these four secondary qualities reflect being set apart from the world and the diabolical in order to exercise a love that re-establishes relationships. Doing so goes to the very heart of a Christian ethics. It is an ethics of both breaking and communicating with the world: each must go hand in hand with the other. There must be holiness, charity, and love. It means that we must break with certain kinds of relationships and establish others. Jesus referred to this when he said that if you have left your father, mother, brothers, or sisters, you will find many others when you announce the good news. The break with the natural relationships of the world means the discovery of more authentic ones that are founded on

God and established through the sharing of the good news. Doing so has nothing in common with becoming a hermit or an aesthete who withdraws from the world and will have nothing more to do with it. This is at best one aspect of holiness. Nor is it a question of simply plunging oneself into the world with love. Breaking with the world in order to establish a new relationship with it is found in many texts. If there is no holiness there will be no love, because simply breaking with the world without bringing it the love of Jesus Christ would make us into Christians who do nothing else but judge the world. On the other hand, if we simply plunge ourselves into the world in order to love it, we will be unable to truly do so because our love must come through our separation, as it were. It is analogous to being judged and forgiven at the same time. To be forgiven without having been judged means nothing, and to be judged without grace would be terrible. In all this we see that not lying against the truth means ensuring that your words and conduct go together. When you live this wisdom of holiness and love, you belong to Jesus Christ.

Verse 18 poses some difficult translation problems. It is possible to translate "the harvest of righteousness" as the fruits that constitute justice, the fruit borne by justice, the fruit that is sown by those who labour for peace, or the fruit for those who do works of peace. I have chosen the translation that appears to best fit the overall thrust of this letter and which is the most meaningful: the fruit of justice is sown in peace by those who search for peace. Understood in this way, this verse poses the all-important question of the relationship between means and ends.

Its continuity with the previous text derives from its being the conclusion to what we may think of as the dialectic between holiness and love. It refers to the common problem of means and ends. Searching for peace signifies the end (the goal or objective). Sowing in peace signifies the means for reaching the end. In other words, it is impossible to search for peace by just any method whatsoever. The means themselves must be peaceful. Those who belong to the wisdom from above must themselves be peaceful. There can be no discord whatsoever between the means and the end. Throughout the Bible, we are told that a good end cannot be achieved by evil means. The ends never justify the means. From a biblical perspective, evil means corrupt the ends. The strategy that will permit justice to reign must be based on the dialectic of holiness and love – having peace as its objective and using means that will permanently establish that peace.

The last detail of the coherence of this text is now within our grasp. We have seen that the wisdom from above is a certain way of conducting our lives in the world, and a certain way of guiding the world. The goal of this wisdom is to establish justice in the world. However, the world cannot bring about justice because its wisdom is diabolical and produces disorder. Justice can only be established by a search for peace through peaceful means; and this is the result of the wisdom that comes from above. Hence, if we seek to bring peace to the world, we cannot use means of domination and violence the way the world does. We must search for justice in peace, the way this has been accomplished in Jesus Christ.

Faced with this text, we as Christians have to admit that, almost throughout its entire history, the church has not practised this wisdom from above. We have almost never done so either individually or collectively, and we have not extended it to every area of life, be it economic, social, political, or any other. It is clear that we ought to have done so. Of course, I am generalizing, but I say that God's plan for the world through the intermediary of the church has failed until now. It shows the seriousness and the importance of the letter of James, addressed as it is to the twelve tribes in dispersion, which signifies the totality of the church from the very beginning until now.

In answer to your questions, I can readily understand your concerns about how we can possibly read and understand the Bible. My answer is similar to the one I would give when we are confronted with many other apparent impossibilities. We can read our Bibles because of grace, and that is all.

I believe that our Jewish brothers and sisters are entirely correct when they point out that, from the perspective of the Hebrew Bible, Jesus really did not say anything new. Everything he said had been said before; but there is one very important and radical difference. Jesus is the one who accomplished everything that had been written. He is the fulfilment of everything. Consequently, as Christians we must live by the intelligence of Jesus Christ. It is the reason why this letter is so profoundly Hebrew in character – James fully understood this.

It would seem entirely hopeless to begin, in this world organized by the technical means of power, to live by peace and justice. Again, I would answer very strongly that it is possible. Christians can act according to justice because they have been justified. We have the justice of faith. If we are sure that God clothes us with his justice, then we can act in that justice. If we do not believe this, then it is indeed impossible. In the same way, we can act peacefully because we are reconciled with God, and in Jesus Christ we are reconciled with our fellow human beings. That is where we must start.

From a theological perspective, the divisions in the church are unacceptable and diabolical. Protestants and Catholics have a great deal in common, and I would say the same thing for the Protestant denominations. What divides us frequently comes down to one or two specific points, which, in comparison to what we have in common, can never justify dividing the church. At the same time, I do not place much confidence in ecumenical councils, where the heads of different Christian institutions learn to get along. Genuine ecumenical actions should begin with the members in the practice of their faith, by reading the Bible together and praying together. This is where we can have genuine reconciliation and reconstitution of the church. It is for this reason that I believe that what we do have in common, such as a certain confessional faith or credo, should never be removed from our services. It is important to recognize that some of the splits resulted when a church completely neglected a part of the good news. For example, in our tradition in France we gradually neglected the teachings about the Holy Spirit, and were taken aback by the rise of the Pentecostal movements. However, we have never sufficiently recognized this. The same kind of thing has happened in the past. The problem with many of these situations is that when a certain neglect is discovered, things quickly get out of hand as a dissident group overcompensates and makes one issue the all-important one. This is wrong even when the original concerns were legitimate. I believe that today many of the older differences have largely fallen by the wayside; and frequently what stands in the way now are the institutions and not our ability to share the Christian life.

Chapter Fourteen

Life in the World

What Is the World?

Chapters 4 and 5 deal with our relationships with the world. I will begin by examining James 4:1–6 to clarify what is meant by the world. This understanding is also found in I John 2:15–17. Within Christianity, there has been a long tradition of contempt for the world, an attitude that has taken a variety of forms. For example, there was the teaching that everything here below is bad and everything above is good, so that Christians should not attach themselves to the things of this world and instead should preoccupy themselves with what is above. Similarly, the body was bad, but the spirit was good. There were many variations on these themes. A strong reaction against all this began to occur in the nineteenth century with the reasoning that what was material was not especially bad. Moreover, theological arguments emerged showing that the soul was not good. There was a growing recognition that the dualism between matter and spirit came from Greek philosophy and was foreign to Jewish and Christian thinking. For Jews and Christians, there was no separate body and soul because these were seen as inseparably intertwined in a human being. A little later, there was a reaction against asceticism and Puritanism. Still later, there were attempts to rehabilitate our scientific, technical, economic, and political endeavours – in short, everything that constituted the world. During the early twentieth century, this led to a theological reinterpretation of what the world was in the New Testament. It became what we mean by this word in a daily-life sense: everything around us, including the world of our society and the natural world. For example, some commentaries on the gospel and the letter of John sought to demonstrate that "the world" referred to the powers that were hostile to God. The material and natural world thus became legitimate, as it were, and was not condemned as such, other than the powers that were in rebellion. Hence, Christians have no problem with their daily-life world but only with the world of these powers. As a result, what is designated as "the world" in the Bible no longer refers to society in general or any human activity in particular. When consulting any contemporary biblical dictionary, you will see that these kinds of interpretations are now mainstream.

These theological developments confront some exegetes, including myself, with an insurmountable problem related to the term "world" itself. All the authors, including John, Paul, Peter, and James, use the word "cosmos." These authors, as we have seen time and time again, chose their language with great care and precision, and even went as far as inventing a new word to designate something new. It is highly unlikely, therefore, that they use the word "cosmos" for two entirely different things: the cosmos as the created universe, which includes all life around us, and the cosmos of which James and John speak in our texts, designating what is rejected and condemned. With theologians such as Niebuhr, Bultmann, and Tillich, this kind of thinking evolved further, leading to the view that the world is essentially positive in character. It leaves us with two cosmoses, as it were, without any way of telling them apart. I believe that we cannot make this distinction, and I also think that our texts make it very clear that our world must be understood in its totality. I find it rather astonishing that a number of commentators and theologians have used the well-known text that "God so loved the world" as showing that the world must be good. I regard these kinds of interpretations of our texts and the theological developments built up with them as being completely untenable. In the Bible, the world seems to appear as one whole, but we must not interpret this as a philosophical or metaphysical concept. In James, the term occurs four times and appears to refer simultaneously to the place where we live and to where we encounter the destructive powers that dominate it. Understanding this in an existential rather than a metaphysical way implies that we are not forced back to the dualism of Greek thought. It is a question of how we must live in and relate to our world, which, from an eschatological perspective, has already come to an end.

We do better by carefully examining what chapters 4 and 5 teach us about this world. In chapter 4, we see that it is closely associated with commerce, wealth, and the accumulation of riches. Chapter 5 deals with employers as well as wealth. The text then turns to the search for material happiness, followed by trials and judgments. Throughout there are statements about pride and the spirit of power. In other words, when the text tells us to separate ourselves from the world, the activities that are condemned are commerce, the exploitation of workers, and other things of that sort. It is because of these activities that we are told once more near the end to break with the world. How is it possible then to claim that the world has nothing to do with society and such things as socio-economic activities? The exact opposite appears to be the case.

We must be in this world but not belong to it. It represents God's creation, and in this respect it is very important to recall what we are told in the letter to the Romans: "The whole creation suffers and groans as in the pains of childbirth and waits to be delivered." Hence, the world within which we as Christians must learn to live also suffers from the domination by evil powers. We cannot simply reject and abandon it, because it is involved in everything we do. The Bible is very realistic on this point. We must learn to live in it.

How do we reconcile this with the radical and total condemnation of the world in James and John? The common theological explanation is that it is because the creation was separated from God when humanity broke with him. I think it has much more to do with the time during which James and John wrote these texts. There was a growing competition between a developing Christianity and a widespread belief in stoicism. I am not referring to the stoicism of the great philosophers developed during the previous two centuries but of a widespread popular stoicism that had become a very influential ideology of the time. It held that the cosmos was the highest spiritual value because it represented the perfect order exhibited by the stars. This perfect harmony was taken to be God himself. As long as people were in harmony with the laws of this cosmos, they could behave as they pleased. The economic and political implications of this view of human life tended to be rather antisocial. There was nothing outside of this cosmos, as it were, and all meaning could be found within it. In contrast, the biblical view is that it is a creation of God, with the result that the meaning of life could not be contained within that creation. Meaning transcends life in this world. Moreover, this creation is not ours since it belongs to our Creator. We are merely the stewards, which means that we cannot do with it as we see fit. In the same vein, there are substantial differences regarding the bringing up of children. According to the stoic outlook on life, it was a matter of clearing away all the obstacles without which children would encounter a meaningful life, because all meaning resided in the cosmos. However, if beyond that world there is a Creator, the children's relationships with him cannot be ignored. This radical contradiction between Christianity and the popular stoicism of that time helps to explain, and may have been at the root of, the radical condemnation of the cosmos. The first generation of Christians tried to make it very clear that nothing good could come of this cosmos, neither as the natural world nor as the social world. For example, observing the natural world in order to learn its laws and follow them had the result that people were pushed by their passions to end up in disorder. In fact, our text shows a connection between our passions and this cosmos. The natural good cannot be a source of salvation. Hence, James and John likely chose the term cosmos for polemical reasons, but also to affirm that the creation of which the Jewish Bible speaks has nothing whatsoever to do with this cosmos and the attitudes to human life so popular at that time. Breaking with the world included a break with the cosmos. I recognize that this is very general, but it may prove helpful in understanding the texts to which we now turn.

In order to understand the significance of the first three verses of our text, we must remind ourselves that this letter is addressed to the twelve tribes of Israel and the entire church. Among them there were fights and quarrels, with the result that the church was not exactly characterized by good relations among its members. The situation is attributed to Christians' attachment to the world. The text asks them whether they do not know that the love of this world means enmity towards God. In other words, an attachment to the things of this world is the cause of hatred and competition among all people, including Christians. This attachment does not disappear just because we have become Christians. There can be no such thing as a pure and sanctified attachment to the cosmos. We cannot live the freedom of our faith and at the same time allow ourselves to be possessed by other powers. It is the activities of the world that induce this divisive behaviour. Ultimately, it is the question to whom or what we are attached. If we are attached to the world, there are a variety of unavoidable facts. When we obey our own nature and tendencies, they will follow the ways of the world. Our passions attach us to the world.

There is therefore a correspondence between our own nature and that of the world. Here, the teaching of this letter is again in complete harmony with that of Paul in insisting that our nature is not good. To obey our passions will assimilate us to the world. A teaching of this kind is important at a time in which we have rediscovered the importance of human desires that must be liberated and not repressed. The question as to why this ought to be the case is not even asked. The result will be an even stronger attachment to the world. In any case, any struggle against repression in order to liberate inner forces cannot detach us from the world in order to lead us towards God. These forces will do the exact opposite. Non-natural behaviour can only come from the Holy Spirit, as we will soon see.

Having affirmed that divisive behaviour comes from an attachment to the world, our text examines the kind of behaviour that was common at the time. It says that people desire but do not possess. Whenever some desires are satisfied, there are always new ones, with the result that we can never have enough. Even when we resort to the most extreme means (including murder), we can never satisfy all our desires. We have already discussed that, in the Bible, covetousness is a significant power. It is described by James as the root of all evil deeds, and the Decalogue concludes with covetousness as the basis of everything else. It expresses itself as a will to power, domination, accumulation, and the exclusion of others. There is a close relationship between the cosmos and the coveting of it. Once we are driven by covetousness, we will never be able to satisfy our desires. We desire but do not have because we will never have enough, and what we have is never secure. This teaching is particularly relevant for a consumer society entirely based on coveting. It tempts us to fulfil our desires in every possible direction, thereby fragmenting our lives in pursuit of the world. Intellectually this is justified by new philosophies of desire.

Our text also explains that we do not have because we do not ask God. I believe this is an important point. Our covetousness pushes us towards conquest, but the things that can really satisfy us are in the hands of God, who freely gives them. He will not allow us to seize them. God gives to those who ask, and this brings out two completely contradictory attitudes. One is exhibited by those who uproot, conquer, and win by whatever means, including violence. The other is shown by those who simply ask in prayer and who await a response. We are told that we do not have because we do not adopt this latter attitude, and instead seek to seize what we desire by means of power. We will never succeed because the one who holds what is genuinely good and able to satisfy us is God, and he will not let us seize it because he only gives it to us for nothing. Even when from time to time we ask, we do not receive because we do so badly, with the aim of satisfying our desires. God does not respond to false requests that are inspired by the world. This is not at all the attitude of someone who recognizes that God is the all-powerful One who gives, and therefore humbly asks for what is necessary, for charity and for God's glory. Rather, it is the attitude of someone who asks in exactly the same way as a person who conquers for the purpose of satisfying his or her desires. It is all about domination, grabbing, and, in the end, diminishing God.

The key point of this text is that God is truly the Lord of all that is good in the world. The people addressed in the letter have an attitude of conquest and possession, and therefore will not succeed. The only acceptable attitude before God is that of prayer and asking. We thus encounter the different possible attitudes of Adam before God. Will he choose what will make him equal to God, or will he continue to ask God and receive what is good without ever seeking to be equal with him? Will he continue to live in communion with God, or will he compete with him? In other words, these attitudes also apply to the Creation. Is the world ours to exploit, dominate, possess, and utilize, even by killing, or will we respect it? It is clear that this text has enormous ecological implications for our world today. Will we be its conquerors in any way we see fit, or will we respect it? If we obey the law of the cosmos and our desires, we will persist to the very end and then ask God for what we have been unable to conquer; but this simply will not work.

We have mentioned the implications of coveting and the will to possess and dominate, both for consumer societies based on mass production, mass consumption, and mass advertising and for the environmental crisis. All this raises the fundamental question as to whether we have the right to possess the Creation in any way possible. Do we have the right to exploit nature to satisfy our endless desires? Can we do anything we deem necessary to matter, plants, animals, and ourselves? Is whatever becomes scientifically and technically possible permitted by God? Today we must ask these questions in relation to the universal strategy for fulfilling our desires and conquering everything on earth and beyond, and heed the warning that in the end it cannot succeed. As Christians we must not surrender ourselves to the will for power that so dominates our world.

Let us take a closer look at verses 4 to 6. The previous verse reaffirms the opposition between the spirit of pride and conquest and that of humility and asking. This part of the text deals with two themes. I will begin with the first. There needs to be a radical separation from the world because love for this world is enmity against God. Being a friend of this world means trying to succeed in it and thus making yourself an enemy of God. It is not a question of God's rejecting us, but of our rejecting God. Any claim that we can be a friend of the world and at the same time be faithful to God is based on an impossibility. Jesus warned us of it when he said that we cannot love God and Mammon. The world demands to be loved. Doing so is not a matter of our attitude towards material things or of our external behaviour. It goes much deeper, to the very core of our being, in the sense that where our love is, there our entire life resides.

That life is either all about the love of this world or all about the love for God. If we love the one, we hate the other.

Because it is a question of love, the letter of James addresses Christians as adulterers who are being unfaithful to God. The Bible frequently draws on the analogy of a marriage between Christ and the church or between God and his people. It is a question of faithful love between the two. If we betray God's love, we become adulterous.

We do not sufficiently appreciate the fact that the world is not satisfied until we love it. Our politics makes this abundantly clear. No democratic or totalitarian state is satisfied with mere obedience. I do not mean this in an abstract sense. Our politicians desire to be loved, as their behaviour in front of crowds and on the media demonstrates. We are told that we must love our country and be willing to die for it. The state would not pose such a problem if it merely organized and managed things for the common good. However, politics never stops there. It ultimately is a question of love.

The second theme in this text regards the Spirit. The text says that God jealously longs for the Spirit he has made to dwell in us. What is so very serious about Christians' giving themselves over to love for this world is not so much the loss of ourselves as it is our trying to make the Spirit stand behind and support our behaviour. I believe this is something that is very difficult to understand. From the moment God reveals himself to us, speaks to us, and grants us his Spirit (and this does not have to be accompanied by spectacular events), he does not withdraw it. When we make mistakes, there is not on the one side the Spirit of God, which is good and intact, and ourselves on the other side because of our mistakes. God so completely stands behind us and is one with us in Jesus Christ that he enters into our life's journey, including our behaviour. This is what is so tragic. As Pascal put it, Jesus Christ is crucified until the end of the world. We continue to crucify Jesus Christ when we draw the Spirit of God into the evil we commit. This Spirit cannot remain pure when we are impure. When we participate in this world, which this letter warns us is defiled, we begin to understand what this involves, namely, that the Spirit is affected by this defilement. When God reacts, it is because he is himself implicated in the human journey. God is jealous for our freedom, in the knowledge that when we pursue our passions and love for the world we become slaves of what we love. It is also with jealousy that God longs for the Spirit that he has made to dwell in us. When we have received the Spirit, it is intolerable that we are covetous, envious, enslaved by our passions, and even murderous, because our being so engages God's Spirit. The writings of Paul say the same thing.

We are thus faced with the question as to what our attitude towards the world ought to be. As the letter of James clearly shows, it cannot be a retreat from the world. We cannot isolate ourselves in a way equivalent to Noah's Ark. Nor does it require some kind of act or behaviour in and of itself, such as asceticism. A third kind of erroneous response to the world consists of beginning with a separation from the world as a point of departure. We must remain in the world and participate in its activities, but we must do so differently. Our behaviour must be different from that of those who belong to the world. As we will see, our text suggests a very different kind of beginning in evolving our relationships with the world.

Although our faith sets us free from the world, we must always ask ourselves whether what we intend to do will glorify God, that is, reveal who he is. Did we glorify him when we converted people by the sword, burned heretics, exploited Native people, and so on? In our daily lives we must always ask whether we do something out of love for God or out of love for something else. The former will set us free, but the latter will cause us to be enslaved by what we love and bring sorrow to God's spirit within us. We have heard the Word of God. This Word has created his spirit within us, with the result that whatever we do involves this spirit. It makes us responsible before God. If we reveal who God is and if his spirit expresses itself in us, then he will grant a greater grace. In other words, renouncing our desires and our coveting does not deprive us, but instead provides us with a richer blessing.

The World and Defilement

In James 4:7–10 we encounter two major themes that may not be immediately evident. First, there is the question of impurity or defilement. The second is that of humility and our approach to God. I will begin with the first.

I would like to go back for a moment to verse 27 of the first chapter, which sets out the plan of this letter. It tells us that the pure religion without fault before God our Father consists of visiting the orphans and the widows in their afflictions, and preserving ourselves from being defiled by the world. In our text, we find the same affirmation regarding our relationships with the world. Immediately after we are told that love for the world is an iniquity against God, verse 8 tells us to clean our hands and to purify our hearts. It is a question of the impurity of the world, and of being defiled by it. What this means is rather complex. For a long time, this business of impurity and defilement was either not taken very seriously or was reduced to something vaguely moral. As more became known about so-called primitive religions, another interpretation began to emerge, which suggested that it was a question of the "magic" of impurity and defilement. As a result, defilement became interpreted in the context of the sacred and the profane. The former was regarded as comprising two opposites: a sacred that may be called pure and a sacred of defilement. Certain objects associated with the latter were believed to bring evil or a curse on anyone who touched or took them. This is the concept of defilement based on magic.

Using these insights, a number of commentators on the Old Testament argued that it contains two concepts of guilt: defilement and debt. Many theologians continue to interpret the former in terms of magic, following the ethnologists and sociologists. As a result, the need to wash your hands, eat kosher food, and observe the rituals of purification such as those involving a red heifer (Numbers 19:1–10) and relying on a scapegoat to carry away defilement were interpreted as being essentially magical in character. In contrast, debt involved being a debtor before God. The priests were supposed to have introduced the original conception of guilt as defilement, and the prophets the conception of it as debt. It was also thought that the New Testament had done away with defilement in favour of debt, as the Lord's Prayer appeared to show. In fact, Peter's vision of the cloth filled with impure animals, which he was commanded to eat, was used to demonstrate that nothing was impure anymore. Jesus touched lepers as well as the dead, who were all impure, and he did not purify himself afterwards. It was concluded, therefore, that in the New Testament the concept of defilement had completely disappeared. In turn, this led some commentators to suggest that the letter of James could not be taken seriously because it spoke of defilement, which was no longer considered an issue.

I believe that much of this fails to take into account that the people of Israel, from very early on, had succeeded in dissociating what was impure and defiled from magic. The reasons are simple and clear. First, contrary to what is often asserted, almost nowhere in the Old Testament do we find statements to the effect that this or that object or person is impure. Instead, the text almost always declares, "you will hold (something) as impure" or "you will regard (something) as impure," and so on. This is the case, for example, in the book of Leviticus when it speaks of impure animals or lepers. It is not a question of something being impure in itself but of our considering it as such. It represents a commandment from God to regard certain things as impure. As a result, the defilement that comes from touching something that is declared to be impure is not a result of contacting it, as it is in magic, but of disobeying God's commandment. Consequently, touching something declared to be impure is an act of disobedience, and a person becomes impure because of it. It is not a question of magic but of debt.

Second, impurity can also result from the mixing of elements that are regarded as being mutually incompatible and should therefore not be brought into contact with each other. In some cases this incompatibility may be obvious, while in other cases it is simply a question of God's having declared this incompatibility. For example, it was not permitted to cook a lamb in the milk of its mother. This concept of impurity was developed in relation to a unique conception of the creation. The opening chapter of Genesis describes the process of creation in terms of acts of separation.[1] Beginning with the *tohu bohu* (the chaos), God separates day from night, the waters above from the waters below, the waters from the land, and so on. From what was without form, a confusion, as it were, God creates something that is ordered. From this perspective, defilement and impurity may be regarded as resulting from an act that is the opposite of those of creation. It involves a mixing and a return to a confusion of elements that are incompatible, such as night and day, for example. All this leads to what I regard as a central theme in the Old Testament, that of impurity resulting from bringing into contact incompatible elements. Whether these elements are incompatible in themselves or whether God has declared them to be so makes little difference: they represent acts of de-creation and a partial return towards the *tohu bohu*. Hence, the separation from the world referred to in our text has nothing whatsoever to do with an idea of the world as unclean or impure in itself. Instead, it is a question of the incompatibility between God's Spirit and the spirit of the world, which should never be confused. Conducting life by the Spirit of God can under no circumstances be assimilated into conducting life by the spirit of the world. In sum, all this has nothing to do with the world being defiled in itself but of its being dominated by an ensemble of powers that must not be related to or confused with the Spirit of God. I believe this constitutes the essential element of what is meant by defilement. The fundamental theological issue is that God is not identical to his Creation and, reciprocally, the Creation is not God. If we allow the spirit of the world to enter into our churches, for example, we mix and confuse God and his Creation. Paul makes it very clear that our bodies are the temple of the Holy Spirit, with the result that if we behave in conformity to the spirit of the world, we mix and confuse the Spirit of God and the spirit of the world and thereby reduce God to his Creation. Jesus also sheds light on this by declaring that we cannot serve God and Mammon. It is impossible to love both at the same time. It is also the reason why James declares that the love of the world is enmity against God.

Defilement is thus related to a very different conception of the world. God's forming and ordering of the world implies a classification, in the sense that certain things are compatible with each other, and this is what constitutes purity. In other words, what is pure is what corresponds to God's creative act itself, which forms and orders things. Impurity in the Old Testament has nothing whatsoever to do with magic because impurity is the chaos: the non-form, and what has been mixed together. Hence, there is an establishment of elements of which each one is compatible with all the others, and the establishment of other elements of which each one is incompatible with all the others. Impurity and defilement thus constitute the opposite of the Creation. The demonic is this order of confusion, as we see with the possessed man living in the tombs, symbolizing a confusion between life and death. As a result, the separation from the world as referred to in the letter of James has nothing to do with the world being unclean or bad in itself. There simply is nothing that is pure or impure in and of itself, as we saw with Peter's vision, because freedom now reigns in this matter. Paul speaks of these issues in the same way.

What we do have is an incompatibility between the world and the Spirit of God. We must not confuse the one with the other. Nevertheless, throughout the entire history of the church, including our own time, there has been an ongoing tendency to either eliminate the world to the benefit of an absolute spirituality, resulting in a confusion caused by a certain absence of the world; or the inverse, where the Spirit is eliminated, making the world and our presence in it all-important and thereby producing another kind of confusion.

The differentiation between the world and the Spirit is fundamental in the context of the Creation. In the same vein, purity and defilement are fundamentally tied to the Creation. It is a question of: Is God within his Creation in a way that intermingles the two (leading to one kind of confusion), or is he entirely other than that Creation? Must we regard society as being intermingled with God, or is he entirely other? Here we are once again confusing God with society. The letter of James strongly warns us against these kinds of confusions.

The world in itself is not damned, but Christians are called to be separated from that world, as God is separated from his Creation. If Christians are the bearers of God's Spirit, they must be distant from the world, as God himself is distant from his Creation. This has nothing to do with being a stranger, being on the outside, or having little or nothing to do with it. God continues to have a relationship with his Creation, but there can be no identity between, or mixing of the two. In other words, impurity is a matter of not maintaining that distance. As we have already discussed, it is a matter of loving the world instead of the Creator of that world, and trying not to confuse the two. We are back to what Jesus taught, namely, that we cannot serve both God and Mammon; we serve one or the other, which implies a distance. Mammon as a deity will be destroyed, but money in and of itself is not necessarily evil. However, we must establish a distance. The same issue occurs with respect to wealth. We must establish a distance to avoid defilement, and any defilement requires purification by re-establishing that distance.

In order to understand the text referring to our being divided people, and to the work of the Devil as dividing us, we must place it in the context of creation and de-creation. In his act of creation, God establishes distinctions, gives form to things, and clarifies things. The Devil also produces distinctions and divisions in his work. However, when God divides, he does so in order to establish relationships of love. When the Devil divides, he does so to establish relationships of hostility. It is the kind of diabolical work that undoes the Creation through the making of divisions in hate. In contrast, God divides for love to become possible: there must be two, and hence a division. When the text tells us that we are divided, it must be interpreted in the context of the preceding texts, namely, that we as Christians quarrel, covet, and even murder. All this and more show the diabolical divisions within each one of us.

As I noted earlier, I believe that the second theme in this text concerns humility and our approach to God. When we have understood that love for this world is an iniquity against God, and that befriending this world turns us into his enemy, our first reaction is likely to be to separate ourselves, or at least distance ourselves from the world in order to be God's friends. Doing so has always tended to lead to either a kind of moralism or a kind of asceticism. However, this is not in accord with what the Bible teaches. We back ourselves into this corner whenever we put our own initiatives first: we ourselves decide to separate from the world. This is not at all how we should proceed. Once again, we need to pay close attention to how carefully this text is constructed. Having warned us, it shows us how to move forward: by submitting ourselves to God. The first step is not to reject the world but to submit. James is not addressing society at large but fellow Christians who have heard the Word. He does not say that we must submit to God's will by constantly asking ourselves whether he would want us to do this or that. Instead, it is a matter of recognizing that the very meaning of our lives comes from the living God, who loves and saves us. It is then possible to resist the demonic because God is the one who reconciles and not the one who divides by undermining and breaking the relationships between himself and humanity or those among people. In other words, if we submit to God we cease to be opposed to him and to others. The text tells us that, when we do this, the Devil will flee far from us because he will be unable to break the unity lived in love and freedom. When we do this, the world will cease to be the active and aggressive power that it is. In other words, breaking with the world is not a question of doing certain things or not doing others but of submitting to God.

We become responsible for this resistance, and we must not expect God to do this for us. We are not "off the hook," so to speak, when we attach ourselves to his will. In the same vein, just because the Holy Spirit exists does not mean that our own spirit has disappeared. We encounter this kind of reaction over and over again.

The reasons for this reaction can now be readily understood. We are not submitting ourselves to the power of God. We submit to the God who is love; hence, we submit our lives to his love. The love of God does not manifest itself by violence, constraints, or external interventions. We must respond to this love, and in so doing, we resist the Devil. His flight signifies that all powers of dividing people, breaking up relationships, and outbursts of hatred or tensions will disappear from within our individual selves, and from our relationships with each other. The reverse is also true. If we are attached to the world, and we love this world more than God, then our lives are not really submitted to his love. These are our points of departure.

The text then continues with a kind of burst of commandments: to approach God, and he will approach you; to clean your hands, to purify your hearts, to sense your misery, and to humble yourself before God, who will lift you up. This text is also carefully put together, and is not at all a set of pious or moral platitudes. The elements are tied together to form a clear progression. It begins by telling us to approach God, and thus not to try to do these things by ourselves. Remember that this epistle is addressed to us as Christians, and to the whole church. What this means is that we, and the church, are not necessarily or constantly close to God. The people who believe in Jesus Christ need to approach him. There is no constant and automatic relationship with God. There are times when we are close, and others when we are not close at all. From the perspective of this letter of James, to approach God refers to meditation, contemplation, reading the Bible, and worship services. It is in moving towards God that he approaches us. As an aside, this was one of the many texts that angered Luther, and this is why he did not really like this letter – for him there was no question of our approaching God, but only of God approaching us. Otherwise, we would be back to the ziggurats and other religious attempts to reach him. For him, the initiative was exclusively God's: God simply decides to approach us regardless of what we have decided. I disagree with his interpretation because of the way this text unfolds. We cannot take a phrase such as the one about our approaching God and he will approach us out of the context of submitting ourselves, resisting the Devil, approaching God, and so on. This approach is integral to something much larger. Moreover, it corresponds exactly to what Jesus told us: when I present myself before God, he is there, and when two or three are gathered in my name, I will be among you. It is the same kind of movement or development that begins with our getting together in his name. When we say that God is always there, we are not really saying anything. It is not a question of our having some kind of feeling that God is present, or that we go to church to be a little closer to him. In the context of our text, approaching God is a question of humbling ourselves before him so that he will raise us up. It is not the religious act of attempting to ascend towards God.

Within our proximity to God, and God's to us, what was impossible before now becomes possible. We can now clean our hands, purify our hearts, sense our misery, and so on. We are back to purifying ourselves from defilement, which involves both the exterior and the interior, as it were: our relationships with the world and the divisions within ourselves. We cannot live and act in the world without getting our hands dirty. It simply cannot be avoided. At the same time, it is also unacceptable to keep our hands clean. All this presents enormous difficulties to those who are deeply engaged in some kind of action in the world. That it cannot be otherwise does not make it any easier to accept. It is the exact opposite of the position taken by people such as Jean-Paul Sartre, for example, who claimed that it was perfectly all right to have dirty hands. For Christians, having dirty hands is a part of the order of evil, and yet we cannot do things differently. It belongs to the order of necessity, and not the order of freedom. In other words, we must undertake the reverse journey: we are engaged in the world and get our hands dirty, so that we must also disengage from it in order to approach God, and then clean our hands and get back into the world. From a biblical perspective, there is only this kind of movement in our lives, as opposed to distinct and separate situations in which our hands are either clean or dirty. Once we have cleaned our hands, we are not done. The movement of our lives continues.

The same can be said regarding the purification of our hearts. This purity is the opposite of the divisions discussed above. Moreover, this purity is not moral in character. When we undertake what is good, it is not a question of our hearts being good. What constitutes the purity of our hearts is explained by what follows in verses 9 and 10. As we discover time and time again, this text is built up very differently from those of Paul, for example. He proceeds in a more rhetorical manner in which ideas are linked together by "hence," "because," "therefore," in order to fit everything together in a logical approach. James does not work this way. He makes grand affirmations that are explained in the verses that follow. In order to answer the question of what is meant by the purification of our hearts, we must refer to what comes after: sense your misery, be in tears, and humble yourself so that your joy changes into sadness. This is what is meant by purification. If we translate the text somewhat differently, we would speak of an awareness of sin, an appeal for forgiveness, and repentance (sense your misery, be in mourning, and shed tears). These are the elements of purification. It reminds us of a great many texts in the Old Testament, especially in the Psalms and the prophets, where it is written that God does not desire sacrifices and burnt offerings for our purification but instead a repentant and humble heart (Psalm 51, for example). In other words, purification from defilement is achieved by an awareness of sin and an appeal for forgiveness.

The misery to be sensed within us refers both to the evil within us and to our weakness. It is the equivalent of being sinful, that is, of not being free, and thus having our lives diminished in the sense of being less full, or of even being empty. Doing bad things is just a symptom, as it were. It is a matter of weakening our lives, and thus diminishing them. It cannot be reduced to a question of morality. Nor does the Bible ever see it as being accused. Becoming aware of our sins is an appeal for mercy because God sees us first and foremost as people who are unhappy, weak, and helpless. This is what sinfulness is all about, and this is what we are asked to feel as we hear God's call and offer of grace.

All this becomes even more evident when we recall that the overarching theme in the preceding verses was that everything in the world was dominated by a spirit of power, domination, and conquest. We were told that we covet but do not possess, that we can become murderous, and that we quarrel all the time. All this was associated with our sinfulness, which is now followed up by a call to recognize our misery. This appeal is

a reaching out by the One who loves us and knows how unhappy we often are in the world. It must not be interpreted as an accusation. This
argument reminds us of the book of Revelation, in which the churches
who believe themselves to be rich are told that they are really very poor
and naked. I believe these texts describe the way God sees us. We have
been so focused on the moral aspects of sin that we have come to believe
that God sees us first and foremost as people who do evil. That is part of
it, of course, but I think it has much more to do with our unhappiness,
misery, and helplessness. When we become aware of this, we will be in
mourning and in tears because of who we really are.

This brings us to the call to humble ourselves before God, in this
"movement" that began with cleaning our hands. The important phrase
in this text is that we must do so *before God*, which means before the cross.
It is the only place where we can realize the depth of our compromise
with the world, the corruption of our hearts, and our misery. It is only
there, where we are responsible for Christ's death, that we can truly cry
because of this absolute evil. It is also before this Lord that the full awareness of our misery will not end in complete despair. In other words, our
mourning and tears are not an expression of despair. This situation is
thus radically different from existentialism, for example, where becoming aware of the limits and weakness of humanity leads to despair. Being
before the Lord is to be before the one who died in order to save us. It
brings us back to the relationship between God's justice and love. This
all-powerful God shows that he desires to save us through the love of Jesus
Christ. At the same time, this God crucified in Jesus Christ is the all-
powerful one who can do so. This is the mystery of the theology of salvation, namely, the relationship between the power and the will of God: he
desires to save us and he is able to do so. We can thus humble ourselves
before the Lord as the one who brings us the only true response. It is not
he who humiliates us, contrary to the way this would happen in the world.
In the world we are humiliated, but here we humble ourselves because
God never humiliates anyone. God never seeks to diminish us in any
way. We, having become aware of our finitude and weakness, humble ourselves before the Lord, who raises us up – the verb is the same as the one
used for the Resurrection. Having raised and resurrected us, the Lord
brings us into his forgiveness; but before this happens, we have to traverse
the desert of purification, as it were. It is in this desert where our spirit of
power, domination, and conquest is taken away.

The journey described by the text may be summarized as follows. It
begins with God's revealing himself to us. As believers we approach, and

God approaches us. We humble ourselves before God, who raises us up and resurrects us. However, once completed, the journey does not end. We undertake it over and over again during our lives. Again, these four verses contain an entire theology.

These verses open up two new themes, which will preoccupy us for the remainder of this study. The first deals with the way the separation from the world expresses itself in our lives. It occupies the remainder of chapter 4, and chapter 5 up to verse 12. We will see that the separation from the world results in an abandonment of the spirit of power by not judging others, not claiming to be in control of our future, not exploiting others, not accumulating wealth, and much more, because these are only some examples. The second one deals with the way the Christian life expresses our reconciliation with God. It takes up the remainder of chapter 5, and thus takes us to the end of the letter of James.

In answer to your questions, I would like to go back to what we learned about sin in the book of Genesis. The sin of humanity was our taking in our own hands the determination of what is good and what is evil. This is the literal meaning of the Hebrew phrase, usually translated as "the knowledge of good and evil." In this way, humanity sought to appropriate what only God can do, and thus put itself in his place. The impossibility of a Christian morality stems from our not having the right to put ourselves in the place of someone else in order to tell them what to do. It amounts to providing them with a kind of system that they have no choice but to follow. There can then no longer be any freedom and love. For this reason, morality is the diametrical opposite of Christianity. In the same vein, the commandments are a guarantee of what and how we can live, by tracing the limits of where and how we can be free – limits that lie within what deprives us of our freedom and our life. In other words, if you wish to live, do not steal or kill. In the book of Deuteronomy, God says that he puts before us *the good and life* as well as *the evil and death,* and urges us to choose the former. Of course, every society has no choice but to create a morality for its members. However, this morality is of the order of necessity, of obligation and evil, while Christianity is of the order of freedom and love. Since Christians are members of societies, they constantly face the temptation of transforming their faith into a (cultural) morality and religion, thereby surrendering their freedom to another enslavement.

The World of Judgments and Planning

Once again, the text of James 4:11–17 appears deceptively simple, and little more than moral advice: not to judge, and to live knowing that our lives are limited and that we do not know our future. If we go no further than these superficial impressions, we will not understand anything about these texts. They are of an existential and not of a moral character.

I will begin with the first two verses (4:11–12) concerned with judgment. They provide us with a first example of the implications of being separated from the world and the differences in behaviour that should come with it. The world is a place largely organized by the classification that results from judging everything around us, including people. Everything is separated and divided by these judgments, as is evident in the vocabulary of our language. Clearly, this goes much deeper than moral judgments. We judge everything: the world, society, social categories and classes, races, nations, and much more. It is a totality that is global in its scope. At the same time, the judgments we make have a reciprocal character: As we judge others, they judge us, and this creates all manner of social barriers that continue to be extensively studied in sociology. Our entire world is based on judgments of all kinds. No society can exist without these judgments, which determine whether someone is accepted or rejected by a group.[2]

This interdiction of judging contains two aspects directly related to what preceded this text and what follows it. The warning to separate ourselves from the world, clean our hands, purify our hearts, and so on, leads to the subject of not judging. The significance is clear. Separating ourselves from the world must not provide us with the position for judging those who are not separated from the world. Doing so to purify ourselves from defilement does not give us the right to judge others. The separation from the world must never create a place for judging the other. I believe this is the link between our text and what went before.

The interdiction, not to judge, also relates to everything that follows it in this letter. By arranging the text in this manner, James implies that there cannot be any judgment in what follows, and yet what follows is occasionally extremely harsh. For example, he attacks the rich but is careful not to judge this or that person who is rich. He does not call into question their person or their life. What he attacks is a social category of people. Any one of us could belong to this category or identify with it. Any one of us can receive the Word regarding the rich as directly concerning himself or herself after having been warned that it is not a question of judging others. When we read a biblical text like this one, we have to receive it for ourselves, and we must not use it against someone. The relationship between not judging and what follows is therefore very clear.

Having put our text in the context of what went before and what went after, we must now attempt to understand what the Bible means by not judging others. I do not believe it has anything to do with a spontaneous and natural reaction, which attracts us to some people and not to others. The Bible does not ask us to have the same affection or sympathy for everyone. It reminds me of Jesus, who loved and preferred his disciples over others. Jesus clearly had his preferences. Nor do I believe that this judgment is of an intellectual character. Not to judge others is always a question, and in a sense, a final question, of the sense or lack of sense of someone's life. What we are not allowed to do is to prejudge the damnation of anyone or whether his or her life is conducted in evil. Such a judgment would result in a separation from, break with, or destruction of someone, because it essentially judges his or her salvation. Jesus tells us how important all this is – we will be measured with the measure we use to judge others. The kind of judgment he is talking about is a final judgment of sorts regarding the whole of a person's life. We cannot make such a final judgment regarding the salvation or damnation of others.

A judgment concerning an evil done by a brother or sister is not a discernment of the Spirit. It is the opposite of love and charity. Recall 1 Corinthians 13, which deals with love. This text essentially tells us that if we see and judge the evil within others, we do not love them.

Our text speaks of judging other Christians who belong to the church. Belonging to the church has little to do with the church as organization and institution – it refers to the church constituted by God as the body of Christ. Hence, if we condemn anyone by our judgment, we break the unity of this body. Since this kind of judging goes on all the time within churches, we do well to recognize how serious this is. It is not a question of morality but of breaking the unity of the body of Christ, which is the role and work of the Devil. The *Diabolos* is the one who divides and breaks apart, with the result that judging other Christians introduces him into the church.

Our text furnishes several arguments for not judging others. Who are we to judge others? There is only one lawgiver and judge who can save or set free. The parallel argument Jesus makes for not judging others also questions who we are. Are we really so different from the people we judge? Since none of us can escape God's judgment, is there any room for claims of superiority? If someone is a little more moral, serious, or better at doing God's will than someone else, will such relative differences be significant under God's judgment? The answers are clear.

An argument not found in our text but present in others has to do with a lack of charity. To love your neighbour forbids judging him or her.

Another argument in this text affirms that there is only one lawgiver and judge. The implication is that when we judge others, we put ourselves in God's place. Only God can define what is good and what is evil, which is why he gives the law and judges according to it. What this means is that God establishes the good. I know that this can trigger an endless theological discussion as to whether there is a good other than the one God has declared. I believe, however, that the good cannot exist in itself. What is good corresponds to what God has declared to be so. We have already discussed this in our study of Genesis.[3] There we read that when God declares that something is good, it is good. There is no point looking for another foundation for the good, nor for another definition. The implication is that when we judge, we repeat Adam's mistake when he wanted to decide by himself what was good. The knowledge of good and evil has often been interpreted as an absolute knowledge. It is not even a question of knowledge but of a decision about good and evil. Adam substitutes himself for God when he decides that this is good or this is evil. It also means that any morality determining what is good or bad belongs to the break with God and everything that comes with it. We speak of Adam's original sin, but then let us recognize how easy it is to reproduce it over and over again in our own lives.

A final explanation of the interdiction against judgment appears to be ambiguous and difficult to explain. The text tells us that anyone who speaks against a brother or sister or judges them speaks against the law and judges it. If you judge the law, you are not keeping it but judging it. I think that this statement contains several aspects. The first relates to the promise that the Holy Spirit will place the law in your hearts. Until now, the law had remained exterior, as it were, but this changes with the coming of Jesus Christ and the Holy Spirit. The law now becomes interior to people. Living within the law means in conformity with the will of God. It is the same teaching as the one from Paul when he says, "Your bodies are the temple of the Holy Spirit." From then on, when we judge brothers or sisters we judge their conduct, and this may be in conformity with the law of God because of its being in our hearts. We are no longer talking about the Mosaic law with its two tablets, which are exterior to us and which everyone can read. With the coming of Jesus Christ and the Holy Spirit, the law is now within all of us Christians, but it is not necessarily identical in us all. This interpretation is confirmed by the letter of James when earlier we examined the law of freedom: speak and act as being judged by this law of liberty. Now, in the fourth chapter, James says that when you judge others, you judge the law, this law being the law of freedom. Those whom we are tempted to judge have been liberated by Jesus Christ, which means that the free conduct of their lives does not

concern us. We may not judge them because they are free. They obey the
law of freedom; hence, if we judge them, we may well be judging the law
that God has placed within them. If we judge others, we create an obstacle in the way of their freedom. When brothers and sisters have been
set free by Jesus Christ, we have no right to place them under some commandment or judgment. If we did so, we ourselves would not be following the law of freedom.

Is it really possible to live without judging? Is this judging so integral to
our lives that we cannot get along without it? These kinds of questions
must not lead us into moralism. We cannot understand and receive this
text if we regard it from a moral perspective. However, if we have understood how serious the judging of others is, then we have no other recourse but God's grace. If we are honest with ourselves, we will have to
recognize before God that we have hindered the freedom of others, that
we judge them in an ultimate way, that we even judge their salvation, and
that we break the unity of the body of Christ. When this is recognized in
our confession of sin, then there is no other way out for us except through
grace. This text, therefore, which at first may appear to be little more
than moral advice, leads to the very foundation of the good news, which
is our salvation by grace, and also the root of our being (in an ontological
sense, as it were), in a very deep way.

If we may not judge others, what practical steps can we take in place of
judging? If the behaviour of a brother or a sister concerns us, what we
must do is to attempt to enter into a dialogue to see if they obey the law
of freedom or some foolish fantasy. We must try to establish a relationship with him or her. It means sharing the daily practice of our faith, with
its joys, difficulties, disappointments, and doubts. Doing so will confront
us with our own shortcomings. We can then share the experiences of
having been forgiven and being loved, and this can go very far. In doing
all this we must remember that we must put ourselves on the level of the
other just as God has done for us. I recognize that all this is very difficult
and time-consuming, and that it is much easier to judge others behind
their backs or dismiss them by means of a convenient label such as fundamentalist, liberal, or even heretic. We thus divide the body of Christ,
contribute to the demonic, glorify God as the opposite of who he really
is, and bar the road to the kingdom of heaven for many.

The remaining verses of our text (4:13–17) are specifically addressed
to Christians. They tell us that we speak just like everyone else as we plan
what we will do today and tomorrow in order to make money. There are
two elements: the undertaking of daily-life projects, and a certain spirit of

pride. The undertaking of daily-life projects is not the problem. What this text speaks of is our behaving as if we are masters of our time, activities, and lives. It is the question of deciding for ourselves what our life will be. It is the mistake of not recognizing that God is the master and thus placing our lives in his hands. The consequence is that our intentions, decisions, and choices can (and often do) get in the way of God's actions with regard to us. These actions are not always evident and clear. They are often hard to discern, because they leave us with the possibility of making our own decisions and choices. If I plan my entire day with not even fifteen minutes to spare, I will not know when I have a certain availability to listen to something that may come from God and is likely to be very subtle. Remember, for example, the way God spoke to Samuel. In other words, with all our planning and decisions, we could be blocking a possible action of God in our lives. Of course, this cannot be remedied by paying lip service to God as our Lord. For example, beginning in the seventeenth century, it became customary for Protestants in France to end their letters with an acronym that meant "God willing" (DV – *Dieu voulant*). This is a matter of writing whatever you like and then saying, "God willing." In the same vein, we pay only lip service to acknowledging God as our Lord if we then proceed with our daily lives like everyone else. Living in recognition that God is our Lord implies a certain renouncing of the running of our lives as we see fit. It is not a question of making our own plans while telling ourselves that if God wants he can upset and change them. These kinds of approaches are condemned in our text, which reminds us that we do not even know what will happen tomorrow.

Our text tells us that we must abandon our pride by voluntarily submitting ourselves. Doing so greatly affects our private and public lives. For example, it also concerns our research into what may happen in the future in order to plan for it. I am convinced that the double element of our insisting on our planning everything and on forecasting everything as much as possible is directly related to a loss of faith. To the extent that we can no longer collectively entrust our world to a God who is good puts us in the situation of trying to make up for it by planning and forecasting or by non-technical means such as astrology and horoscopes. However, these passionate interests in the future often lead to an attitude of despair, and this concerns me a great deal. For example, attempting to predict the evolution of public opinion by polling has caused some observers to warn us that this is a bad development because it could fundamentally change our elections and thus democracy itself. Another example of our anxiety is the proliferation of insurance for everything and anything in order to assure us that we are secure. Clearly, this is something entirely different from entrusting our future to God. I recognize that it is not easy to give up on insurance. You have to take God's assurances pretty seriously. Nevertheless, there is no point talking about putting our lives in God's hands and at the same time having all kinds of insurance, as if God counts for nothing. We cannot have it both ways: take charge of our own lives until we die, at which point we put it all in God's hands. When we take the will of God seriously, we are always confronted with very difficult decisions, to go one way or the other. For those of you who know me well, when I say these things, I begin by seriously calling my own life into question.

Our civilization gives this text another dimension. During the days of James and Paul, it was entirely obvious to everyone that there were limits to the extent to which you could plan life and death. As a consequence of our ever more powerful means, we live as if this kind of control is becoming feasible. We have been planning the life and death of animals for some time, and there is a continuous advancement in our ability to do the same for human life. It continues to raise some of the deepest and most troubling questions regarding our civilization. Collectively, we live as if we are the masters of all life on this planet. Nevertheless, our experiences with planning and forecasting have borne out our text. Few if any plans have ever been realized, and not a single forecast has ever proved accurate. Even the forecasting of the evolution of our technical capabilities has proved impossible. Human life remains a great deal more unpredictable than we are generally willing to acknowledge. The text from Ecclesiastes referred to in these verses reminds us that our lives are but vapour (also translated as smoke, mist, or vanity) that appears for a limited time and then disappears. Attempting to control this vapour is a folly against which our text warns us. As Christians we are placed before a choice: either live by your plans or trust God.

To be open to and available for God's will has generally less to do with interventions or miracles from above than with our relationships with others. This is often where we encounter God. Recognizing this takes on another dimension when we realize that these others frequently constitute an obstacle in our way, as recognized by the commandment to love your neighbour as yourself. The Sermon on the Mount tells us that if we love only our friends we are no different from anyone else. Our neighbours are not the kinds of people we get along with. They are the opposite, thus constituting an obstacle in our lives. This is exactly how Karl Barth defines who our neighbour is in his *Church Dogmatics*.[4] Our text implies it, coming as it does after our being told not to judge others and to be available to them. After all, judging others is an easy way to dismiss them and put an end to the relationship. It is also directly related to how we use our time. If I am master of my time, I am also master of my relationships. Consequently, verses 11 and 12 are closely related to our text. By judging others I decide who is in and who is out of my circle of acquaintances and friends. Similarly, by thoroughly planning my daily-life activities, I essentially decide who will be within and who will be outside my social circle. In contrast, if I go about my daily life with a great deal of flexibility, this fluidity will translate into my time and relationships, thus leaving opportunities for the Holy Spirit to express itself.

What our text condemns is not planning or acquiring insurance themselves, because God has the power to upset this and more. What is condemned is our pride, expressed in our boasting about ourselves and putting ourselves in God's place by planning our time, engaging in commerce, and making money. We claim to be able to decide the purpose and goal of our lives. In other words, we decide to whom or to what we will consecrate our lives. That is exactly what the text says. We go to a city, pass some time there, engage in commerce, and make money. We are thus consecrating our lives to this. These choices, which we as Christians make all the time, are those of the world all around us. Christians talk like everyone else, as James reminds us. We think the same way, and we make the same choices. We believe ourselves to be separated from the world, but we are not. Verse 17 tells us that they who know how to do the good but do not undertake it commit a sin. It is clearly addressed to Christians. Once again, a choice has to be made as to whom or what we consecrate our lives to. Is it to what everyone else thinks and does, or is it to what is good? In the latter case, we must remember that it is God alone who declares what is good.

If we have not discerned the will of God, and have not heard and understood what he has declared to be good, we will do something else. Even if we do what is good, we still do not have the right to judge those Christians who do not. Knowing what is good, we as Christians have a much greater responsibility than anyone else.

I would like to say two more things about this text. First, those who know how to do good but fail to do so commit a *sin*. We must make an important distinction between a sin that we commit and the condition of being sinful before God. It is this latter condition that has been transformed as a consequence of the pardon we have received in Jesus Christ, but this does not mean that we no longer commit any sins. Doing so is no longer the result of having been conditioned by sin or by our sinful nature, if you like. Having been forgiven eliminates this conditioning, with the result that we can now get on with our lives in freedom. When we do so, we are bound to make many mistakes, and these will constitute our sins. Dreadful as these may be, they do not change our fundamental condition.

The other matter has to do with knowing what it is to do good but failing to do so. In conventional moral theology, this was referred to as sinning by omission, and this was frequently considered as less serious than sinning by commission. I do not believe that this is what the Bible teaches at all. For example, in Matthew 25, which deals with the judgment of the nations, Jesus tells us that each time we fail to provide the necessities of life to one of the least of us, it is to him that we have done this. I take this to be the parallel of our text: what is most important is not so much hating someone but failing to love him or her. It is ultimately on the basis of this failure to love that we will be judged. Once more, however, we have to recognize that this is absolutely impossible. How many times in our lives have we not failed to bring the love of Jesus Christ? We are brought to this recognition because it will bar the road to a new legalism. Recognizing how impossible it is for us to live as bearers of the love of Jesus Christ will also make it impossible to say things such as "God willing." All we can do is to ask for forgiveness, because there is no other way out. This supposedly moralistic epistle has been put together in such a way that our moralistic way of talking and living is constantly redirected back to the very heart of the good news, namely, forgiveness and grace.

Chapter Fifteen

To Whom or What Do We Belong?

The World of the Rich

James 5:1–6 continues to deal with our separation from the world and the need to purify ourselves from being defiled by it. It now turns to the issue of riches. I propose to discuss four themes: the scope of this issue, the reason for the dire warning, the description of this warning to the rich, and the reference to "the just" in the last verse. The text follows the prophetic tradition that we examined in Amos, but it is unique in the sense that it focuses on one form of riches, that related to money.

In the Bible, the scope of the subject of wealth is enormous. Although money and gold are used as symbols of all forms of wealth, wealth also includes every way in which one person may be superior to another. The Old Testament speaks of riches that can take many forms. A person can be rich in children, happiness, reputation, years (a long life), knowledge, intelligence, craftsmanship, and work. From a biblical perspective, anything that gives a person a certain superiority or advantage over others is considered to be riches of some kind. For example, we have become well aware of how knowledge can provide someone with a certain power over others. Furthermore, the drama of the Jewish people has everything to do with having received the revelation from God, which is another form of riches. Christianity has a great deal of difficulty understanding that it also has these riches. To some non-Christians it seems perfectly obvious that what is referred to as having faith is a form of riches. The very term implies having something that others do not have, which can open the door to behaviour similar to that of the wealthy in this regard. This latter form of riches is well illustrated by the Pharisees. They were not the kind of people whom we can easily criticize. They were extremely virtuous and pious, and observed the commandments much better than most of us do. Nevertheless, for them, this constituted a form of riches, which was their justice and justification.

When we think about riches in this way, very few of us remain unaffected by this teaching. It certainly is not simply a matter of not having money, given that any form of superiority is a form of wealth. We do well to recall what happened after a young man left Jesus deeply saddened because he could not give up his wealth (Matthew 19:23–30). Jesus followed up by telling his disciples that it was easier for a camel to pass through the eye of a needle than for the rich to enter the kingdom of God. Every person of that time would have understood the meaning. The "eye of the needle" was a small door through which a single person could be admitted to a walled city at night. A camel could also squeeze through this door provided that everything it carried was taken off, including the saddle. When Jesus' disciples heard this, they were greatly astonished and asked, "Who then can be saved?" Jesus replied that only God can do this. In other words, these people, who had given up a great deal in terms of riches in order to follow Jesus understood very well that they still had other forms of it (family, good health, etc.), and wondered how they could possibly shed it all to enter God's kingdom. They clearly grasped the scope of people's riches.

Why do the rich deserve such a dire warning? According to our text, riches lead to certain kinds of behaviour. As far as money is concerned, there is always the desire to have more of it, referred to as accumulating treasure. However, it is the same for other forms of wealth. Every intellectual seeks to accumulate his or her knowledge and skill.

A second form of behaviour that flows from having riches is to place our confidence in it as a kind of security for the future. We desire to be the master of our future, and wealth is an important means for doing so. It reminds us of the parable of the person who has accumulated a great deal of wealth but does not live to enjoy it.

The third kind of behaviour that flows from having riches, according to our text, is the oppression of others. A superiority in any form of riches implies competition with those who have less, leading to a form of domination.

Finally, riches can provide a certain happiness. Our text talks about living on the earth in luxury and self-indulgence. In other words, wealth can bring you a certain kind of happiness. However, in his letter, James warns us of the misery that will come, and he advises the wealthy not to rejoice in their riches. After all, doing so is to behave as the world does.

There must be a break with this kind of behaviour. This parallels the warning Jesus gave to the Pharisees. However, unlike Jesus who tells the rich young ruler to give his wealth away, James does not discuss this break with the behaviour of the world in these terms. James advises the rich to weep and wail because of the misery that is coming. When we understand riches in the broader sense that we find in the Bible, it is frequently impossible to give your riches away. Of course, at one point the church defended the view that if you were intelligent you had to give up being so if you wanted to be a true Christian. You had to become stupid, as it were. James recognizes that, in most cases, it is impossible to stop being wealthy. For example, each time you read the good news you become richer, whether you like it or not. It would do us no good to become poor in this respect. James therefore advises us rich people to break with the behaviour of the world by crying because of the misery that is coming. Instead of the usual rejoicing, we are asked to deplore being rich people, regardless of the form taken by our riches.

Why does James advise the rich (in money) to deplore their being rich? Is it really because of the coming misery? It is not likely that this misery is damnation, since James is talking to Christians. The nature of this misery is not specified. For example, is it a misery on this earth? Is it a spiritual condemnation, or something else? The text provides us with three elements to help us better understand this.

The first is that their riches have rotted, their clothes are moth-eaten, and their gold and silver are corroded. James knows very well that gold and silver do not corrode. What he is undoubtedly referring to is that this gold and silver have already been destroyed on the inside, so to speak. This is borne out by the verb in Greek, which is in the present tense. It is not a question of something that will happen later, when riches may disappear during their lives, or that they cannot take their riches with them when they die. What the text tells us is that these riches are rotted and dead at this very moment. Their situation is so serious because they have riches as a consequence of desiring them. When it comes to life or death, the Bible makes it very clear that we are attached to what we love: if we love Jesus Christ, we are attached to his death and his resurrection, while if we love something else, we share the destiny of what we love. For the Bible, our love is the most fundamental attachment, and it can be to God, people, or things. In the Old Testament, God expresses his fury against idols and false gods because he cannot accept that humanity, with its love of these false gods, will disappear along with them. It is not in the least a question of a competition between the true God and these false gods.

We find the same idea in our text with regard to money. Their corroded gold and silver will testify against them, and it will eat their flesh like
fire. This is not the fire of damnation, but it destroys the riches to which
they are attached, and that will be a painful business, as we shall see.

A second element deals with how money is obtained. The wealthy always
enrich themselves by taking something away from others. The text complains that the wages owed to the workers who harvested their fields are
crying out against them. Moreover, the cries of the harvesters have reached
God's ear. We encounter this theme throughout the Bible, especially in
Isaiah and Amos. However, in those texts it appears to be more a question
of the honesty of the employers. James goes much farther by claiming a
certain necessity or inevitability, because the wages are crying out against
the wealthy. It is as if they have no other choice. The workers are deprived
of the value they produce, since gold and silver affect far more than wages.
Money gives the rich a certain superiority over others, which either implies
their inferiority, or that in one way or another the rich have deprived these
people of something that they have used to build up their own superiority.
James is not speaking merely of social justice. He is also dealing with it as a
disobedience of the law, because there are two texts (Deuteronomy 24:15,
for example) that explicitly forbid depriving workers of their wages. The
entire salary must be paid before sundown. It does not say that you must
pay whatever wages are promised but the entire value of the work produced. If this is not done, the employer commits a sin. This commandment, along with the one found in Jeremiah, makes it clear that where
there is no love for your fellow human beings there is no love for God. Our
text appears to go a little farther. There is an opposition of sorts between
the ways of the rich, who deprive others with a measure of violence, and
the ways of the people who are oppressed and who cry out. The difference
is that the latter express their situation in words. Perhaps I am taking this a
little too far, but I could not help thinking as I read and reread these texts
during the last few days, that there is a kind of opposition here between
riches and the Word. Riches imply an appropriation and an accumulation
by acts of violence, while the Word cannot be owned, cannot be accumulated, and communicates with others by recognizing them. In contrast, violence always denies the other. If this is so, it is fundamental for a theology
of the Word. Since this Word is at the very centre of the revelation, the
condemnation of wealth is even more fundamental than I had previously
thought. So often we have made the problem of the rich into a moral and
social issue, while this goes much deeper. Since all forms of riches imply a
measure of violence, they constitute the opposite of the Word.

According to our text, the oppressed have no other means than their words. However, God hears their cries. The name used for God in the Greek text is the one we encountered before in Amos, namely, the Lord of the Armies. One of the explanations found in the Talmud is that God is at the head of an army that cannot be numbered, with the result that even the smallest and least significant are a part of it. In referring to the Lord of the Armies, James reminds us that this is not only the God who is all-powerful and who judges, but also the God for whom the poor, the miserable, the humble, and the rejected count. He will gather them and bring them into his army. It is a clear reference to the ultimate intervention of God, who has heard their cries and is coming with his army. It is hope for the poor and the oppressed but a disaster for the rich. This interpretation can never be used to justify a revolt against the rich and powerful. In our time of increasing poverty and despair this is hard to accept. Some may wish to accuse us of helping to keep the poor in their place. I am well aware of how often the Christian church has used biblical arguments against groups of agricultural or industrial workers, their demonstrations of protest, or their unions. Worse, Christian churches have rarely protested when even industrial leaders use the Bible in this way. Once again, we none of us have any right whatsoever to use biblical texts to justify ourselves or to reinforce and strengthen our social position. We must humble ourselves before the Word and submit ourselves in obedience to what is good. Having said this, we must be mindful that nowhere in the Bible, neither in the Old or New Testaments, do we read that the poor must revolt to obtain justice for themselves. Nor do I believe that any of these texts regarding the poor can be used to justify a violent revolution, as a few liberation theologians have done.

Even though these kinds of texts focus on one particular form of wealth and its consequences for the poor, they must not be separated from the general teachings regarding all forms of wealth. As we have seen, all riches create a power for the wealthy to dominate others. Such domination diminishes them, since riches tend to possess those who have them. They love their riches and place their confidence in them, thereby becoming incapable of loving their true Lord. The exploitation of the poor by the rich continually deepens because the latter always covet more. Christians are frequently tempted to turn their faith into a possession, and this is often perceived by non-Christians as a justification of a certain social and moral superiority. Those who do so frequently also use texts to judge and condemn others, which shows their lack of submission to the good that God wills.

Some non-Christians have observed these kinds of things in their societies. For example, Karl Marx observed that, in his day, the less people spent the less they existed. At the same time, the more people had the less they existed. In this way, the economic system possessed people's lives and being. Today we are still a very long way from understanding that under the current system and its mass societies it is still true that the more we have the less we are as human beings and, in the case of us Christians, the less we are the human beings we are called to be.

A third element suggests that on this earth the wealthy have a certain happiness and reward. The Greek text is very strong. The rich have lived on the earth enjoying great pleasure and every delight, and they have satiated their hearts in the days of slaughter. The parallel text is found in Matthew 6:2–4, where we are told that the rich already have their reward. They have their riches for now, and this is exactly what they desired. This line of argument, which occurs throughout the gospel of Matthew, is not easy to understand or accept. The judgment he makes of this is that we cannot have two goals or two purposes for our lives. We simply cannot serve God and Mammon, for example. Hence, if our goal in life is to be rich and happy, we may achieve it, but we must not expect that we can add to this an accumulation of justice, as it were, or an accumulation of spirituality, knowledge, or intelligence. If we acquire happiness through riches, we will have "satiated our hearts in a day of slaughter." I believe this text is closely linked to a kind of apocalyptic thinking of the time, although the book of Revelation itself had probably not been completed in James's day. From this perspective, all of human history must be regarded as days of slaughter because of the presence of diseases, wars, and everything that destroys. Human history is an immense slaughter. How do the rich respond? Instead of supporting others and standing with them, they separate themselves from everyone else in order to enjoy what they have and live a life of luxury. I am reminded of what some of them did during the Black Plague in 1340, which in two years killed two-thirds of the population in a large part of Europe. For example, the population of Limoges dropped from around five thousand to six persons. The rich fled the towns where the conditions were worst to go to their villas in the country, taking with them enormous quantities of provisions. They shut themselves in and enjoyed themselves while the world perished. This is the image I always have in my mind when I read this text. In other words, what the rich do by satiating their hearts in the middle of slaughter is at the heart of evil.

What is so important here is that the text explicitly addresses itself to Christians, as we have seen. In other words, we are not talking about evil rich people outside of the twelve tribes, and thus outside the church. The text speaks of Christians. It means that this letter was written during times when the Christian church had become more affluent, and wealthy people joined it. However, these wealthy new members were not particularly well regarded. The church certainly did not aggressively attempt to win over the elite. Since they were also pardoned, there was no reason to reject them or expel them, but they were not exactly received with open arms either, as is clear from the book of the Acts of the Apostles and the letter of James. When rich people became Christians and joined the church, they were clearly told what was involved, but they were not told that they were damned since they were received as brothers and sisters.

Another important detail is that the rich are told that they are accumulating riches in the last days. This latter phrase refers to the time following the death and resurrection of Jesus Christ. In other words, they have not discerned what the life, death, and resurrection of Jesus Christ really signify. They were not behaving as if they were in the presence of the Kingdom of God, which was imminent. As James tells them: These are the last days and you are wasting your time accumulating riches that have already rotted. As a result, they will serve no purpose in these last days. Clearly, saying anything of the kind to pagans would not be understood by them. The text clearly speaks to the rich who have become Christians.

Having described the meaning of riches, and having examined on what basis James condemns these riches, we now arrive at the third theme. The judgment against the rich is not a moral one. It is not a matter of their being bad rich people. For James, there is no such thing as good rich people versus bad rich people. Nor is it a question of good or bad behaviour or intentions, in order to counsel rich people to adopt a better morality. It is not a question of morality – the letter of James simply speaks about the rich.

Instead, the message to rich Christians is all about waiting, in an eschatological sense. They are in the last days, and their riches are rotten (the verb is in the present tense). The judgment of the world and the kingdom of God are coming, and everything must be interpreted on this basis. Being rich means participating in the powers of this world (which will be destroyed) instead of in the love of God and his kingdom, which is coming and already among us. The letter of James refers to the kingdom of God in a way that reminds us of the parables of the kingdom of heaven in the gospel of Matthew. The sixth verse confirms this interpretation.

The final theme I would like to discuss is the reference to "the just" in verse 6. It informs the rich that they have condemned and killed the one who is just and who did not resist them. There have been many interpretations of this text. One is that the poor simply do not have the means to go to court and plead their cause. Another is that the wealthy always manage to legalize their violent actions against the poor. I have some difficulties with these kinds of explanations because the text does say that the poor were unable to oppose the wealthy. Moreover, the Greek text refers to the one who is just, and not to "the just" in the plural. Clearly, this is a reference to the only one who is just, namely Jesus Christ. Since this letter is addressed to Christians, there can be no doubt about this. It means that the rich within the church have condemned and killed Jesus Christ. The evil of the rich, whatever form their riches may take, leads to these consequences. The reason is that Jesus Christ was killed as a result of the break with God, the desire to dominate the whole Creation, the will to possess every form of power, and the intention to shut God out of his Creation. The text that confirms this is found in Matthew 21:33–41, which is the parable of a person planting a vineyard and renting it out. Later, he sends his servants to collect his share of the harvest. The servants are beaten, stoned, and killed; he sends more servants, and they are treated in the same way; and finally, he sends his son, thinking that they will respect him, but his son is killed as well. The traditional explanation held that the two rounds of servants represented the patriarchs and the prophets. God then sends Jesus Christ. However, I would add that this kind of behaviour is a permanent feature of the relationship between God and humanity following the break. With the Tower of Babel, humanity seeks to exclude God altogether in order to possess and dominate the Creation. These developments paralleled the processes associated with wealth. As a result, the rich are responsible for the death of Jesus Christ.

Verse 6 also tells us that the one who is just did not resist. He allowed himself to be condemned. In other words, he did not use his power, and hence there was no power struggle between him and the rich. The depth of the evil of the rich comes out when they do not hesitate to kill the one who was weak and did not resist.

The mirror image of this interpretation is that Jesus Christ takes on himself the condition of the poor. Clearly, this is a fundamental text for contemporary theology, which associates Jesus with the poor. Another text that has been used for this is Matthew 25, but I do not believe that this constitutes a good interpretation. However, James is very clear. The rich deprive the workers of their wages, and they also kill the one who is just. The connection between the poor and Jesus Christ could not be any clearer than that. Jesus Christ took on himself this poverty. Some interpretations take this a step farther by concluding that Jesus *is* the poor. I do not agree with this. This is not to say, however, that Jesus Christ is not the one who is poor, nor that whenever we mistreat the poor or exercise any form of superiority over others, we do not touch Jesus. When we encounter a poor person, Jesus Christ is not entirely in that person. He is not identical to that person, and this has rather important implications. It is as if there were two commandments: each time we attack the poor, we attack people who are poor, and thus we attack God, who knows these persons. Such would not be the case if Jesus Christ were entirely within these persons.

Our text appears to end on a tragic and condemning note. Jesus Christ's way of being just is his following the way of non-power and refusing to compete with any power. It is for this reason that he is the one who is just. He acts in ways that are other than those of power. The reason he identifies himself with the poor is out of love. Since the poor have been the most deprived of their humanity, they are loved more than anyone, as we are told in the Old Testament. In other words, the one who is just and who identifies himself with the poor is also the one who loves and who saves. The opposite of riches and the accumulation of wealth is when everything is free (gratis). The law of riches is buying and selling, while the law of love is everything being freely given. Therefore, verse 6 warns us that we as the rich have condemned the very one who grants grace and pardon. It is not a question of his being the just one for himself, but of being the just one for the poor, the one who pardons. If we now go back to the beginning of this text, we see that it tells the rich to weep and wail because of their wealth, and because they cannot behave in any other way than that of the rich. Hence, they are driven towards the one and only possibility for salvation, and that is to appeal to the one who is just and whom they have killed. The text leads them back to grace, not to damnation.

We can now understand the logic of this text, as it were. The one who is just identifies himself with the poor; he does so out of love and because they are most in need of that love. Because he loves the poor, he has only one way of approaching them, which is that of non-power. The only law he has is of grace, but this grace is not limited to the poor. The rich can become poor when they weep and wail because of their wealth. When the rich begin to truly understand their real wealth, they can gain access to it through pardon and grace, and the one they have crucified will grant it. I believe this is how the sixth verse refers back to the first one. These texts are extremely dense and rich, and I am sure that I am far from having dealt with all of it.

In response to your questions, the happiness desired by the rich is very different from the happiness referred to in the Sermon on the Mount. What constitutes happiness in a society varies a great deal. Generally speaking, it is what most people desire, namely, a little more comfort, money, ease of life, and so on. In a modern mass society, happiness is strongly associated with consuming and with material well-being.

As I mentioned, Christians have sometimes been envied by non-Christians because their faith can provide a great deal of consolation during times of suffering. In other words, there is a certain recognition that we are rich in this regard, and I believe that to be the case. However, along with this come the temptations associated with being rich. In the case of spiritual riches, this takes the form of appropriating the Word of God when, instead of speaking God's Word, we speak what we desire to do with it. In this case (and this is very common), we behave as the rich do. We would do well to remind ourselves of the warning issued near the end of the book of Revelation, where we are told that if we add anything to that prophecy, God will add to us the plagues described in it, and if we take away from it, God will take away from us our share in the tree of life. It is the reason why some great theologians have refused to prepare commentaries on this book, but I believe that this warning applies to the entire prophecy, and to anyone who preaches on it. It is probably something we should think about whenever we prepare a sermon. We must never appropriate God's Word to hide behind it or to influence and exercise power over others. Throughout its history, the church has done so to make itself into a kind of fortress. From the perspective of our text, we have been on the side of the rich, and not on the side of the poor. We have to learn to use our riches in ways that are other than those of the world.

For example, when we do something that is free and gratis with our money, we are disobedient to the banks and the entire monetary system. It constitutes a desacralizing activity with regard to money. The same is true if we burn the money received in the collection at our services. People may object that this money could have been put to better use, and that is undoubtedly the case. However, every time we are obedient to the utility of our money, we obey the law of Mammon. The only way to deal with Mammon is to get away from everything having to be paid for. Every time we give freely, without any goal or objective, as an act of pardon and grace in Jesus Christ, we engage in an activity that desacralizes Mammon. All this is very difficult. For example, someone who is extremely good at making money and who does so like any other wealthy person cannot compensate by giving most of the money away. As an intellectual, I confront the same kinds of problems. How can I avoid acting as a rich person in the intellectual world? Perhaps the most difficult situation arises when a politician wielding a great deal of power is converted. It is not easy to see how faith can act in the world of political power.[1]

Being possessed by riches of any kind raises the question of human freedom. The texts regarding riches must be read in the context of the whole letter, whose entire structure is centred on human freedom. We are fundamentally and essentially free under the law of freedom dominated by mercy. There is another aspect of all of this which you have picked up in your questions, and which I should have dealt with. Because we are free, the focus is constantly on what threatens that freedom, and on what could destroy it entirely. We have already discussed how this happens when we claim to be masters of our time, and thus want to plan our daily lives and our futures. We have seen how the same thing happens with riches. Paul puts it this way: everything is permitted, but not everything is useful. In other words, you were emancipated in order to be free; therefore, do nothing which could alienate that freedom. There can be no other foundation for a Christian ethics. It cannot rob us of the joy of living, but instead, it must ensure that in this joy of living, we remain free. For example, someone has expressed this issue very well in relation to cigarettes; the only question we need to ask ourselves is whether we smoke cigarettes or whether these cigarettes smoke us. The joy of living is not limited to God, the kingdom of heaven, and salvation; it includes all of life and our relations with others.

The issue of humility is endlessly misunderstood. We must make a clear distinction between humility and humiliation. Humiliation is an action that comes from outside, as it were, and that oppresses and destroys us. Humility comes from within and does no such thing. However, the problem of humility is that practically every intention to be humble is an occasion for pride. As long as we are preoccupied with the question as to whether or not we are humble, we are trapped, because we are preoccupied with ourselves. Freedom is the opposite of being preoccupied with yourself, through relations of love. In the Old Testament, humility and humiliation are closely interrelated. It is as if it is impossible to be truly humble without being humiliated. All this once again reveals that, ultimately, we are totally dependent on grace.

One of the bitter disappointments regarding the behaviour of the Christian church during the last two thousand years is that it often sought and exercised power. Faced by economic and political powers, it desired to be a counter-power of the same magnitude and kind. As a result, it became contaminated by the powers of the world.

Finally, there is no doubt that the Bible forbids the charging of interest. It may be helpful to understand why the Christian church opened the door to doing so. In western Europe during the Middle Ages, the customary interest rates amounted to 12 per cent per month or 144 per cent per year. Beginning with the sixteenth century, a distinction was made between this kind of usury and a more acceptable lending of money at a rate of 8 to 10 per cent per year. A significant economic transformation aided this distinction. Increasingly, money was no longer lent to the poor for their subsistence, a practice that had been the case almost everywhere. This usury had amounted to literally stealing their lives. With the gradual development of capitalism, money was lent to affluent entrepreneurs for the purpose of making more money by, for example, investing in ships for expeditions and trade. At this point, money began to play a very different role in human life and society. Especially among the Protestants, the attitude towards money became increasingly more positive, to the point that in 1830, when young Christians approached a French Protestant leader to ask how they should live their lives, they were advised that the best they could do was to become wealthy. Generally speaking, when the Protestants became wealthy they tended to accumulate their wealth because they did not spend much of it on possessions.

Divided Loyalties

A rapid reading of James 5:7–12 creates the impression that we are dealing with little more than two items of moral advice; to be patient and not to swear. Careful attention must be paid to the motivation of the text as well as its many details in relation to the full argument. Our text concludes the third part of this letter dealing with purifying ourselves from the defilement of the world, which means separating ourselves from the world. This separation had not occurred in the lives of those who claimed to be masters of their time (referring to the rich), thus permitting them to plan their lives. We now come to the third part, in which patience and refusing the oath represent an opposition to the world.

What we have learned is that breaking with the world is itself very different from the way the world breaks relationships. We may never judge, curse, or condemn others or the world. For example, James, as a disciple of Jesus Christ, cannot go as far as Jesus does when dealing with the rich.

He cannot say "woe to the rich" (literally, cursed be the rich). In the beginning of chapter 5, James tells the rich to weep and wail, because of the misery that will come their way. In other words, it is a warning and not a curse. I believe this is fundamental and decisive. All too often, Christians have pronounced curses of all kinds, such as "the world is cursed" and "humanity is damned." This is what characterizes virtually every sect: everyone is damned, but we alone are saved. Much the same behaviour occurs in the face of ideological and political differences. For example, the Communists are evil and damned, but we are on the good side. The Fascists are monsters, but fortunately we are not. It is more or less how everyone in the world operates. Hence, if we are to be separated from the world, we must do things differently.

Our text is linked to the one dealing with the rich in verse 7, which advises us as follows: "*therefore* be patient." Apparently, there is a link between this discussion and the advice to adopt the attitude of patience, as indicated by the word "therefore." As we have seen, the rich are possessed by an attitude of conquest and domination. They cannot stand the situation as it is. They simply cannot wait. Any situation must be faced quickly in order to achieve success. The Bible frequently speaks of this impatience of theirs.

We have also learned that the rich cannot accept suffering. They live on the earth in luxury and self-indulgence, according to our text. They will not accept suffering, but immediately reach for a remedy, and this remedy is money. Their attitude is therefore one of impatience; and if we wish to separate ourselves from the behaviour of the world we should adopt the opposite behaviour, which is that of patience.

There is another way in which the ways of the world as exhibited by the rich are contrasted to how we must break with that world. The Greek text in verse 5 accuses the rich of *fattening* their hearts. In verse 8, James tells his fellow Christians to *strengthen* their hearts. This kind of terminology refers back to the prophets, who used the word "fat" to describe Israel's condition of having strayed so far from the task for which it was elected that it was no longer of any use in this respect. The opposite condition is that of having a strong heart, and it is for this reason that James advises us to strengthen our hearts. Many modern translations completely miss this opposition in the Greek text.

The Greek word usually translated as "patience" therefore represents an attitude to the world that is the opposite to the attitude of the rich. It is a question of the heart. The rich are wealthy because they are in the grip of an attitude of conquest instead of one of patience. Our text may well imply a reference to a group of people of that time who were called the poor of Israel, as we noted in our study of Amos. They were regarded as a model of patience: they patiently bore their poverty in the knowledge that they had chosen the right path. Jesus may also have been thinking of them when he pronounced the beatitude "Happy are the poor." However, the patience of which the text speaks has nothing in common with what we usually mean by it. It does not refer to the human attitude of standing patiently in line, for example. Nor is it a kind of wisdom, and above all, it is not at all a question of being passive in our lives. In other words, patience does not exclude fervently stirring things up or actively expressing our eschatological faith. It certainly is not getting on with our lives with a "business as usual" attitude until Jesus shows up. We are encouraged to actively pray for his return. I would largely agree with those who say that resignation is the greatest possible sin. It is difficult to understate how much our text is weakened by translating the Greek word as "patience."

To make things even more complicated, there are two Greek words that are both commonly translated as "patience." The word used in the first chapter as something that results from the testing of our faith is *hupomone*, which means with firmness, steadfastness, and endurance. All these meanings have little in common with patience. The other Greek word translated as "patience" in our text is *macrothumia*. It means a largeness of passion or a largeness of courage. It can also mean a big heart or a largeness of spirit. It has also been translated (in French) as the breathing of a long-distance runner. None of these meanings comes even close to what we mean by patience, and what is even worse is that the church has often used these texts to counsel resignation.

Once again, this confusion can be traced to the translation of the Greek text into the Latin Bible, which resulted in many misunderstandings and even opposite meanings from the original text. In this case, the Latin word for patience has a sense of passivity and resignation. As a result, some translators have retranslated the Greek word for patience as literally "having a big heart" or a great passion for things, which I believe renders the original meaning.

The entire Old Testament speaks of the patience of God. For example, Exodus tells us that our God is patient, full of goodness, and slow to anger. This does not mean a kind of "laissez-faire." It means that he leaves time – that is, time for people to act, and to let things develop. God accompanies people without imposing himself. His patience is one of being present, as we see clearly in the life of Jonah. God accepts what Jonah does, even to the point of disobedience, and he remains present in his

attempt to recover what Jonah has done.[2] In his patience, God also intervenes in our lives, not to mechanize or model them, but to allow them to
recover and flourish. Without these interventions, our lives would slump.
God's actions are highly moderated and designed to fit into people's
lives in order to allow them to live.

Hence, our patience must be a response to and a reflection of God's
patience. He allows us to live, but the one thing that God does not appear
to tolerate is our becoming inhuman and thus no longer being in his image. Examples of this are found in the accounts of Cain and Abel, and
Sodom and Gomorrah. The models of patience provided by our text are
those of Job, the prophets, and perhaps Jesus. There are two possible
ways of translating the Greek text. Following the reference to Job, the
text may be translated as "and you have seen the end the Lord gave him,"
or "and you know the end that our Lord (Jesus Christ) had." Either translation is possible.

Keeping these translation problems in mind, I believe there are three
aspects to patience. First, this patience is directed towards the coming of
the kingdom of God. The letter to the Hebrews tells us that patience
gives birth to hope and provides us with a solid anchor. Hope makes us
steadfast and vigilant as we await and pray for the Lord's return, in the
knowledge that this is God's decision to make. In the meantime, we have
a reliable point of reference for our lives as Christians. As we await God's
decision, we have time, which is now a duration of hope. This attitude
towards time is in sharp contrast with that of the world, as illustrated by
the rich, who seek to dominate time by planning it in order to accumulate wealth and power. Our text illustrates this with the example of the
farmer who patiently waits for the fruits that will follow the first and later
rainfalls. The early rain would cause the first crop to grow very rapidly,
but the complete returns on all the work would not be known until more
rain had produced a second crop. Hence, the farmer would patiently
wait for it. Similarly, Christians must not judge the results of their decisions by their immediate effects but discern everything in the long term
to see what the further rains bring, as it were. We must be patient because the Lord's coming is at hand. We usually think of this in terms of
being close in time and the end of world, but it can also mean that the
Lord is close to us here and now.

The example of the farmer teaches us that we must be patient with
respect to waiting for nature to take its course. We do well to reflect on
this as we are doing everything we can to speed it up! Next comes the
example of the prophets, who patiently but actively waited not for nature

but for faith to take its course. Waiting for the fruits of their witness often involved a great deal of suffering and even persecution. They patiently persisted in the knowledge that the results of their announcing and the people's listening to the Word might take a long a time, and many died before ever seeing any results of what God had promised. Abraham died long before the Promised Land was given: all he owned of it in the end was the grave of his wife. We do well to think about this, given how accustomed we are to everything being instant in our civilization.

A second aspect of patience is to be so in relation to other people. Verse 9 tells us not to grumble against others so that we will not be judged. It also tells us that the Judge is standing at the door. God is patient with us and we must be patient with our neighbours. They too are called to repent, and we must leave them time by enlarging our hearts. God does not pressure or rush us; hence we must be patient with others. Doing so is hardly a question of tolerating everything and anything, as we have discussed earlier. The difficulties that we encounter in our relationships with others must not make our hearts fat and divide the church.

It reminds me of the parable of Matthew 13, which describes how the servants, seeing that wheat and tares are growing together in the field, propose to their master to take out the weeds. Their master replies that this is impossible because if they attempt it, they will also uproot the wheat. When the servants propose to get rid of both the wheat and the tares and start again, the master replies that this is not a good course of action because the wheat is not yet ripe. In other words, the moment has not yet come. We must not rush things but wait until they are ripe. We must act at the pace of human history and not rush it, neither in our own lives, the lives of others, nor our world. God alone is the judge of the maturity of the fruit. We are not its masters and we must not accelerate things, an idea accompanied in the text by the encouragement to strengthen our hearts (the equivalent of active vigilance) because the coming of the Lord is near. There is a certain proximity, which is not necessarily a proximity in time.

The third aspect of patience is found in verse 11, which tells us that we count as blessed those who patiently suffered. We must be patient in suffering. We have heard of Job's patience in hope, and what the Lord brought about at the end because he is full of mercy and compassion. This last term makes it very clear that it was not because of Job's merit that he received what he did. It was a gift of mercy. The compassion of the Lord responded to Job's patience. This example is astounding because Job was hardly a model of spiritual patience. He is not only the person who at the very beginning declares, "The Lord has given and the Lord has taken away, blessed be his name." He is also the one who, during forty-five chapters, never ceases to protest and complain against his God and against what he has done. This example of patience brings us back to what we said earlier about this patience, which does not take things lying down when it comes to what we believe are God's decisions. There is a constant dialogue with God about things that Job holds to be just until God shows him that they are not. Our patience can be of the same kind, and we can uphold before God what we believe to be just, as long as we do so in hope and the complete certainty of the coming of the Lord. We must evaluate our suffering, beginning with this. Doing so is completely different from patiently suffering without complaining. Conducting ourselves in this way separates us from the world because it is a world without hope.[3] It also separates us from it because this patience is the opposite of the impatience of the rich. The latter are also without hope, for which they attempt to compensate by instantly acquiring everything they possibly can.

In answer to your questions: As parents, we can be very close to our children, for example, even when they are far away. Proximity is not first and foremost a question of distance. In the same way, the coming of the Lord may be near without necessarily being close in time. This coming has several dimensions. For example, there is a coming of the Lord in our hearts whenever someone converts. It also is an event. Similar events occur wherever and whenever the kingdom of heaven appears, as was explained in an earlier study.[4] It is true that we no longer live in the kind of ecstasy experienced by the early church, believing that the Second Coming would be very soon. It was based on, and continues to be based on, certain sayings of Jesus in the Gospels that his return was near. However, this does not mean that it would happen just like that. Besides, what we believe to be the case about early Christianity is an interpretation that may or may not be correct. Moreover, there certainly was no unanimity among the early Christians. We have the idea that the alpha and omega the Bible speaks of are the equivalent of what in physics would be $t = 0$ and $t =$ end, respectively. When God speaks about eternity, we have no corresponding experience and thus only a vague idea of what this could possibly mean. When it comes to an intervention of eternity into our passage of time this becomes even more difficult.

As to the exercise of patience in political decision making, I have often asked myself the question: What would I have done if I had been a minister in the French government during 1957 and 1958? In 1954, just before the Algerian war, I would have known what to do, but once it had started,

I believe I would have had no option but to resign. In other words, there are times when things are fluid, with the result that a Christian is able to intervene in the course of political events. However, the situation is usually so heavily constrained that even a Christian with the best intentions in the world can do absolutely nothing. I believe this is exactly the situation in which President Carter found himself during his term in office. I am convinced that, because of his faith, he would never have pushed the red button, so to speak. However, if other politicians had become convinced of this, the United States would have been delivered into their power. Hence, he could have been faced with a situation in which he had no choice but to trigger the nuclear catastrophe, and yet this would have been impossible. It is easy to criticize Christian politicians, but I have often asked myself the question: What would I do if I were in their place? I believe that I would not be able to do very much, and that appears to be the same for others. Hence, the question of separating ourselves from the world remains one for which there may be frequently no recourse other than through God's grace.

I will now turn to verse 12, which tells us that, "above all else," we should not swear, not by heaven or by earth or anything else; and instead let our "yes" be yes and our "no" be no, so that we will not be judged. The phrase "above all else" warns us that what follows is more important than anything else within this theme of having to purify ourselves. Moreover, James is summarizing a parallel text from Jesus' Sermon on the Mount, found in Mathew 5:34–7. Swearing an oath raises two profound issues: hypocrisy and religion.

Swearing continues the theme of patience, as indicated by the opening words "above all else." We have seen that patient people have a big heart. However, the Bible regards those who swear as having a divided heart, because they cannot be themselves in their words. As a result, they need to add something to their words in order to make them believable. Their words do not come from their hearts. Their actions do not correspond to their words. What they have broken is the unity of their being. It is a matter of their hearts and their words because the Bible tells us that our words come from the depth of our hearts. If, in order to establish the truth of what I am saying, I must appeal to something other than myself, then I, within myself, am not taking it seriously. By myself, I do not suffice to take full responsibility for what I am saying. I refer what I say to an authority other than myself, with the result that I hide behind the oath and what I swear by in the oath, be it heaven, the earth, or something else. The very act of taking an oath is bad precisely because it attests that I will not commit myself. My words become something else, and thus an expression of hypocrisy.

It is important to recognize that hypocrisy is not the same thing as a lie. I am lying when I am saying something that is not exact or true. When the Pharisees are accused of hypocrisy, it is not because they are lying. They are convinced that what they are saying is true, and that they are acting in good faith. Hypocrisy is the dissociation between what a person appears to be and his or her being. I believe this is what Jesus refers to when he says that you wash the outside of a cup and a plate, but you leave the inside dirty. However, it is not a question of hiding oneself behind an exterior behaviour, as it were. The Pharisee is convinced that in doing everything required by the law, he does so with his entire being. However, he has only achieved the appearance of doing so by his external behaviour. If we are satisfied with our behaviour, with the way we appear, and with what we say, then we also are hypocrites. We will have to learn that when we stand before God, we do so with our entire being, without the possibility of disguising anything. In the same way, we must not conceal anything in our dealings with other people. We must be entirely present before them in our love for our neighbour. This presence must not be any different from the one before God. Our text refers to this as our being "yes" or our being "no" and doing so with our whole life. When we are "yes" we can say "yes"; or when we live "no," we can say "no."

It is clearly extremely difficult, if not impossible, to be entirely true in who we are. In part, this is because, deep down, we are not very proud of who we are; hence, we may not be ready to put our entire selves into our words. Moreover, it is also because this may appear as being proud or lacking charity in our dealings with others. Being entirely who we are without any reservation is next to impossible. We have all experienced Christians who are constantly glowing with excitement, and how this becomes embarrassing and profoundly uncomfortable to others.

There is the possibility of conducting ourselves with a measure of reserve, of which Paul speaks when he says that he has been "as under the law" with people who live this way, "as being without this law" with others who live that way, as a Jew with Jews, as a Greek with the Greeks, and so on. What this means is that Paul is free, and he attests to this. He does not have to swear an oath to the effect that he is free. On the contrary, it allows him to say what his freedom is. In other words, to be entirely with the other does not mean putting our personality on display. It is a question of a complete unity of what we say and how we live. This recognition points us back to Jesus Christ, who was fully "yes" before God, and who was fully "no" before Satan, and who is anew fully "yes" with regard to us. It may be helpful to reread 2 Corinthians 1:19–20, which is exemplary in this regard. There is a complete unity between Jesus' being, which is a "yes," and his words, which are also a "yes." It is this unity that would be broken by an oath.

These teachings have enormous implications for propaganda. It was Goebbels who said that anyone who creates propaganda must never believe in what he or she is saying. This recommendation goes to the very heart of what propaganda is. We must also ask why this phenomenon was so widespread and influential throughout the twentieth century in both democratic and non-democratic regimes, and why this is not likely to change.[5]

These teachings also remind me of a theological debate that raged for much of the seventeenth century. The Jesuits had developed the doctrine of the so-called mental reserve. It meant that you could tolerate something or someone as long as in the depth of your heart you told God that of course you could not do so. Many opposed this vigorously, including Pascal. To love others and to be with them does not mean accepting what they do or think. We can and must be firm in our hearts.

The second issue involved in the swearing of an oath is that of religion. Every religion has made use of, and to some extent depends on, the oath. Only Christianity forbids it. I know very well that for centuries, Christians were obliged to cooperate with the demands of society to swear an oath in a court or when accepting a public office. The Catholics swore on the cross and the Protestants on the Bible. In the United States, the swearing on the Bible continues. Nevertheless, doing so manifests a profound lack of understanding of what is involved, including the religious implications to which we now turn.

By refusing to take an oath we accept that everything we do is relative. Nothing we say or do can be made into something absolute simply by swearing an oath. It gives a religious value to what I say or do, and this is strictly forbidden in the Bible. Following the previously cited text in Matthew, we cannot swear by heaven, by earth, or by Jerusalem because, by means of this religious act, we endow them with a religious character. For example, if we swear by heaven, I transform it from what the Bible tells me over and over is something created by God into something religious.

We swear by something we hold sacred, and this involves two things. In the gospel of Matthew, we are told not to swear by the heavens because it is God's throne, nor to swear by the earth because it is his footstool. In other words, swearing involves an appropriation of what is not ours.

What are we doing with these heavens and this earth when we take them as witnesses to the truthfulness of our words, when these are no such witnesses at all? They are the throne of God and his footstool, which we cannot use in whatever way we see fit. We cannot take them as a kind of guarantee for ourselves.

The corresponding text in the letter of James is a little different. It tells us not to swear by the heavens, the earth, or by any other kind of oath. This text probably does not have the same motivation because it is likely related to the religious context of James's time. It made heaven and earth into religious values and sacred powers that are supposed to give value to our words. This is more or less how an oath always works: we swear by a value that is sacred. The swearing of oaths must be radically and completely eliminated from the Christian life because it is a fundamentally religious act. Whenever we are tempted to take an oath, we risk entering the religious sphere, which the God of the Bible rejects because what is religious is not biblical. There is no other way to swear an oath. If we do not swear by the religious power of a sacred idea, our oath has no weight whatsoever.

There are thus two dimensions to the commandment not to swear an oath. When I swear an oath, what I attest to is not my truthfulness but my hypocrisy: my being in life is different from my words. Also, when I swear an oath, I am engaged in a religious act. Whether it is seen from the perspective of the gospel of Matthew or the letter of James does not change the fact that it is unacceptable. As Christians, we cannot enter into the domains of pagan religions. With this double aspect, it becomes clear that the swearing of an oath is not as trivial a matter as we might have believed. This is especially true for the time and cultural context in which James lived, but it is of equal importance for our secular-religious mass societies.[6]

As was the case with the previous issues, the swearing of an oath exposes us to being judged. We can now understand why this subject was introduced with the warning that, above all else, we must not swear an oath. Doing so involves hypocrisy and religion, which characterize human behaviour in the world. When our societies compel us to take an oath, we must become conscientious objectors and carefully and patiently explain why we can do no such thing. In so doing, we must place our confidence in the presence of the Lord, who is close to us.

Chapter Sixteen

Our Christian Lives Together

Following a long discussion of how Christians must not behave in relation to the world, James now reaches what may be regarded as the conclusion of his letter in chapter 5:13–20. It represents the positive side: how Christians ought to behave together. It is this behaviour that constitutes the church, as opposed to an organization or a social group. This is no "theory of the church" but only the practices of its members, and it is these practices that constitute it and set it apart from the world. Of course, James has already made it clear that he is well aware of what happens in real churches. There are four main themes, each embedded in the context of prayer. Verse 13 deals with relating everything in our lives to God. In verses 14 to 16 we encounter the struggle against evil, be it physical or spiritual in character. Verse 16 concerns the trust for one another. Finally, the remaining verses deal with our struggle for the truth, which is also a struggle for life.

Before getting into the details of our text, I would like to make a general observation. There are many calls for modernizing Christianity and for rebuilding our churches. Usually this involves playing down or dismissing texts that appear to us to be too simplistic for our times. Generally speaking, these efforts are guided by good intentions, which acknowledge that in the past, when life was assumed to be simpler and more straightforward, certain practices or advice given may well have been excellent for the time. Alternatively, it may be argued that certain texts address a set of local customs of the time that have little relevance for us. In the same vein, a text may be regarded as being intertwined with beliefs or assumptions that no longer hold. Our biblical commentaries are full of these kinds of arguments. It is as though we have stopped believing in the possibility that the words we read in the Bible can still be turned into the living Word of God. I firmly believe that this is possible and that, for our part, we must make every effort [to make this happen] by reading these texts together, interpreting and discussing them together, and studying them further until we have exhausted all our joint resources. We must trust that the Holy Spirit will turn the words we read and meditate into the living Word. It is the exact opposite of setting ourselves up as judge and jury of what we read, thus prejudging this entire process. We must probe the depths of each text with all our collective resources. From time to time we may come away with very little, but if we do not make this effort, the Holy Spirit will not turn the words we read and share together into a living Word. Let us now turn to our text, which once again will not turn out to be as naive and simplistic as a first impression may suggest.

Verse 13 introduces us to the central role that prayer plays in the Christian life. It is mentioned seven times in the first five verses of our text. Its centrality is hardly surprising because it constitutes a relationship with God, and through it a relationship with others as well. A purely individualistic prayer is impossible. Through our prayers we must make ourselves available to God by first and foremost listening, and only then speaking. The importance of doing so has been pointed out by many, including the prophets and the church fathers. The effectiveness of prayer is also mentioned in the text, and we will return to it.

Prayer is related to our suffering and our joys, which jointly represent our entire lives in all their circumstances. Because prayer is related to our lives, which constantly change, it must not be repetitive. Jesus says as much when he tells us not to multiply endless repetitions. Nor can our prayer be ritual in character because it concerns our personal lives. For the same reasons, it cannot be institutional in character. For James, prayer is the centre of an individual's life of faith and also, together, the most complete expression of the church. It must be renewed in every new circumstance as an act of bringing everything in our daily lives to God.

Although this teaching is straightforward and practical, it is not easy to live. For example, when we suffer we find it easy to complain, and when we are joyful we readily credit ourselves. As a consequence of these kinds of reactions we tend to close up our lives instead of opening them up. Most or all of us have experienced that in suffering we are all alone. However, through prayer we can open up to God and to others. For example, in a situation in which everyone, including the patient, knows that death is near but no one dares to talk about it openly, they are compelled to act as if the situation were different. It is as if walls were erected between the people; and when death finally comes, they continue to experience a terrible isolation from one another. Hence the importance of bringing suffering to God.

It is for the same reason that we must bring our joy before God in prayer. Doing so is represented in our text by the singing of hymns through which we give thanks and glorify God (i.e., to reveal who he is). The singing of the Psalms originally meant revealing the presence of God, but this notion of glorification has been all but lost in our congregations. Our joy allows us to reveal who God is to others and to show our thanks to him. When we ask God to give us our daily bread in the Lord's Prayer, we are asking for life because that is what the bread represents. It implies our thanks for another day of life and a request for another tomorrow.

Paul explains that the Holy Spirit brings our prayers before God in a form that far transcends what we are capable of expressing. It is also important that we are on the alert for a reply because if we are not, we are likely to miss it. I recognize that it is difficult to pray the Lord's Prayer in a manner that is non-formulaic. This is why some have counselled people to meditate on each phrase in the context of their lives before speaking it. For example, did I forgive anyone today? How exactly did I attempt to live out the good as the will of God? How did my activities with which I was preoccupied hallow God's name? Another example is furnished by Job, who struggled with God in his prayers. All this clearly shows us that prayer is the centre of the Christian life, with its suffering and its joy.

Verses 14 to 16 take this all a little farther by considering illness and sin as representing the presence of evil. In the Bible, sickness is always related to sin, but not in the sense that a particular sickness corresponds to a certain sin, nor in the sense that the person who is ill is more sinful than the one who is healthy. Especially in the Gospels, sickness is a manifestation of disorder and our separation from God. In the Old Testament, illness marks the potential presence of death. A sick person was considered almost as good as dead. It may well be that this corresponded rather well to people's daily-life experiences in a society with little medical knowledge. In any case, in the Old Testament illness is a sign of death and, as such, of the victory of the void and of evil over Creation.[1] The very possibility of sickness and death arises from the reality of sin. As a result, neither sickness nor death is tolerable before God, as signified by the miracles of healing performed by Jesus. These miracles amount to a promise that, following the Resurrection, as the book of Revelation says, there will be no illness, no tears, or any kind of separation.

We are thus faced with the question about healing through faith. The text tells us that if people are ill they should call the elders of the church to pray over them and anoint them with oil, and the prayer offered in faith will save them. I believe that we must not minimize healing by faith. Nor should we make it the only true benchmark of a spiritual life. It must not become the criterion of spiritual gifts, as is common in some charismatic groups. It continues to be a reality, but when we are faced with illness, we must pray and also ask for healing. As we will see, healing should not become the primary objective of this praying. The fundamental relationship remains the one between illness and sin. Remember that in reply to requests for healing, Jesus frequently says, "Your sins are forgiven." There may also be healing afterwards, but the essential matter is clearly that of sin, of which illness is a sign.

When confronted with illness, we commonly exhibit an attitude and approach centred on efficiency – the doctor is there to cure us. In the same vein, when we speak about or engage in prayer for the sick, we are focused on healing. All this is understandable, but this is not what the text has in mind, as we will see. If translated into Hebrew, the Greek verb rendered as "being ill" would, in one form of the corresponding Hebrew verb, mean "to soften God's anger," and in another form mean "to pray." In other words, for the Jews, praying and softening God's anger are inseparable. The exegetes have found an explanation that is rather amusing. The original term was being ill. The Hebrew *halat* means to (be) weaken(ed). This verb is often used with God as the object, in which case it means to weaken God or to soften him in terms of his anger. Such softening of his anger can only be accomplished by prayer. This is how all this is connected, using a kind of play on words. Prayer is a kind of weakening of God, almost a kind of illness, as if we make God weak through prayer. Such is the supposed etymological connection between praying and being ill.

This text is also important in relation to the organization of the church because it is the sick person who must ask the elders to pray for him or her. It is the responsibility of the elders to do so, and they do this together. The implication is that the communities James speaks about were organized more along the line of the synagogues than those described by Paul, which had diverse ministries acting more or less independently. Moreover, these elders were not regarded as having the gift of healing, which was one of the gifts recognized by the communities Paul dealt with. The elders in this text simply represented the community, and praying for the sick who asked for it was one of their responsibilities. It was a way in which the sick entrusted themselves to God's power.

Next, the text speaks of anointing the sick person with oil. All this is extremely complex. I will give you three explanations, and I see no reason why we have to choose among them. The first is that oil was a common remedy used in antiquity. Jesus used it, as described in Mark 6:13. It is not a question of a holy oil, but simply of a remedy. In this case, there was first a prayer and then the anointing with oil, meaning that first the sick person was entrusted to God and then there was a turning to medical means. It turns our usual approach on its head, because we begin with the available medical means and then accompany it with prayer because it certainly cannot hurt to do this. However, it is a kind of supplement in which we have confidence up to a point. I must confess that this first explanation troubles me somewhat. The pharmacology of that time was well developed and complex. Oil was but one of many remedies. Given this situation, why does the text single out the use of oil? The only explanation given for this is that oil was most commonly used by armies to treat cuts and other wounds. I do not find this explanation very convincing.

A second explanation holds that the unction of oil is a sign of joy experienced at a banquet and a way of honouring a person. Scented oils and oil-based perfumes were used in this manner, as described in Psalm 23 and in Matthew 6:17, for example. In contrast, olive oil was generally used for medicinal purposes. In addition to being used as a sign of a joyful communion and a way of honouring someone, as Mary did to Jesus, there is another interpretation of the use of oil based on a commentary by Augustine on Psalm 23. The person who is in the shadow of death (and thus very ill) is invited to a banquet and anointed with oil by God. Despite illness and death, oil is a sign of joy here.

A third explanation holds that the unction of oil is a sign of royalty. All kings were anointed with oil, and this practice continued almost to Jesus' day. From this perspective, the text means that the sick person must be considered by the church as royalty, representing Jesus Christ himself in his church. As a result, the sick person was accorded the sign of royalty. This approach to sick persons, where in the healing communities sick people were spoken of as "our lords the sick," endured until the Middle Ages. It reflects the same kind of perspective and approach.

As we can see from these three explanations, the meaning of the unction of oil is ambiguous. Personally, I have no strong preference, although I find the symbolic explanations more appealing than the one that considers oil as a remedy. However, this is something that is purely personal.

Verse 15 tells us that the prayer of faith will save the sick, and the Lord will lift them up; and if they have committed sins, they will be forgiven. The text is clearly referring to healing, consolation, and the Resurrection. The verb in "the prayer of faith will save the sick" is used five times in the letter of James. Each time it is used it refers to a person being saved spiritually and not medically. In the first chapter, it is the Word that is capable of saving our life and soul. In the second chapter, it is faith that can save. In the fourth chapter, we encounter the judge who could save us or condemn us. We may assume, therefore, that in our text this verb has the same meaning. It is not so much a question of regaining our health but of being saved, in the double sense of right now and (eschatologically) for eternity. Hence, I do not believe that this text first and foremost refers to the sick being cured. I believe this interpretation also fits with the Lord lifting up the sick. The verb is ambiguous. In some contexts it can mean to resurrect, in others to lift up, and in still others to awaken. In our text it is impossible to know which of these three meanings was intended. It would appear, then, that the prayer of the elders for sick people aims to give them absolute confidence in their salvation, in their resurrection, and possibly in their healing. The prayer for the sick is a prayer for their entire life and being, which may include their healing – but it can also include their death, with the absolute certainty of their resurrection. The role of the elders is thus to accompany the sick, to entrust them to God. It is a prayer of faith that saves in the name of the Lord. We must remember that it is not faith itself that saves us. God saves us by grace through the means of faith. In Protestant circles, it is common for people to believe that they are saved by faith, but that would give the wrong meaning to these texts.

In verses 15b and 16a, James turns to the subject of sin. The text makes it very clear that there is no link between sickness and sin, because it says "*if* the sick person has committed a sin." Once again, this shows that there is no necessary link between the two. From the biblical perspective, every person is a sinner, but as a result of God's grace we are saved from this condition. However, we remain responsible for any particular sinful acts we may commit. When the person who is sick has committed a sin, the text advises us to pray for him or her. At the same time, since we all commit such acts, this advice concerns not only the sick but the entire community. We are all to confess our sins to one another. Moreover, each and every member is given the authority to forgive the sins another member may confess to him or her. There is no longer any mention of the elders. Nor is there any mention of a particular ministry that corresponds to confession and forgiveness. Any member has the authority to hear my confession and forgive my sins. All this should hardly surprise us because this forgiveness of sins is no different from announcing the good news that we are saved and that our sins are forgiven. That is what we can and must say to a brother or sister. In this way we sustain each other and bear each other's burdens.

I believe there is another important reason why we must confess our sins to each other and not directly to God. Beyond supporting one another, the person to whom the confession is made acts as a witness, and this is of fundamental importance for the life of the church. We only need to think of the gossip, worries, feelings of guilt, accusations made behind people's backs, and so on, to realize how important it is to be two instead of one in this confession and forgiveness of each other's sins.

There is one very important detail in this text. It says that we must confess our sins to each other so that we will be healed. The Greek verb used here and translated as healed refers to a healing of a medical nature, while the Greek word used in the context of sick people refers to healing of a spiritual kind. I believe it drives home the point that sin does not manifest itself in our lives only as disease but also as what has sometimes been referred to as the "sickness of the soul," as long as this is understood in the Jewish and Christian sense and not in the Greek one. Sin involves *not* doing what is good and unto life according to the will of God, and *not* loving him and our neighbour. Sin creates a debt in terms of what we owe God, and we become ill in a physical or spiritual sense.

This raises the question: To whom should we confess? I believe that this is a matter of opportunity involving the confidence we have in the other person, the friendship we may have, and the circumstances we may share. We confess what is in our hearts to someone with whom we have a certain affinity or friendship. I do not think that this can ever be a question of principle. Of course, we must treat the confessions of others in the strictest confidence. If we love the other person, we treat them in the same way we would want to be treated, and we support each other in love. Such confessions are a continuation of the kinds of communal and reciprocal relations described before, with everything being centred in prayer: confess and pray. Also, the Christian life as a whole is marked by prayer.

In answer to your questions, there have been times in the history of the church when strong measures had to be taken that were contrary to the kinds of texts we have been reading. For example, from the fourth to the tenth centuries, things were so indescribably bad in the church that eventually the bishops decided that confessions would only be heard by one person, namely, the priest. However, many of these priests were a big part of the difficulties. There are records of many polygamous priests and others who were illiterate. The latter problem contributed to the development of a liturgy, which these illiterate priests were compelled to memorize to make sure they would not talk nonsense. When you read the documentation we have of these five hundred years, it is hard to believe that the church was able to recover at all.

If what I have attempted to explain is correct, the flow of the text is as follows. Having shown that it is necessary to break with the world (to submit to God and resist the Devil, clean your hands, and purify your hearts, and so on) and that the love for this world is enmity with God, prayer emerges as the sign of all of this. Prayer is the opposite of an adaptation to the world, and the opposite of the kinds of works this world demands. I strongly believe that prayer is an act without means and without efficiency.[2] In other words, our non-conformity with the world is not first and foremost a question of acting differently. In the final analysis, I would say that it is a question of praying rather than acting. Our world solicits us to act every step of the way, and to do so with the greatest possible efficiency. Prayer is the most radical and total divergence from this orientation. It is not a question of using other means and using them differently. It is ultimately taking an entirely different path, which does not depend on any means whatsoever. Prayer is never a means.

I recognize that we frequently transform prayer by ritualizing it and incorporating it into liturgies. It often becomes an instrument for obtaining what we desire.[3] Nevertheless, I believe that prayer is about renouncing all means and giving up on the notion of efficiency. It is about admitting my powerlessness and submitting myself to the power of God. It is truly the inverse of the efficiency of our world. The people who pray submit themselves to the free sovereignty of God. They are not attempting to get results.

Let us now consider all this in some detail. Verses 16 to 18 speak of the prayer of a just person having a great power in its effects. We have already noted that the entire Christian life in all its aspects is formed and sustained by prayer. Prayer can intervene at any time, and it must not be reserved for some special occasion in a service or a mass. We must not conform to the world, where religions divide time into the sacred moments dedicated to the gods and the remainder devoted to people's own lives. Our whole life must be holy, that is, set apart. We are told to pray ceaselessly, to give thanks to God in all things, and to drink, eat, and do everything to the glory of God (to reveal who he is). The result has often been that these kinds of teachings are taken literally: so we say thanks before a meal, before we go to bed, before a church meeting, and then we're done. The point that Paul makes is that the entire meal must reveal who God is, and so must everything else. Everything we do should be inspired and induced by prayer. In other words, we must *live* our prayers, and this is hardly a question of formal, ritual prayers. Our churches have completely lost this.

Prayer is thus the mark of the Christian life, which does not divide time. It is the opposite of adapting to the world. Ultimately it is this prayer that ought to differentiate us from the world, much more than simply behaving differently. I would almost say that it is better to pray than to act. Augustine told the example of the second king of Rome who, in the middle of a religious celebration, received a messenger urging him to assemble the army because the enemy was approaching. This pagan king replied, "The enemy may be coming but I am praying." According to Augustine, this showed that already during that time there were people inspired by God. The world always invites us to act but we are asked to pray above all.

Individually and collectively, we must bring everything before God. I believe strongly that many of our communities could benefit from praying more and talking a lot less. It is not only a matter of our services but also of our meetings, where we have our little formal prayers and then we get on with the more serious business. The Greek word James uses for prayer in this context is not the same as the one he used when speaking about praying for the sick. *Deesis* means the prayer of requests or of asking. It is quite astonishing that when James speaks of praying for the sick and for each other he uses the normal Greek word for prayer, while in this context of the prayer of a just person having a great power in its effects, he speaks of the prayer of asking.

Since all religions depend heavily on prayers, we do well to ask how ours must be different. Our prayers are not to be a religious act in the sense we spoke of earlier. To guide us in this, James refers to three characteristics: prayers must be fervent, prayed by those who are just, and made in the name of the Lord. A fervent prayer has nothing to do with its being superior to others but to the engagement of the person's entire being. We have encountered the importance of the unity of a person's being and life when James spoke of not swearing an oath. Our entire being must be engaged in our words, so that there is no difference between the two. Nor must there be any difference between our faith and our works. Our one being must live in faith and do our works. In the same way, our prayers must engage our whole being and life. This is true not only for our prayers with words but also for our active prayers expressed through our relationships with others, for example.

When James speaks of the prayer of a just person, it raises the question as to who or what is just? It is not a question of the person being good or acting in a way that conforms to a notion or theory of justice. James made this clear in the second chapter, where he counted the prostitute Rahab as being justified by her works. Abraham was justified for the same reason. It is a question of these people having been justified by God, that is, they expected justice from him and in faith trusted him to justify them. This is fundamental in the Bible as another instance of the interpenetration of human actions and those of God. I believe that the biblical answer to the question as to whether human beings are free or not would be that they are enfranchised (or set free), which is different from their being free. In the same vein, we are not just in ourselves, through our own actions, but we are justified.

Finally, praying is done in the name of the Lord. Doing so implies that these prayers are in line with God's project for humanity. As a result, these prayers are evoked by a love for others. James affirms that under these conditions, prayer has a great power in its effects. We need to recognize the ineffectiveness of our own actions and the complete effectiveness of God's actions. Doing so means that we submit ourselves to the free sovereignty of God; and we are able to do so with confidence because he is the God of love.

Our text then turns to the story of the prophet Elijah. James insists on the fact that he was not an exceptional person. Throughout the Old Testament the people called by God were ordinary people. Paul explains that God chooses what is weak to convince the strong. There can be no ambiguity about what God does. When ordinary people accomplish tasks that normally would be beyond their capabilities, they are inspired by the Holy Spirit. According to the first book of Kings, Elijah prayed for what he needed to accomplish the mission God had entrusted to him. He was able to pray in the name of the Lord because his prayer was oriented and directed by this mission. Our common reaction is that we could never do anything of the kind. That is precisely why James tells us that Elijah was a person like us. We cannot let ourselves off the hook in this way, so to speak. I am convinced that each member of a Christian community has received a mission or vocation. Our prayers must be oriented and guided by this vocation and by the gifts we have received.

The enormous difficulty regarding Elijah's prayer is that it would do a great deal of harm to his people. As a result of his prayer, no rain fell for three and a half years, and many people starved during that time. All this was happening because the king had drawn all the people into idolatry. It surely was not something Elijah took lightly. In fact, we are told that he put himself in the same condition as everyone else. He was not like Jonah, who was rather keen to see the destruction of the city of Nineveh from a safe distance. God sent Elijah to a poor widow whom he asked for a little to drink and a morsel of bread. She replied that all she had left was a little meal and oil, which she was going to prepare for her son and herself and then they would die. Elijah told her to first make a cake out of it for him, but that the meal and the oil would not run out until the drought was over and the rain fell. He put the three of them in the position of await-ing God's grace day by day for whatever would happen. When Elijah fi-nally brought the king to his knees, he prayed for the rain to fall again and for the earth to bring forth its fruit. This account warns us that our prayers may involve us in a very difficult struggle. We may get into a lot of trouble from the church, as Elijah did from his people, the Jews. These kinds of prayers require a complete humility and a non-judgmental atti-tude. Otherwise we will be tempted to say that we are just and thus able to condemn others. It is something Elijah never did. Neither must we ever appropriate God's Word to tell us that we are right. I believe that this is fundamental when we pray these kinds of prayers before God.

In answer to your questions, I do not believe that the mission we have all received can be discerned by means of psychological tests, or that we can define it ourselves. However, in our relationships with others and in the milieu in which we find ourselves, possibly in the political life of our society (if necessary), there will sometimes come a moment when we rec-ognize that something must be done that is absolutely essential. In faith we must then discern if this is the mission God is entrusting to us. On the other hand, we must also pay careful attention to the talents we have re-ceived. This also is extremely important. In both Protestant and Catholic congregations, we recognize a variety of ministries. However, we have be-come accustomed to approaching these kinds of questions in a manner that I believe is the wrong way round. My friend Jean Bosc always strug-gled against the way we deal with these situations. We have certain minis-tries, and when there are vacancies we look for people to fill them. Instead, we ought to discern the gifts of each and every member, and create the ministries that correspond to what is available in terms of gifts. For example, if in a particular community there is no one who has a gift of speaking, then there would not be a pastor. If there is someone who is very gifted in approaching poor and humble people, then a ministry should be created for bringing these people the good news. Never should we do the opposite: make a list of all the ministries we must have and then attempt to find people to fill them. I recognize that for the church authorities this is unacceptable. They are too accustomed to the bureaucratic models of our society. However, since every person in the community has received spiritual gifts, it is the task of the head of a congregation to discern the gifts of its members and put them to work.

On this point, I would like to add my own personal experience. When I was converted, I wanted to study theology and become a pastor. I spoke about it to someone who had my confidence and trust. He asked me to give him a few days to think about it. He then advised me not to do this because he felt I would be much more useful as a committed lay person. He told me that as a pastor I would have a ready-made function while as a lay person I would have to invent it, and this would likely have a much greater impact. I obeyed, and here I am.

Today the people who have offices of responsibility in our churches are preoccupied with balancing the budget, filling all the vacancies, maintaining or constructing buildings, and so on. However, that is not what they should be doing. As I mentioned, they ought to be discerning the available gifts and finding ways of putting them to work. Each and every community will be different in this respect. There are no formulas, no organizations, and no institutions that can take care of this.

In the same vein, I do not believe in large congregations. I think that we must practice our faith together in small groups, and that jointly these groups may possibly constitute a congregation. Small groups in which people know and live their faith together should be the base of any larger grouping. We appear to be reinventing the idea of house churches, and this may well be the best way forward. After all, *paroisse* (the French word for "congregation") means the neighbours, the homes that are side by side. Any leader of these groups must discern the available gifts and put them to work, and no institution can ever do anything of the kind. There are many ministries in which there is room for everyone.

We now turn to verses 19 and 20, which abruptly end this epistle. The usual kind of ending is absent, and this undoubtedly contributed to the arguments for not including it in the canon. These verses deal with a touchy subject that has been referred to as the admonition of a brother or sister. It constitutes the last example of what the Christian life in the church should be. We have dealt with our yes being yes and our no being no in our words and commitments, our accompaniment of those who are sick, our prayers, forgiving one another's sins, and now the pastoral concerns we ought to have for one another. Paul says exactly the same things in his first letter to the Thessalonians when he tells his fellow

Christians to warn those who live in disorder, console those who have been beaten by life, support the weak, be patient with everyone, take care not to repay evil with evil, and pursue always what is good among themselves and towards others. In sum, we ought to take care of one another in a pastoral sense. These two verses are addressed to brothers or sisters who have wandered far from the truth. They are called brothers and sisters even when they have wandered so far as to have broken with Jesus Christ. This pattern follows the one we encountered earlier: it was the sick who had to call the elders.

What is interesting about this text is that it is addressed to those who have strayed away from the truth. James does not say: you who follow the truth, pay attention to the people who wander away, and bring them back. Instead, the text warns the person who is about to make a mistake, and warns that if someone comes to bring you back, know that he or she is attempting to save you. I believe that from a biblical perspective, this dynamic or sequence of events is fundamental. Recall the numerous texts which never say that a husband has authority over his wife, but instead always tell the wife to be obedient to her husband. The same is true for the relationships between parents and children. The Bible tells the children to obey their parents. In other words, the biblical exhortation is always addressed to those who find themselves in the situation of weakness or inferiority, sickness or sin, in order to put them in the place of the just with respect to others. We have seen the same thing with regard to the sick: it is not the elders who must take the initiative. The exhortation is to those who are sick, and thus in a position of difficulty and weakness, to take the initiative and assume responsibility for others. This is completely upside down and backwards from what is normal in the world. The world always affirms those who have power, and it is in relation to this power that we assess the situation of those who are subordinated to that power. The approach in the Bible is the opposite. It speaks of the people who have an obligation, so to speak, and from there we reach out to those who have power. In the world this is abnormal. We see the same kind of abnormality in the text. When you think about people who stray from the truth, and others reaching out to bring them back, the normal reaction is not at all what we find in the text. It reflects the drama of how heretics are usually dealt with.

When our text refers to wandering away from the truth, this does not necessarily mean being lost, being spiritually lost, or being lost for eternity. I believe it means being lost in the trajectory of life, and in the reality of the world. It certainly is not a question of a theological truth. It is a matter of being lost in your life, and finding yourself in a situation of fear, anxiety, hopelessness, loneliness, meaninglessness, or the like – situations that we know very well. In such cases, people can no longer recognize where and who the truth is. The Gospels talk about these kinds of situations, as, for example, when Jesus saw the crowds as sheep without a shepherd. They were wandering and lost. Once again, it is not a matter of a dogmatic or theoretical truth but of bringing them back to the one who can lead them in the way of life. This good way is found through Jesus Christ, to whom the text implicitly refers.

These verses make it very clear that those who have strayed away are brothers and sisters, saying, "*My* brothers and sisters, if someone among you wanders from the truth ..." They imply another way of understanding what hypocrisy is. Those whom we may consider as doing evil, having moved away from the truth, or having become outright heretics are brothers and sisters and nothing else. Nowhere does it say that these people have ceased to be brothers or sisters. I am tempted to say that it is the opposite, in the sense that they are even more our brothers and sisters because, more than all the others, they need to be treated as such because it is a matter of straying from life itself.

The practices of the early church make this very clear. When, for the first time, the decision was taken to excommunicate people, it meant barring them from communion. There was no question of socially or spiritually excluding them from the church. The opposite was the case. These people had to be supported, sustained, and healed even more than before because they were even more intensely brothers and sisters by virtue of having been sanctioned. I personally believe that all this involves an incorrect interpretation of the role of communion, but that is another matter.

All this is clear from the text, which has the truth at its core. It speaks of those who have wandered from the *truth,* of those who bring a sinner back to the *way,* and of saving a soul from death by returning a person to *life.* In other words, it deals with the truth, the way, and the life, referring to Jesus' saying that *he* is the way, the truth, and the life. The text therefore speaks of those who have lost the only way, the only truth, and the only life, who is Jesus Christ. It is a question of having been separated from the person of Jesus Christ and not from a theological, doctrinal, or philosophical truth – a mistake that the church has made over and over again. In the Bible the truth is a person, and I do not understand why we have so much difficulty receiving this message. Hence it is not a question of those who have become heretical with respect to what is taken to be the correct theology or doctrine. There can be no mistake about this because James uses this interpretation of the truth three times in his letter. For example, in James 1:18 we are told that "Of his own will he brought us forth by the Word of truth that we should be a kind of first fruits of his creatures." This verse refers to the saving power of the Word, which we know is Jesus Christ. For us to be in communion with him implies a certain way of living our lives and of dealing with others. When the behaviour of a brother or sister appears to deviate from this way, it is possibly a sign that this person has separated himself or herself from Jesus Christ. It may plunge his or her life into despair, misery, and all the troubles that may come with no longer choosing what is good and unto life.

James tells us that bringing someone back to the truth is to save a soul from death. The Greek text is ambiguous because we do not know whose soul it refers to. It can be the soul of the person who has wandered away and who is brought back to Jesus Christ, but it can also be the soul of the one who approaches him or her and by doing so saves his or her own soul. It can be translated either way. Ezekiel 33:7–9 sheds light on this text as follows. If someone is given the responsibility of being a watchman for the people in the name of God and the people do not listen, they will die in their sin, but the watchman will have saved his life. However, if the watchman fails to warn the people, he will be held responsible. This text has the same double meaning as the one in James.

There is also the constant confusion regarding the meaning of the soul. We continue to interpret this as the Greeks did: the immortal and eternal soul, which is superior to the body. The Jews never had such a conception of the soul: "I" am a body, with the soul designating my psychological activities, as it were. Consequently, the Greek word for soul could just as well be translated as the *being* of a person. When our text speaks of saving a soul from death, it refers to recovering a person's being, that is, this being that was lost in the journey of his or her life. It certainly does not refer to saving a person's eternal being from an eternal death. Like everything James writes, what the text refers to is practical and immediate: a death already present in the life of a person. It is a question of saving a person from everything that is deadly or unto death: anguish, despair, hopelessness, solitude, rebellion, the absence of meaning, the absurdity of the world, and so on. It is from all this that we must protect our brother or sister. After all, their being is already saved in Jesus Christ, but this does not take away the possibility that they may be terribly unhappy and suffer from feelings of hopelessness and insignificance that are deadly in their daily lives. It is from this that we are called to save them. To bring them back to Jesus Christ is to enable them to rediscover a meaning and a hope for their lives. I believe that this is what our text speaks of.

The reference to covering a multitude of sins may appear surprising since it is speaking of one person. We can immediately rule out the idea that this person is a greater sinner and therefore has accumulated more sins than anyone else. It is more likely that this refers to a world in which a multitude of sins await us, as it were: despair, hopelessness, insignificance, solitude, rebellion, and much more. It is this multitude of sins from which a person will be relieved. The text says that these will be covered, which is exactly how this would be expressed in Hebrew by the verb *kasah*. It means to hide and forget sins. In other words, to bring back a brother or sister who has strayed away is to bring about a pardon from God, who covers these sins and sees them no more because Jesus Christ stands between this person and God. We must be totally convinced of this when we attempt to reach out to others with the good news, in the knowledge that this pardon is always available to them. Jesus Christ has saved them and is able to give a new meaning and direction to their lives. God never refuses to pardon a multitude of sins for those who repent. It should be noted that the expression translated as "a multitude of sins" can also refer to "the sins of the multitude." When a single person goes to his or her death it concerns all of us because it is an expression of the multitude of all our sins. As a result, when one person finds the way back to Jesus Christ, joy reigns in the church and in heaven, as proclaimed in one of the parables. It is on this note that our text ends, which corresponds very well with the universal character of this letter of James. The sins of all are covered, and forgiveness is permanently present, a reference that harks back to the opening address to the twelve tribes in the dispersion. The same greeting that opens the letter also closes it.

Where does this leave us with regard to admonishing a brother or sister? This last detail is so difficult to carry out that most of us simply do not bother with it. You really have to love someone if this is not to turn into a judgment on your part and if it is not going to be taken as such by the other person. We cannot put ourselves in the place of the just when faced with the person who has distanced himself or herself far from Jesus Christ. We must imitate Jesus, who goes and looks for the lost sheep simply because he loves it. In the same way, we must announce a free pardon and love from God instead of talking about the harm the person has done and the risk of damnation. This means putting ourselves exactly on the same level as the other person. It must never be a question of separating myself, as a person who is on the side of Jesus, from the other, as someone who is on the wrong side, as it were. I would say that we would have to go over to the side of the one who has strayed, in order to accompany him or her where they are and not where we are.

I can go no further with this other than through my own experiences with the Club de Prévention, which worked with the *blousons noirs* (black jackets), who are delinquent youth. Our advisers constantly had to be on their side and live within this delinquency, as it were. We knew very well that the clubhouse frequently acted as a place where stolen goods were received following a burglary. Being on their side was a condition for attempting to reach and convert them. You can well imagine all the problems that this got us into. At one point we were even working with a murderer, who was hiding in the club. We did so in the conviction that maybe he would repent and change his life and then give himself up to the police, but now accompanied by our promise and assurance of forgiveness. In any case, the advisers who worked at the club had to almost live on the side of these youth; and for twenty years it was my job to make sure that all this would not get completely out of hand. Fortunately, I could protect these youth somewhat because I had the complete confidence of a judge and a police chief, and we were constantly working things out. I remember that one evening I was telephoned at home by one of the advisers of the club, who informed me that he did not know what to do about the situation with which he was confronted. There was a gang who wanted to burn the home of a very well-known person in Bordeaux because this man was a homosexual. These youth despised and hated homosexuals to a degree that is difficult to describe. They had discovered that this person had attracted a lot of young boys, and they were going to expose this and burn his house, preferably with him inside. The adviser told me that they were about to leave and asked what he should do. I told him to accompany them and do everything possible to change the situation. Fortunately, the adviser had the presence of mind to take along a camera, and he photographed everything, from the moment that the black jackets broke down the doors and discovered an orgy of indescribable decadence. I saw the photos involving about a dozen men, a dozen women, and some twenty young boys. It was truly indescribable. Fortunately, the adviser told the gang that since he now had the evidence, they should leave. I will never know why the black jackets listened, but obviously they implicitly trusted their adviser. All the same, we came very close to a fire and possibly murder. We turned the photos over to an examining judge, and I can assure you that the orgies never reoccurred. I must confess that that was a very difficult night. I knew very well that this gang was capable of anything, and the situation could have deteriorated into something extremely serious. I am certainly not proud of this, but it does illustrate the kinds of difficulties we can get into in this business of admonition.

In answer to your questions, I must confess that in this case I feel that the gang was not altogether wrong. I observed the same kind of thing for many other things they did. Rarely did they undertake a break-in for reasons other than to punish someone for doing something they thought was absolutely wrong. It drew us all into a permanent state of illegality. Nevertheless, I do not see how we could have done anything else in our attempt to give these young people some hope and confidence for their lives, in the knowledge that they were not alone and that deliverance was possible. I believe that the good news is indispensable in all of this.

There is another important thing I learned from these experiences. Among the approximately one hundred and fifty advisers (literally, "educators for prevention") whom I have worked with, two groups stand out. For the one this was just another job, but for the other it was a vocation. The first group never achieved anything of significance, but the second group managed to establish a genuine existential rapport with the young people, an achievement that from time to time led to amazing situations. It reinforced the distinction between a job and a vocation.

In order to underline the difficulties in all of this, I will share one other experience. One of my close friends told me that I got on his nerves because I acted like a spider who waited to pounce on him. We enjoyed each other's company, but it is true that I was waiting for the right moment to approach him with the good news.

Postscript: The Poverty and Riches of Jews and Christians

The Flesh, the Law, and the Spirit

What we have learned thus far still has an important missing element, namely, the relationships between Christians and the Jewish people. When James speaks of the law of the Spirit, the question arises as to what happens to the Torah and the Jews. For answers, we turn to Paul's letter to the Romans.

The first two chapters of the letter to the Romans explain that the gospel is the power of God, which brings salvation through grace by the means of faith. It is granted to anyone who comes to believe upon hearing the good news. In chapters 3 to 7, Paul tells us that God freely grants his salvation without giving any consideration to merit, fault, or works (including works of the Law). Once granted, this salvation cannot be taken away by anyone. Chapter 8 explains the interrelationships between the Law, the Spirit, the flesh, and the law of freedom and liberation in the lives of Christians. This raises the question as to what happens to the Law and the Jewish people. It is dealt with in Romans 9, 10, and 11. The role to which Christians are called is closely related to that of the Jewish people, which is why these three chapters introduce a Christian ethic elaborated in the remainder of this letter.

Paul is tackling an issue that has divided the Christian community from the very beginning. There are those who believe that everything will change with the coming of the Kingdom of God. In the meantime, Christians have to go on living as before except that they now have hope because of their faith in Jesus Christ. Other believers claim that everything has changed. They have become entirely new people, with death behind them and eternal life before them. To the first group of believers, Paul said that because the Spirit lives in them, they will already be able to do some things that please God. As a result, to go on living as before is to in effect expel the Spirit. To the other group, who believed that the Spirit had changed everything, Paul warned of their continuing life in a mortal body that was still an instrument of the flesh. Hence, they would experience suffering and death. Of his own life, Paul observed in the closing verses of chapter 7 that he failed to do the good he desired to do and instead did the evil he attempted to avoid. He also expressed frustration with his "body of death." In other words, Paul acknowledged the presence of a power in human life that he referred to as the flesh. The flesh lives within our bodies as a power that opens the door to sin. It is by the intermediary of the flesh that sin dominates people. It becomes our very being.

The situation in which Christians find themselves must therefore be understood in terms of the interplay between the Law, the Spirit and the flesh. The flesh must not be confused with the body. It designates our entire being. Following humanity's separation from the only Living One, our being has become a non-being. Our being in the world is lived by means of what may be called an existential project aimed at succeeding in that world. It motivates both our individual lives and our joint efforts in making history. The one thing this power of the flesh cannot do is to provide human life with true meaning, and this weakness turns this power into one that covets everything that exists in the world. We saw this in the letter of James. For example, the flesh covets to do by itself what the Law does, as shown by the proliferation of moralities in human history. Humanity clearly regards these moralities as being superior to the Law of God. In the same vein, the flesh covets access to God, a desire that has resulted in many religions, each claiming exclusive and privileged access in opposition to all the others, as well as a superiority to the revelation. It is probably for this reason that the opening chapters of Genesis launch an attack on morality, religion, and magic as being antitheses of the revelation.[1] Paul makes it very clear that all those who live by the flesh use their actions, thoughts, and lives to satisfy it, and that this results in their detesting God. The love of the flesh (the non-being) is the hatred of God (the only One who lives). Genesis deals with the beginning of the non-being of the flesh.

The flesh is in opposition to the Law given by God to Moses. The Law teaches humility and the meaning of life. It shows what God has declared to be good; it therefore reveals the sins within us, and in turn compels us to acknowledge that we cannot fulfil the Law. God's justice must be satisfied according to this Law. There is a kind of impasse: the Law cannot be eliminated, while at the same time it cannot conquer the flesh to make it possible for humanity to obey it.

We are thus confronted with a fundamental question. How do Christians get from the Torah, which condemns the sin within us, to the law of freedom? If salvation is through grace by means of faith, what happens to the Torah and the Jewish people? Both these questions tackle the same issue. God's justice must be satisfied with regard to the sins revealed by the Torah. It prescribes a variety of sacrifices for different sins but it does not provide the sacrifices themselves.

In order to save the humanity that God loves, he must conquer the flesh; but he cannot do so by the means of power, which are means of the flesh. God is going to follow the Law. It demands specific sacrifices for particular sins, groups of sins, or the sins of each year. What we are dealing with now is the totality of the evil committed by humanity. An absolute sacrifice is required which once and for all must destroy the power of the flesh. Doing so would mean the condemnation of all of humanity, but this goes against God's love. The dilemma may be described as follows. The Torah brings to light a host of sins, but the roots of this sin remain in the flesh. If sin is to be uprooted, it must be done in the flesh. There must be a sacrifice in the flesh. This sacrifice cannot come from animals because it must be absolute. There is only one solution: God decides to take this condemnation on himself. It is important to recognize the scale of what is involved. All we need to do is to listen to the news reporting on all the wars, disasters, accidents, and all manner of suffering in the world and recognize that all this happens despite the best efforts of many people pitching in to reduce the impact. We may then begin to have some small appreciation of the scale of the sin of humanity. Only God can act on that level and take upon himself the totality of the condemnation that falls on humanity. This absolute sacrifice must be made on the level of the roots of sin in the flesh, but by the means of humility or non-power. God gives himself in his son, Jesus Christ, who became flesh and conquered it by his weakness. In other words, in the life of the son of God the power of the flesh must be dominated by a greater power, which is that of the Spirit. In this one aspect, the emphasis on the historical Jesus is correct. He experienced everything we do and shared everything with the members of his generation and time. He spoke their language, he knew what they knew, and he experienced the trials of the flesh and the suffering that accompanied them. However, by the Spirit he did not succumb to any of that. He took on all that is flesh, including all its pride and covetousness; but never did he covet the place of his Father, as is so well explained in the second chapter of the letter to the Philippians. It is worth noting that Islam claims this to be impossible. There cannot be a father and a son without the latter coveting the place of the former.

It was in this manner that Jesus conquered the flesh. He was the servant who came incognito and was despised. This provoked unimaginable tensions in Jesus' life. He was not to covet to be as God is, even to the point of being abandoned by God. It was in this way that all the pride and covetousness of the flesh were overcome and destroyed. Hence, the cross was the beginning of the forgiveness of our sins and the beginning of our forgiving others. At the same time, it is before this cross that we come face to face with the results of the totality of our sins. Once the flesh was destroyed, the enslavement to the flesh was broken and freedom became possible. It even changes the way believers read the Bible and reflect on it. They can only do this once the flesh is conquered by the Spirit, which means that they renounce their own cultural and intellectual resources to submit themselves to reading by the Spirit. It also means that there is no point in attempting to improve the flesh by a morality, or a religion – or anything else, for that matter. What Christians need to do is receive the Holy Spirit of Jesus Christ within themselves. In the meantime, as the last verses of chapter 7 clearly indicate, they continue to live in their bodies of death (non-beings going to their death), and yet the Spirit now lives within them. When they hear the Word and listen to it according to the Spirit, they no longer live according to the flesh. If Christ is within them the body is dead, and yet they will die because of sin. As we have seen before, when they hear the Word, something new is created within them and the miracle takes place. They can begin a life of freedom.

One of the implications of all of this is worth emphasizing. Christians have somehow become accustomed to turning all this around: they read the Law, the Law reveals their sins, they confess these sins and ask for forgiveness, and they are told that they have been forgiven. It is the exact opposite of the sequence we find in the Bible. They should begin with the announcement that God loves them, and they have been forgiven. It is only then that they learn that they are sinners and that they must live differently. In other words, they must begin with life, and it is only then that they learn that they are dead in their flesh. God's decision about humanity had already been taken in eternity: there were two trees in the centre of the Garden of Eden.[2]

As far as understanding the Spirit is concerned, Christians find themselves in the same situation in terms of their understanding of God. They can neither define nor grasp him to a satisfactory level of understanding, and yet they are asked to bear witness of him. The Spirit *is,* just as God *is.* Christians do not *have* the Spirit, because they do not possess it. Yet this Spirit transforms their lives. They may not even be aware of it when they are inspired by it. For example, something one person may say to another may become a turning point in his or her life, but the one who has said it may not know this until later, if at all. Even then, what exactly happened cannot be explained. In eternity, God made a decision in favour of humanity. He would grant it his Spirit, which would lead humanity to make a decision in its turn, a decision in favour of God, by responding to his love. The kingdom of heaven (as opposed to the kingdom of God)[3] is among us. Those who work within it know the road Jesus travelled and seek to overcome the flesh in their lives. In the meantime, the Law continues to exist, and obeying it can only be done through the Spirit. In Jesus Christ they have died to their flesh and the Law and have been reborn. They now live in the law of freedom, which is the law of the Spirit.

Christians cannot separate people's actions in the Spirit from those of the flesh. Only God can do so in the final judgment. When Christians hear God's Word, they live simultaneously in the present age and in the eternity of God. In other words, they must live in the economic, social, political, and religious conditions of their time as well as in eternity, and this creates a life full of tensions. There is no longer any place for a morality or religion on which humanity relies for guidance for living in the world. Believers will have to get along without the false sense of security that these elements of a culture provide. Nor is there any place for the Law, because the law of the Spirit in Jesus Christ has delivered them from the law of sin and death. They now have to figure things out for themselves and discover how to live this new freedom in the Spirit. Christians thus become engaged in a struggle against their non-being in relation to the specific conditions in which they find themselves. It is the world they have been given, but at the same time they must not give themselves entirely to that world. They must seek to liberate what they can in the Spirit. Doing so is profoundly dialectical and cannot be transformed into any moral, theological, or philosophical system for guidance. They will live in a constant state of conflict, torn as they are between living according to the flesh and living according to the Spirit. Within it they must seek to make the world as liveable as possible because people's lives must not be dominated by poverty any more than they should be dominated by riches. This effort is integral to their helping to create the conditions under which people are able to hear the good news.

The Refusal of the Jewish People

The fulfilment of the Law raises the question of the Jewish people. The only part in the New Testament where this is addressed is in the letter to the Romans, chapters 9 to 11. No comprehensive study of these chapters was made by the early theologians, although Calvin made some use of them. It was not until 1918 that Karl Barth published his commentary on this letter, of which a major portion is devoted to these three chapters. In 1940, Wilhelm Visscher[4] also studied these chapters, and it is his introduction that I will briefly summarize.

Following Paul's theology set out in the first eight chapters, he turns to the question of what happens to the Jewish people because of their refusal to accept the gospel. This situation poses an enormous theological problem. If the Jewish people choose not to believe, salvation no longer depends on God's grace and instead now depends on a human decision to believe or not. Salvation would then depend on the moral and religious capabilities of humanity; and people would be free to accept or reject the grace God gives. The implication is that following the break with God, humanity has been able to retain the power to do the good that God wills without the need for grace. If human beings have a free will that permits them to do the good on their own, there no longer is any need for grace, and God's limitless power of liberation would have no effect. We now begin to see the problem. God made his promise to the Jewish people. They did not believe it; hence, God's promise is void, which means that people have the power to do this. Can we leave it here and accept that people's refusal, their expression of free will, represents both the ability to do good and to render void God's promise? Of course, this is impossible.

When we examine the revelation made to the Jews, it is clear that they were chosen by grace from among all people. Within the Jewish people, there was always a remnant that bore this grace for everyone. However, without going into detail, the people wanted to do the good on their own without opposing God. Because of this, they failed to understand God's intention and the significance of their election. Visscher argues that, as a result, the Jewish people found themselves in a situation similar to that of the oldest brother in the parable of the prodigal son. The younger brother asks for his inheritance, departs, and squanders it all, but eventually returns to be received by his father with open arms. The father then holds a big banquet. The older son rebels and points out that he has always been a good son and has done what his father asked but has never received anything in return, and certainly not this kind of banquet. For Visscher, this is exactly how the Jewish people must feel. They cannot understand how people who have never served the way they have by performing the religious services, keeping the commandments, and so on, are now the people called by God. It is not possible to simply cancel out the promise God made to all Israel. For now, they are not going to receive the salvation granted by grace in Jesus Christ, but as a consequence, Christians now have to bear the good news for everyone. They have no choice but to turn to the non-Jews and announce to them the good news. In other words, the refusal of the Jews shows what Barth regards as the ·total seriousness and severity of grace. Salvation by grace is not easy at all because it demands a total engagement of our being, puts us with our backs against the wall, and is a question of yes or no. We are not going to get away with a few good works here and there and a few engagements of our choice. Hence, the refusal of the Jewish people attests to this radical seriousness. They have said no, and have been rejected. However, this rejection opens the door of God's truth to all other people. The unbelief and powerlessness of the Jewish people show that God's grace in Jesus Christ is now God's only course of action. Faith remains a free gift from God and is never the work of people. It is this way of God that we encounter again and again – a way that takes into account the decisions of human beings, takes charge of them, and uses these decisions in his own plan. When the Jewish people refuse, God accepts their refusal and uses it to have the gospel reach everyone. There is thus a unique but rather strange cooperation between God and people, where God uses human disobedience for the good. However, when the good news has been brought to everyone, the Jewish people will no longer be able to bear being excluded and, in their turn, will accept God's free gift of grace in the recognition that they cannot save themselves by their works.

God's Strategy

In chapter 9, Paul asks whether Israel's refusal to believe in Jesus Christ implies that God's Word was without power. Clearly not, because God's Word is Jesus Christ, who himself affirmed this. Jesus has accomplished everything God had announced with regard to Israel, and this does not depend on whether Israel believes or not. As Visscher pointed out, the entire history of Israel is the constant choice of a remnant, and when that remnant became disobedient, another one was chosen to bear the Word for all.[5] Eventually, the only one who was left was Jesus Christ, who then bore the Word for the entire Jewish people, past, present, and future. So the unconditional "yes" of God in Jesus Christ cannot be cancelled out by the "no" of the Jews who do not believe. There was refusal throughout the history of the Jewish people, and it was the children of the promise and not those of the flesh who were considered as the descendants of Abraham, as Jesus himself confirmed. God himself elected the children of the promise to represent him to everyone. However, the Israelites constantly attempted to take things into their own hands, beginning with Abraham. Despite God's promise, he and his wife had no children; he therefore decided to do what was customary and involve a slave, who bore him a son. God intervened by telling Abraham that his son Ishmael was not the one chosen to bear the promise but another son, whom Sarah would conceive.

This kind of behaviour is the key to understanding the history of Israel. The people wanted to keep the covenant and the Law and be such good servants that God would have no choice but to save them. However, God fulfils his promises by extending grace without taking into account fault or merit. He is entirely free to choose the ones who will bear his promises of the covenant, the Messiah, and his kingdom; and these bearers will be entirely free in his service. From generation to generation the question always is: Who will bear God's promises among humanity?

It is essential to recognize that the choices God makes are not unto salvation or damnation. As the text says, "I have loved Jacob and passed over Esau."[6] The choice may appear arbitrary to us, and yet it is a choice made in love. It is the same for us. Why do we love one person instead of another? In any case, it does not mean that the person we do not love is bad or any less human. Those who are chosen are the ones who have a job to do for the benefit of all humanity – it has nothing to do with salvation or damnation.

Christians have become so preoccupied with their individual salvation that it has become almost impossible for them to understand this message. Nevertheless, the question of salvation or damnation is entirely the wrong issue. In the Bible, the true question is the kingdom and how they can serve it. How do believers serve their God? – in such a way that his promise will be heard by everyone around them. For example, in church meetings Christians assume themselves to be good servants by starting with a prayer for the guidance of the Holy Spirit, and then they immediately get into strategies, budgets, and finance. They are so full of their own organization and plans that they leave no flexibility or openness to this guidance. If Christians are going to be true servants, they must

constantly ensure that, individually and collectively, their lives are open
to God's guidance.

The text then addresses the question that most of us probably have
wanted to ask: Is there injustice in God? People are always tempted to
judge God by their own standards, as if we are capable of inventing abstract principles by which we can judge God. From a practical standpoint,
God is God, and if he chooses to do something, there is nothing we can
do about it. Posing the question in this way is entirely foreign to the
Bible. God assures people of his love, and he wills them to respond to
that love, live in that love, and relate to their neighbours in that love. God
freely chooses those who will bear his promise. The others not chosen
will simply not have that mission, but they will still be held in his love.
Luther explained that God holds those whom he calls in his right hand,
and those whom he does not call in his left. One of the most dreadful
mistakes we can make is to read these texts in terms of God's election being for salvation or damnation. The Bible is quite clear. The people God
does not choose to bear his promise succeed in other ways. Ishmael was
promised to become a great nation, but it would not bear the promise.
Of Esau we are told that he became rich and powerful, and in the end he
reconciled with Jacob. There is no question that it is hard to understand
God's choice of Jacob over Esau, because Jacob cheated his brother, his
father, and probably everyone else, and yet he was the one chosen to bear
the promise. Being the second son, he had no rights whatsoever, but God
chose the weaker one, and proceeded to make him still weaker as a consequence of his struggle with an angel.

God chooses freely, but he also respects the choice of his human creatures and takes into account the possibility of their refusal. In other
words, there is no good God and bad God, as it were. Nor is the good with
God and the evil outside of God. Texts like Isaiah 45:7 do not please us
very much. God tells us that he forms both the light and the darkness and
that he creates prosperity as well as adversity. Similarly, in the Lamentations
of Jeremiah 3:37–8 and throughout Ecclesiastes we find similar declara-
tions. The freedom of humanity to refuse God does not limit his sovereignty, however, nor restrain his actions. It is because of his limitless
power that humanity's refusal can be respected by God, since it does not
call him or his design to save humanity into question. For example, the
"God is dead" theology rendered us the tremendous service of destroying
some false images of God – we might almost say that it was a good thing
to do this evil as a kind of house-cleaning. In the Hebrew Bible, this is apparent when we recognize that things frequently happen in pairs. A good

and a bad go together, as it were. There are Ishmael and Isaac, Esau and Jacob; and in the New Testament, Judas is the disciple who betrays Jesus, and Paul is the one who replaces Judas. Opposite to the person who is elected to bear the promise we find one who is passed over. In Israel there always remained a remnant who bore the blessing for all the people. Hence, God's strategy always includes the negative, and it serves a purpose. The text explains that the refusal of Israel is accompanied by the appearance of the gospel among the non-Jewish people. This is why the church cannot be separated from Israel, as we will see. The two are tightly bound together: it is not a question of the Christians being right and the Jews being wrong. Similarly, the struggle between Moses and Pharaoh cannot be interpreted as the former being good and the latter evil. Only God is good. When he extended his grace to these wretched Hebrew slaves, he showed his power. This power collided with the one who was most powerful at that time, namely Pharaoh. Pharaoh inadvertently was made to proclaim God's power and make his name known throughout the world at that time. As such, he played a role in the history of salvation; but it is important not to confuse God's power with his justice. Pharaoh was also within God's love, and God took his refusal into account in his strategy to reconcile himself with humanity.

When humanity decided to break with God, there were two things God could have done, given his power. He could have annihilated the entire creation or he could have mechanized everything, thereby destroying all possibility of love. Instead, he pursued a complex strategy of non-power and love by which he respected the liberty of his people and used their decisions in his design. Our popular images of God completely overlook his being a jealous God in his love for humanity and the all-out struggle to save us. In God's strategy, the ultimate pair is, of course, the Crucifixion and the Resurrection.

There has been a long tradition of reading the text in chapter 9 dealing with the potter and the vessels as saying that God creates some people to receive his wrath and others to receive his grace. The text says no such thing. What it does say is that God endures with great patience the vessels of wrath formed for destruction. This is not a question of God's punishing these people or making them suffer the consequences of their evil. God endures until the promise of salvation is announced; and when these vessels made for God's wrath hear this promise, they will receive it and learn what his wrath is, because the only one who has borne the fullness of this wrath is Jesus Christ. He is the only one who was fully cursed and blessed on the cross, and all the other vessels are summed up in him.

Jesus Christ thus becomes the key to everything in human history, as the book of Revelation shows.[7] It is through the disobedience of the Jewish people that God elects all the people of the earth. All the people who were previously excluded are now included. When God temporarily shuts people up into disobedience, it is to have mercy on everyone.[8] The text is very clear about this.

Love and Justice

Just as Romans 9 is centred on God, chapter 10 is centred on people. Both chapters begin with Paul's praying for the salvation of his Jewish brothers and sisters. Paul's prayer means that the future of the Jewish people is still open. If the future of the Jewish people had been decided by their refusal, there would be no reason to pray for them because all would be lost. This is not the destiny of his people. To show that what is happening to the Jewish people is not unexpected, Paul uses ten citations of the Hebrew scripture in these twenty-two verses. They all deal with the temporary rejection of Israel. God is prepared to deal with each of the following two scenarios. If the Jews accept and obey God's election for them to present him to all nations, then everyone will be converted by Israel. If, on the other hand, Israel disobeys and refuses the task for which it was elected, things will develop as explained in the text.

The last two verses of chapter 9 and the beginning of chapter 10 deal with the question of God's justice in relation to Israel's temporary rejection. The error of Israel, according to the text, is its justice. It is important to recognize that the justice the text speaks of is not an economic, social, or political concept. It is a justice humanity cannot know by itself. It comes very close to what, in Job 28, is called wisdom, which humanity also cannot find for itself. Justice is what God does. Israel received a law that was God's justice, but the Jews misunderstood this, thinking that the fulfilment of this law to the letter made them just. Hence, they appropriated God's justice, and this is what Paul refers to as justice through works. It caused them to stumble over this foundation stone. The Jews received the Torah as the living Word, which they transformed into a closed writing, leaving them having to interpret what was written and thereby enclosing God into the Torah. In response, God called all the other nations who knew nothing, and who now learned that justice is he who gives justice. Karl Barth suggests that, for God, justice is to give to those to whom you owe nothing; while for the Jews of that time, justice was to give to others what you owed them. It is in this way that God justifies the unjust – by giving to humanity what it does not merit. The only condition is that we must believe it by means of faith. As Paul puts it, although the Jews believe, they have a great zeal that is manifested in their knowledge of scripture and their attempts to work it all out to perfection. However, this is not the zeal of God, which is a love unreservedly given to all people. This love for everyone the Jews did not understand – they made the revelation their own property, as it were. They made it their privilege, forgetting that the Torah came from a God who declared himself for everyone. Their task was not to endlessly study and comment on it but to transmit it to all people. It was this error that led God to the election of others for this task. God continued the Torah by sending Jesus Christ as the "end of the Torah," in the double sense that it no longer has the purpose of expressing God's will and justice. After Jesus Christ, the Torah no longer corresponds to this intention. The end of the Torah in Jesus Christ also means that it is entirely accomplished by him. However, this does not mean that Christians can get rid of this law, because the Hebrew Bible teaches who Jesus is. For example, all the sacrifices pointed to the ultimate sacrifice of Jesus Christ; and by reading Leviticus, Christians can learn how these are summed up in the life of Jesus. Hence, in these and other ways, the Torah continues to enlighten them. Although this is not mentioned by Paul in this text, Jesus instructed his followers to go beyond the Torah. For example, if they did not give more than the requisite one tenth, they would fall back to being under the Law. Hence, there is a justice of the Law and a justice of faith, and the two meet in Jesus Christ on the cross, as Paul demonstrates through his many citations from the Hebrew Bible. The one who was just died for the unjust, and that is the justice of God. The Torah was also on the cross, as Jesus fully accomplished it. It becomes clear that God's love is also his justice. This love has no limits, as the death of Jesus shows.

Did Israel have an excuse for not listening to the many warnings it received according to the Hebrew scriptures? They did not know, because salvation and justice as gifts from God respond to faith; and how could the Jews have lived this faith when they had never heard someone speak of it? Faith comes from what a person hears. There is an opposition between the Jews, who referred themselves to what was written, and the Christians for whom everything came through hearing the Word preached (and it is God who is the origin of this Word). For Christians, bringing the Word to others is of the highest priority. Paul claims that the Jews of his day had heard the gospel proclaimed in their synagogues, but he is probably referring to Psalm 19, which essentially says that the creation is a Word, not because it is a kind of natural theology but because God reveals it as such. The Jews knew this Psalm and should have realized, therefore, that this Word was universal and not restricted to those who had received the Torah. Paul concludes by citing Isaiah, saying that all day long God held out his hands to a disobedient and obstinate people, meaning that God continues to call his people (once again revealing the limits of his rejection of them).

In his commentary on this chapter, Karl Barth applied these texts to the Christian church and found it guilty. It has robbed the Jews of their Bible and the revelation by appropriating them and excluding the Jews. It has transformed the justice of Jesus Christ into a law: you must do this and not do that, and so on. It has made a morality out of faith. It too believes that justice can be obtained through works, and has a greater confidence in its means and organization than in the Word. Just as the Jews did not know how to bring God and his promise of salvation to everyone, the church instead has brought a law and a morality. It also has failed to turn the written Word into a living Word. I would add that Christians have become so used to asking whether they or others have faith that they completely fail to understand that you cannot possess faith. Moreover, churches are so busy planning their actions and finances that there is little time left over for prayer and meditation as an opening up to the Holy Spirit.

When the Jews no longer fulfilled the task of bringing the revelation to all people, God found another way to reach the entire world. Very small churches of Jews and non-Jews accept the revelation, and they must now do the work to which the Jews were called. The Jews are now watching, but they are not likely to convert when the grace they received is greater than the grace extended to the non-Jews. If the rejection of the Jews was the reconciliation of the world, what will their reintegration be but "life among the dead?" This rabbinical phrase does not refer to the Resurrection but to their final realization of the love of God because Jesus was the first to descend towards the dead and to defeat death forever. At this point, the conversion of the Jews will trigger the salvation of everyone, as the book of Revelation makes plain. Paul interprets his work among the other nations entirely from the perspective of the conversion of the Jews, a perspective that is eschatological in character. If God desired that the setting aside of the Jewish people would bring about the salvation of the non-Jews, what God expects now is that their conversion will produce the jealousy of the Jews so that they also will seek his grace and salvation. The work of God began with the Jews, and it will end with the Jews.

As a result, the responsibility for the unbelief of the Jewish people lies with the Christian churches. Their conversion must spur the Jewish people to jealousy. However, if Christians do not arouse the Jews by their liberty, love, justice, and holiness, they are not likely to be interested.

It may well be that for this very reason these three chapters have been ignored for nearly two thousand years: the message that the conversion of the Jews depended on the faithfulness of the Christians was just too threatening.

Grafted onto the Jewish Tree

Paul compares the Jewish people to the roots and trunk of an olive tree. The comparison of grafting a branch from a wild olive tree onto a cultivated one, which bears the olives that produce the oil, is contrary to how olive trees are normally grafted. However, chapter 11:24 explains why Paul did so. The non-Jews belong to their "nature" – the equivalent of the wild olive shoot. Branches were broken off so that these shoots could be grafted in, contrary to nature. It is the inverse of what people do. Hence the olive tree in this story of Paul does not represent nature but grace and liberty. The roots represent grace, and thus the fruits borne by the olive tree are the fruits of that grace. The gardener has taken branches from the wild olive tree and grafted them onto the cultivated tree so that they would participate in the grace of God, which was in the roots and the trunk. It was against their nature that non-Jews became believers. They were the branches from a bad species that did not bear fruit but are now grafted onto the people elected by God and who clearly remain God's people. The oil comes from this extraordinary work of God, who grafts non-Jewish believers onto the good tree, and they therefore depend on its roots and its trunk. As a personal note, I have always felt perfectly at home at the many meetings of Jewish intellectuals and theologians that I have attended during my life. I felt like a person who was grafted onto where I belong.

Since God was strict with the Jewish people and cut off branches that no longer bore fruit, he can certainly do so with Christians if they commit the same error as the Jews. Christians could also be cut off if they appropriate the election and the revelation for themselves. They too could be rejected the way the Jews were. Hence, Christians cannot look down on the Jews and try to eliminate others through their preaching, morality, theology, and behaviour. In any case, the hardening of the hearts of the Jewish people is temporary, and nothing can be judged by what is happening today. In the end, the Jewish people will convert, and it is in relation to this eschatological event that we must interpret the present. Any

ethic or any theology must be eschatological in character because everything will be decided in relation to the end, which will be the love of God
for everyone. This love has maintained the Jewish people and has grafted
the Christians onto them.

What does Paul mean when he says that God has bound everyone in
disobedience so that he may have mercy on them all (11:32)? Does this
mean that God has led everyone into disobedience or caused them to
commit sin? James has assured us that this is absolutely not the case, so
what is the disobedience that our text speaks of? It is the disobedience of
the two great commandments: to love your God and your neighbour. No
one can live in this total and exclusive love for God and neighbour, with
the result that no one is just and that humanity is trapped in its disobedience of living outside this love. God, however, makes this disobedience
into a means for bringing his love to everyone. The Jews disobey, and
God uses this to bring salvation to the non-Jews. In turn, those who convert will bring about the conversion of the Jews. Hence, this disobedience is but a moment in human history since it is God's purpose that
everyone will know his love. The proof of this is that God sacrificed himself. God loves us more than we love ourselves. He loved us first, and it is
only because of this love that we know what love is.

It should be noted that the word "mystery" in the New Testament always refers to a revelation that concerns the end, making it eschatological in character. The history of the Jewish people is in relation to the
end. The refusal of the Jews will continue until the end of time, when
everyone will believe in Christ; and then Israel in its entirety will be saved
and thereby reunited. All of human history occurs on the seventh day,[9]
but when humanity does not live by love, it disturbs God's rest. If love
had reigned, God's rest would not have been disturbed.

What these three chapters (9, 10, and 11) are saying is that if Christians
were truly Christians, then the Jews would be converted. In other words,
it is not because of the theology of grace that Paul exhorts the Christians
to live as Christians but because of the Jewish people. The structure of this
letter is now perfectly clear. The first part explains Paul's theology of
grace, the second part deals with the relations between Jews and Christians,
while the third builds a Christian ethic on all of this. He makes this clear
in the opening verses of chapter 12, where he exhorts the Christians.
Doing so must not be confused with giving commands, because the people whom he is addressing have been liberated. It is therefore a question
of the possibility of living in the compassion God has for everyone. It is
the One who suffers with us, who understands our problems, and who
enters into them when we disturb his rest.

Paul begins the construction of his ethic with people's bodies. We might almost say that we are first and foremost our bodies. In other words, Christian life is not a question of spirituality superimposed on daily life, of Sunday separated from the rest of the week, of the soul in preference to the body, and so on. There must not be any separation between the material and the spiritual life, and this is why the first point of Paul's ethic for Christians is to offer their bodies. This ethic begins in daily life, where the real service of God takes place. Christians cannot be of their world and time because the spirit of this world and time will put its form on everything they touch. It is a spirit of power and covetousness desiring to live human life independently in a world of consumption, which will lead to the destruction of that life and the world. Christians must refuse to enter into the form (spirit) of their age. They must be nonconformists and not follow the fashions of the world. How different a world this would be if Christians were faithful; and yet in the end, the Jews will have shared their riches with the Christians, and the Christians with everyone else, even though now we see a wasteland of poverty. The intelligence by which Christians apprehend the world is in urgent need of reform, to be based not on power and covetousness but on non-power and love. To love God and your neighbour with all your heart, soul, mind, and strength begins with intellectually understanding what all this means. Every Christian must choose to be a nonconformist but must do so in liberty and love for God and neighbour.

Notes

Translator's Introduction

1 By "system" I mean the experience we all have when we say, "That is how the system works," or, "You can't beat the system." For the most comprehensive description of this system as it functioned in the second half of the twentieth century, the reader is referred to the many works of Jacques Ellul, which describe how it functions technologically, economically, socially, politically, legally, morally, and religiously.

1. Introduction to Amos

1 A French journalist has written a book suggesting that Jacques Ellul foresaw almost all the major events of the second half of the twentieth century (Jean-Luc Porquet: *L'homme qui avait presque tout prévu* [Paris: Le Cherche Midi, 2003]). Most of these predictions were based on his analysis of technique and its vast influence on human life and society (Jacques Ellul, *The Technological Society*, trans. John Wilkinson [New York: Knopf/Vintage, 1967]).

2. The Prophecies against the Six Surrounding Nations

1 André Neher, *Amos: Contribution à l'étude du prophétisme* (Paris: J. Vrin, 1950).

2 Wilhelm Visscher, *The Witness of the Old Testament to Christ*, trans. A.B. Crabtree (London: Lutterworth Press, 1949).

3 Jacques Ellul, *The Presence of the Kingdom*, trans. Olive Wyon (New York: Seabury, 1967); *The New Demons*, trans. C. Edward Hopkin (New York: Seabury, 1975) (see especially "Coda for Christians," 209–28); *Hope in Time*

of Abandonment, trans. C. Edward Hopkin (New York: Seabury, 1973); *False Presence of the Kingdom*, trans. C. Edward Hopkin (New York: Seabury, 1972).

3. The Prophecies against Judah and Israel

1 Emmanuel Levinas, *Du sacré au saint: Cinq nouvelles lectures talmudiques* (Paris: Editions de Minuit, 1977).
2 Gerhard von Rad, *Genesis: A Commentary*, trans. John Marks (Philadelphia: Westminster Press, 1972).
3 André Neher, *Amos: Contribution à l'étude du prophétisme* (Paris: J. Vrin, 1950).

4. Intertwining Themes ...

1 Jacques Ellul, *On Freedom, Love, and Power*, comp., ed., and trans. Willem H. Vanderburg (Toronto: University of Toronto Press, 2010).
2 Jacques Ellul, *The New Demons*, trans. C. Edward Hopkin (New York: Seabury Press, 1975); *The False Presence of the Kingdom*, trans. C. Edward Hopkin (New York: Seabury Press, 1972). In addition to the state, science and technique are also worshipped.
3 André Neher, *Amos: Contribution à l'étude du prophétisme* (Paris: J. Vrin, 1950).
4 Jacques Ellul, *The Politics of God and the Politics of Man*, trans. Geoffrey W. Bromiley (Grand Rapids, MI: Eerdmans, 1972).

5. God's Pedagogy and the Evolving Revelation

1 Before we jump on our politically correct bandwagons, I would like to point out that these remarks must be carefully interpreted in the context of a life-long study Jacques Ellul has undertaken of our civilization, closely coupled to a life of activism. It is unfortunate that only the former is attested to by his many writings, while the latter is little known in North America. It is also worth pointing out that with hindsight, we can definitively say that practically everything Ellul foresaw has come true, and this has been recognized by others. This is in sharp contrast with the many intellectual fashions of the second half of the twentieth century, most of which have been passing illusions. The only confirmation of the scientific validity of his social interpretations of where our civilization is going is their confirmation by current and subsequent events. It is for this reason that I believe Jacques Ellul is the most important scientific and Christian thinker of the twentieth century. We do well to interpret these remarks regarding a sensitive subject such as AIDS in the context of the following works by Ellul: *The Technological Society*,

trans. John Wilkinson (New York: Knopf/Vintage, 1967); *Propaganda: The Formation of Men's Attitudes*, trans. Konrad Kellen and Jean Lerner (New York: Vintage Books, 1973; see especially chapters 2, 3, and 4 regarding life in a mass society. My sociology and engineering students have always been deeply struck by this analysis); *The New Demons*, trans. C. Edward Hopkin (New York: Seabury Press, 1975); *Déviances et déviants dans notre société intolérante* (Toulouse: Érés, 1992); (with Yves Charrier), *Jeunesse délinquante: Des blousons noirs aux hippies* (Paris: Mercure de France, 1971); *Hope in Time of Abandonment*, trans. C. Edward Hopkin (New York: Seabury, 1973).

2 André Neher, *Amos: Contribution à l'étude du prophétisme* (Paris: J. Vrin, 1950).
3 Jacques Ellul, *Reason for Being: A Meditation on Ecclesiastes*, trans. Joyce M. Hanks (Grand Rapids, MI: Wm. B. Eerdmans, 1990).

6. Justice and Related Themes

1 Jacques Ellul, *The Theological Foundation of Law*, trans. Marguerite Wieser (Garden City, NY: Doubleday, 1960).
2 Jacques Ellul, *On Freedom, Love, and Power*, comp., ed., and trans. Willem H. Vanderburg (Toronto: University of Toronto Press, 2010).
3 Ibid.
4 Jacques Ellul, *Apocalypse: The Book of Revelation*, trans. George W. Schreiner (New York: Seabury Press, 1977).
5 André Neher, *Amos: Contribution à l'étude du prophétisme* (Paris: J. Vrin, 1950).
6 Wilhelm Visscher, *The Witness of the Old Testament to Christ*, trans. A.B. Crabtree (London: Lutterworth Press, 1949).

7. The Five Visions

1 Wilhelm Visscher, *The Witness of the Old Testament to Christ*, trans. A.B. Crabtree (London: Lutterworth Press, 1949).
2 Karl Barth, *Church Dogmatics*. I have been unable to find the exact reference.
3 Jacques Ellul has devoted an entire book to this topic, in which he contrasts hearing and seeing, truth and reality, the word and the image, and so on. It is the only work in which he examines (in alternate chapters) what he understands about this topic from studying the Bible and observing the world around us. See: Jacques Ellul, *The Humiliation of the Word*, trans. Joyce Main Hanks (Grand Rapids, MI: Wm. B. Eerdmans, 1985).
4 Throughout the Bible, there is an opposition between what we hear (the Word) and what we see (the images and the idols). It so fundamentally calls

contemporary lives and cultures into question that Jacques Ellul devoted an
entire book to this issue: *The Humiliation of the Word.* It is the only work in
which (in separate chapters) his sociological reflections engage in dialogue
with his Christian thought.

5 I have developed the thought of Jacques Ellul on the relationship between
words and images in *Our War on Ourselves: Rethinking Science, Technology,
and Economic Growth* (Toronto: University of Toronto Press, 2011). Briefly
put: everything we see exists in its own space; it can be only one thing; it is
separable from everything else; it is open to measurement, quantification,
and mathematical representation; and it is part of a simple non-enfolded
and non-dialectical complexity. In contrast to the "world" that babies
and children first enter into by language and culture, the visual "world"
expresses the principles of separability, non-contradiction, closed defini-
tions, and applied logic. This is in contrast to an enfolded and dialectical
symbolic universe. The meanings and values of this universe have multiple
dimensions that are often ambiguous and possibly contradictory. The complexity of what we see can be built up one constituent at a time, while the
symbolic universe of individual and collective human life develops through
differentiation and integration. The world of babies and children emerges
out of undifferentiated stimuli. It is a relational complexity that cannot be
assembled one constituent at a time.

From this, it follows that science, technique and everything built up
with them share their characteristics with what we see, while symbolically
mediated social relationships, groups, and societies have all the opposite
characteristics. The collision of these two "worlds" has produced a de-sym-
bolizing influence on human life and society, to the point that our future as
a symbolic species may well hang in the balance.

6 Jacques Ellul, *On Freedom, Love, and Power,* comp., ed., and trans. Willem H.
Vanderburg (Toronto: University of Toronto Press, 2010).

7 André Neher, *Amos: Contribution à l'étude du prophétisme* (Paris: J. Vrin, 1950).

8. Confronting the Religious Establishment, and the Silence of God

1 Jacques Ellul, *The New Demons,* trans. C. Edward Hopkin (New York: Seabury
Press, 1975).

2 Rudolph Otto, *The Idea of the Holy: An Inquiry into the Non-rational Factor
in the Idea of the Divine and Its Relation to the Rational* (London: Oxford
University Press, 1924).

3 Jacques Ellul, *On Freedom, Love, and Power,* comp., ed., and trans. Willem H.
Vanderburg (Toronto: University of Toronto Press, 2010).

4 André Neher, *Amos: Contribution à l'étude du prophétisme* (Paris: J. Vrin, 1950).

5 Jacques Ellul, *On Freedom, Love, and Power.*

6 Our civilization has done everything possible to make it appear that an absence of meaning in human life and society is entirely normal. Functionalism, structuralism, systems theory, and (most recently) post-modernism all imply in one way or another that we are functions, mechanisms, or information processors, which are all aspects of dead machines. It is then possible to dismiss any hunger or thirst for some meaning in our lives. We had better get used to living without these kinds of ideologies of the past. This attitude constitutes what I have referred to as *Our War on Ourselves* (Toronto: University of Toronto Press, 2011). It is the ultimate assault on our humanity. In his sociological and historical analyses, Jacques Ellul has shown that this is the inevitable outcome of technique dominating human life and society. It leads to the desymbolization of experience and culture in general, and our values and reference points in particular. As long as we believe that there are no limits to what science can know, what technique can do, and what the nation-state can politically organize, we will have some reference points or secular idols. However, their desymbolization is fuelling our dependence on various substances to dull the pain and escape from our lives. The so-called war on drugs ought to become an attempt to restore some meaning to our individual and collective lives. "Getting tough on crime" ought to become an attempt to create an economy in which every-one can play a part. Of course, in these kinds of issues, the churches are not to be found. They are slavishly following one fashion after another.

9. Reconciliation

1 Jacques Ellul, *On Freedom, Love, and Power*, comp., ed., and trans. Willem H. Vanderburg (Toronto: University of Toronto Press, 2010).

2 Oscar Cullmann, *Christ and Time: The Primitive Christian Conception of Time and History* (London: Westminster Press, 1964).

3 André Neher, *Amos: Contribution à l'étude du prophétisme* (Paris: J. Vrin, 1950).

4 Ibid.

5 The image of using a sieve to separate wheat grains from chaff was un-doubtedly familiar to everyone during the time of Amos. After the wheat had been harvested and threshed, the wheat grains had to be retrieved from what remained of the plant. The sieve allowed some of the debris to pass through the holes as it was moved back and forth. Also, much of the chaff was eliminated by shaking the sieve in such a way that its contents would be airborne part of the time so that the lighter debris could be

carried off by the wind and not fall back onto the sieve. Like the heavier debris, it would eventually drop to the ground, where it could be collected to be burned. This image has some resemblance to that of the purification of precious metals by heating them so that the impurities would rise to the surface where they could be skimmed off.

6 Jacques Ellul, *Apocalypse: The Book of Revelation*, trans. George S. Schreiner (New York: Seabury Press, 1977). In this study, Ellul shows that one of the four horsemen represents political power. He also shows that during the final judgment this political power will be destroyed along with all the others after the people have been separated from them.

7 For additional insight into Jacques Ellul's understanding of politics see also: Jacques Ellul, *The Politics of God and the Politics of Man*, trans. Geoffrey W. Bromiley (Grand Rapids, MI: Eerdmans, 1972); *The Political Illusion*, trans. Konrad Kellen (New York: Vintage Books, 1972); and *The New Demons*, trans. C. Edward Hopkin (New York, Seabury Press, 1975).

8 Jacques Ellul, *On Freedom, Love, and Power*.

9 The reader is referred to Jacques Ellul's study of the last part of the book of Job in Jacques Ellul, *On Freedom, Love, and Power*.

10 There are various translations published by André Chouraqui. The translation cited by Jacques Ellul is not the one found in Chouraqui's Bible.

11 The reader is referred to Jacques Ellul's study of the opening chapters of Genesis in Jacques Ellul, *On Freedom, Love, and Power*.

12 Ibid.

13 The reader is referred to Jacques Ellul's study of the election to render a service in the kingdom of heaven in Jacques Ellul, *On Freedom, Love, and Power*.

10. Introduction to James

1 Sören Kierkegaard's use of the Epistle of James mainly occurs in two works: *For Self-examination*, trans. Howard V. Hong and Edna H. Hong; in *The Essential Kierkegaard* (Princeton, NJ: Princeton University Press, 2000); and Part One, "Purity of Heart Is to Will One Thing," in *Upbuilding Discourses in Various Spirits*, trans. Howard V. Hong and Edna H. Hong; in *Eighteen Upbuilding Discourses* (Princeton, NJ: Princeton University Press, 1990).

In *For Self-examination*, Kierkegaard endorses James's advocacy of works in a Christian life, although Martin Luther rejected James's discussions of works. Kierkegaard defends Luther, however, in two ways. He explains that Luther's rejection of works was in effect a rejection of the Catholic church's view of earning salvation by works and of its limited view of works. As Kierkegaard notes, "faith is a restless thing" that alters how one leads one's entire life. Luther was closer to James than he realized in his redefinition of works to include witnessing for the truth. The most important point is that Kierkegaard (following James) emphasizes that works are the expression of faith in *everything* one does.

Kierkegaard comments extensively on the metaphor of James, "the mirror of Scripture," also referred to as the "perfect law of freedom." When I look at myself in the mirror of Scripture, I see myself as I really am – a sinner – and not as the good person I imagine myself to be. In order to see myself realistically, I have to hear God's Word addressed to me personally. It is only by treating God's Word as doctrine, as objective and impersonal, that I can protect myself against what Kierkegaard called the infinite demand of God – to be perfect. The infinite demand is set within the perfect law of freedom, however. Consequently, I have to work out my salvation as a free person.

In "Purity of Heart Is to Will One Thing," Kierkegaard meditates on James's term "double-mindedness." To be double-minded is to be both for God and for oneself in a worldly way. But this is impossible because God demands that we die to our worldly self and become an unselfish lover. As a consequence, to be double-minded is not to be for God. To be for God means that one is willing to suffer everything in the love of God and fellow human beings. Examples of double-mindedness include loving God only to a certain degree, or for the sake of a reward, or to avoid punishment. Double-mindedness, Kierkegaard argues, is a kind of sickness, which at bottom is sin. Either one loves God completely or one selfishly loves oneself. We are thus all double-minded, but as Ellul points out, God loves us and saves us despite our selfishness.

2 In order to understand Jacques Ellul's interpretation of the structure of this letter, the reader may find it helpful to recall the role of the kingdom of heaven in human history, that of a yeast or salt that entirely transforms history. The letter of James may be regarded as explaining how some of this occurs in our daily lives. We must take responsibility for working out the implications of our faith, which means that daily-life experiences will put it to the test. At first, we will be like newborns attempting to make some sense of our lives in the world, but this time by faith and less by culture. If we persevere and our lives in the world begin to take on new meanings and values in this faith, we may grow and become like children. Further perseverance may allow us to grow into adults. In other words, we can never claim to *have* faith, as if we could possess it, as it were. Faith can have us, provided that we allow it to grow in our lives.

Jacques Ellul elaborated his interpretation of the kingdom of heaven in *On Freedom, Love, and Power*, comp., ed., and trans. Willem H. Vanderburg (Toronto: University of Toronto Press, 2010).

3 Louis Simon, *Une éthique de la sagesse* (Geneva: Labor et Fides, 1961).

11. Overview of the Christian Life

1 The insistence of Kierkegaard, Ellul, and others that the letter of James has
nothing to do with moral advice may be more fully understood by interpreting the role of faith in our daily lives as something utterly concrete and
practical. Faith is non-natural and thus non-cultural as well. Throughout
human history, groups and societies have lived by means of very different
ways of life and cultures. We are all people of our time, place, and culture.
Our cultural dimension involves implicit commitments to ultimate reference points, which make human life liveable in an ultimately unknowable
reality. According to cultural anthropology, we are committed to myths as a
kind of spiritual orientation of our culture. Simply put, these myths make
certain things so self-evident and obvious that the very possibility of human
life and the world being otherwise becomes unthinkable and unliveable.
The result is that they are experienced and lived as absolutes during a
particular historical epoch of a culture. The fact that these myths are not
absolutes only becomes apparent over time, when it becomes evident that
the world (and, consequently, human life lived in relation to it) is very different. However, for a time this remains hidden.

When God delivered the Jews from Egypt (meaning the double anguish
of life and death), he commanded them not to have any false gods. The
Jews were asked to put God at the centre of their lives rather than the idols
of their neighbouring cultures, which amounted to nothing but smoke
and vapour. When you needed rain, these vanities could do nothing for
you. The Jews were encouraged to participate in their liberation by adopting God's way as expressed in the law and the covenant. Doing so implied
a constant struggle against their own cultural way. Most of the time, the
necessities of their culture won out, with the result that the law and the
covenant functioned more or less like any cultural morality and religion,
as we have seen in Amos.

Today we live in so-called secular mass societies. We no longer have gods
of any kind, and hence all the biblical teachings regarding false gods appear
rather strange. It has encouraged an extreme dualism in which Christianity is practised as if it were a complement to a secular life by bringing some
morality and spirituality into it, as if there were none. However, what if there
are secular myths in our cultures: a symbolization of entities in our daily lives
making them into much more than they really are, along with the expectation that they can do much more for us than they can really deliver? What
if there is a great deal in our daily lives that science cannot know? What if
there is a great deal that technique cannot help us accomplish? What if the

nation-state is fundamentally impotent to deliver on our values and aspirations? Obviously, if this is the case, then our rush to entrust our knowing to science, our doing to technique, and our political organizing to our nation-state will get us into trouble and could potentially end life on this planet.

By participating in the kingdom of heaven, Christians are called to exercise their responsibilities by putting Jesus at the centre of their lives. This is certainly not a matter of attending worship services and insisting on not doing some of the things our culture engages in. It has to do with a faith-based participation in being the yeast that will transform the "dough" of human history. To do so we must live by faith: what is self-evident in our cultures is not what it appears, and through faith we must discern this. In other words, putting Jesus at the centre of our lives and living by faith turns our daily-life activity into a test of whether we live and deal with it according to our culture or according to the ways of the kingdom of heaven. Do we discern the limits of science, technique, and the nation-state or do we treat them as omnipotent? If so, we need to develop ways of knowing and doing and organizing our communities so as to live as free people who are loved by God and who trust him to know what is good and what is not. Every single situation and every decision we take will be unto death or unto life, and we are invited to do what is unto life. Jesus shows us how to do this. From this perspective, faith acts as an anti-morality and an anti-religion – something we already encountered in Jacques Ellul's study of the opening chapters of Genesis in his book *On Freedom, Love, and Power* (Toronto: University of Toronto Press, 2010).

In sum, if the letter of James is read with a biblical perspective as opposed to that of a so-called secular mass society, it is not only deeply rooted in the biblical message of the Old Testament, it also helps us to engage in the kingdom of heaven and join the struggle between God's way and our cultural way of life in every detail.

2 Jacques Ellul, *On Freedom, Love, and Power*, comp., ed., and trans. Willem H. Vanderburg (Toronto: University of Toronto Press, 2010).

3 Louis Simon, *Une éthique de la sagesse* (Geneva: Labor et Fides, 1961).

4 Jacques Ellul, *Reason for Being: A Meditation on Ecclesiastes*, trans. Joyce Main Hanks (Grand Rapids, MI: Eerdmans, 1990).

5 Jacques Ellul, *The Humiliation of the Word*, trans. Joyce Main Hanks (Grand Rapids, MI: Eerdmans, 1985).

6 Jacques Ellul has devoted an entire book to this theme: *Living Faith: Belief and Doubt in a Perilous World*, trans. Peter Heinegg (San Francisco: Harper and Row, 1983). Unfortunately, the English title *Living Faith* does not at all capture the French title, which literally says "Faith at the Cost of Doubt."

7 Jacques Ellul, *Money and Power*, trans. LaVonne Neff (Downer's Grove, IL: Inter-Varsity Press, 1984).

8 Jacques Ellul, *The Meaning of the City*, trans. Dennis Pardee (Grand Rapids, MI: Eerdmans, 1970).

9 Jacques Ellul, *The Politics of God and the Politics of Man*, trans. Geoffrey W. Bromiley (Grand Rapids, MI: Eerdmans, 1972).

10 Jacques Ellul, *False Presence of the Kingdom*, trans. C. Edward Hopkin (New York: Seabury, 1972); *The Political Illusion*, trans. Konrad Kellen (New York: Knopf, 1967); *The New Demons*, trans. C. Edward Hopkin (New York: Seabury, 1975).

11 Jacques Ellul, *On Freedom, Love, and Power.*

12 One of my anonymous readers put the problem as follows: "here, Jacques Ellul argues that James' reading of Job supersedes all previous readings, and that the question of temptation has been a misreading all along. At the same time, Ellul seems to be desirous of resolving the apparent breaks and contradictions between the books of Job and James. Why? … Does Ellul understand the Bible as a divine text that is a coherent whole, that contains no contradictions (other than the ones that our own bad hermeneutic practice put there), or is Ellul's Bible a human document formed over centuries, and so not subject to the problem that each part of it must support, agree with, and relate to the other parts of it?"

    Jacques Ellul's interpretation of the Bible is much closer to the Jewish than the Christian position. The latter has made the subjection of the Bible to scientific and historical criticism a priority over the hermeneutic question. For example, in his preliminary remarks to the opening chapters of Genesis, Ellul's real question is: Given the obvious contradictions between the two accounts of the Creation, why did the rabbis retain them both as contributing something essential to the revelation? Similarly, the contested part of Job does fit extremely well, from a hermeneutic perspective, and cannot therefore be rejected on historical grounds, such as not being part of the original manuscript, or having been added later by another author. The bottom line is that the Jewish people discerned all this as being part of the revelation. Later in this book, Ellul makes a similar remark regarding Romans 9–11. Issues of translation have added to the confusion. For example, in the Lord's Prayer, "Do not lead us into temptation …" is a very bad translation, as Ellul explains in his book on the temptations of Jesus, entitled *Si tu es le Fils de Dieu* (Paris : Éditions du Centurion, 1991). It is a question of not putting us to the ultimate test, since we are rarely capable of discerning the good, which only God can do.

13 Jacques Ellul, On Freedom, Love, and Power.

14 Yves Charrier et Jacques Ellul, Jeunesse délinquante: Des blousons noirs aux hippies (Paris: Mercure de France, 1971).

15 On page 29, Jacques Ellul acknowledges that organic causes can also play
    a significant role. Philosophers like to speak of our free will, thereby com-
    pletely ignoring the massive scientific evidence showing how deeply we are
    influenced by biological, genetic, economic, social, and ideological factors.
    Our "free will" is that of an alienated being, or to put it biblically, that of a sin-
    ful person who is like a slave and thus has only limited control over his or her
    life. Salvation is the message of the eventual liberation of our entire being.
16 Jacques Ellul, The Judgment of Jonah, trans. Geoffrey W. Bromiley (Grand
    Rapids, MI: Eerdmans, 1971).
17 Jacques Ellul, On Freedom, Love, and Power.

12. The Other

1 See chapter 4 in Jacques Ellul, *Perspectives on Our Age: Jacques Ellul Speaks on
    His Life and Work,* ed. Willem. H. Vanderburg (Toronto: House of Anansi,
    2004), 2nd ed.
2 Jacques Ellul, *On Freedom, Love, and Power,* comp., ed., and trans. Willem H.
    Vanderburg (Toronto: University of Toronto Press, 2010).
3 Ludwig Feuerbach, *The Essence of Christianity,* trans. George Eliot (New York:
    Harper and Row, 1957).
4 I have been unable to locate the source of these remarks regarding faith.
    For an overview, see Jürgen Moltmann, *An Autobiography by Jürgen Moltmann,*
    trans. Margaret Kohl (Minneapolis, MN: Fortress Press, 2008).
5 Unfortunately, Jacques Ellul's explanation of the first few elements of faith was
    lost during the time the cassette was turned over during the recording. I was
    able to reconstruct it by interpolating between what was recorded and another
    recording of a previous study of James that I made when I was in France.
6 Jacques Ellul, *On Freedom, Love, and Power.*
7 Ibid.

13. The Word

1 Jacques Ellul, *Propaganda: The Formation of Men's Attitudes,* trans. Konrad
    Kellen and Jean Lerner (New York: Knopf, 1965); *The Humiliation of the Word,*
    trans. Joyce Main Hanks (Grand Rapids, MI: Eerdmans, 1985); *The Political
    Illusion,* trans. Konrad Kellen (New York: Random House/Vintage, 1972); "De
    la signification des relations publiques dans la société technicienne," extrait
    de *L'Année Sociologique 1963* (Paris: Presses Universitaires de France, 1963).
2 Jacques Ellul, *The Humiliation of the Word.*
3 Jacques Ellul, *On Freedom, Love, and Power,* comp., ed., and trans. Willem H.
    Vanderburg (Toronto: University of Toronto Press, 2010).

4 Jacques Ellul, *The Humiliation of the Word.*
5 Ibid.
6 Ibid. See also *Apocalypse: The Book of Revelation*, trans. George W. Schreiner (New York: Seabury, 1977).
7 Jacques Ellul, *The Humiliation of the Word.*
8 Jacques Ellul is reading from a French translation by Louis Segond, which I have translated into English.
9 Jacques Ellul, *On Freedom, Love, and Power.*
10 In further developing Jacques Ellul's interpretation of our civilization dominated by technique, I have referred to our current situation, in *Our War on Ourselves* (Toronto: University of Toronto Press, 2011). It shows how technique is desymbolizing our language and hence what has made us human until now.

14. Life in the World

1 Jacques Ellul, *On Freedom, Love, and Power,* comp., ed., and trans. Willem H. Vanderburg (Toronto: University of Toronto Press, 2010).
2 I believe that what Jacques Ellul is referring to in this paragraph is the role of culture in human life. It is an aspect of his thought about which he has written very little. His reaction to a draft manuscript of my first book, prepared when I worked with him as a post-doctoral fellow from 1973 to 1978, sums it up. After reading it, he asked me if I did not think he had already worked this out. I responded by asking him for the references, admitting that I had not yet read everything he had published. A few days later, he returned and acknowledged that indeed he had not developed it. He did acknowledge that much of it was implicit in his work, with which I entirely agree. The theory of culture was originally published as *The Growth of Minds and Cultures* (Toronto: University of Toronto Press, 1985), with a foreword by Ellul.
3 Jacques Ellul, *On Freedom, Love, and Power.*
4 Karl Barth, *Church Dogmatics, Vol III: The Doctrine of Creation, Part 2* (Edinburgh: J. & J. Clark, 1960).

15 . To Whom or What Do We Belong?

1 Jacques Ellul, *The Politics of God and the Politics of Man*, trans. Geoffrey W. Bromiley (Grand Rapids, MI: Eerdmans, 1972).
2 Jacques Ellul, *The Judgment of Jonah*, trans. Geoffrey W. Bromiley (Grand Rapids, MI: Eerdmans, 1971).

3 Jacques Ellul, *Hope in Time of Abandonment,* trans. C. Edward Hopkin (New York: Seabury, 1973).
4 Jacques Ellul, *On Freedom, Love, and Power,* comp., ed., and trans. Willem H. Vanderburg (Toronto: University of Toronto Press, 2010).
5 Jacques Ellul, *Propaganda: The Formation of Men's Attitudes,* trans. Konrad Kellen and Jean Lerner (New York: Knopf, 1965); *The Political Illusion,* trans. Konrad Kellen (New York: Random House/Vintage, 1972).
6 Jacques Ellul, *The New Demons,* trans. C. Edward Hopkin (New York: Seabury, 1975).

16. Our Christian Lives Together

1 Jacques Ellul, *On Freedom, Love, and Power,* comp., ed., and trans. Willem H. Vanderburg (Toronto: University of Toronto Press, 2010).
2 Readers may not appreciate the full weight of these observations unless they familiarize themselves with Jacques Ellul's extensive study of our civilization dominated by technical means, efficiency, and a technical orientation to everything it does. For an introductory overview of his thought, the reader is referred to *Perspectives on Our Age: Jacques Ellul Speaks on His Life and Work,* ed. Willem H. Vanderburg, 2nd ed. (Toronto: House of Anansi, 2004). For further details, the reader may consult Jacques Ellul, *The Technological Society,* trans. John Wilkinson (New York: Knopf/Vintage, 1967); *Propaganda: The Formation of Men's Attitudes,* trans. Konrad Kellen and Jean Lerner (New York: Knopf, 1965); *The Political Illusion,* trans. Konrad Kellen (New York: Random House/Vintage, 1972). See also Jacques Ellul, *Prayer for Modern Man,* trans. C. Edward Hopkin (New York: Seabury, 1970).
3 Jacques Ellul, *Prayer for Modern Man,* and *Living Faith: Belief and Doubt in a Perilous World,* trans. Peter Heinegg (San Francisco: Harper and Row, 1983). The literal translations of the French titles are: "The Impossible Prayer," and "Faith at the Cost of Doubt."

Postscript: The Poverty and Riches of Jews and Christians

1 Jacques Ellul, *On Freedom, Love, and Power,* comp., ed., and trans. Willem H. Vanderburg (Toronto: University of Toronto Press, 2010).
2 Ibid.
3 The distinction between the two has been developed in Part 3 of Jacques Ellul, *On Freedom, Love, and Power.*
4 Wilhelm Visscher, "Étude biblique sur Romains IX à XI," in *Foi et Vie,* 1988. See also "Le Mystère d"Israël," in *Foi et Vie,* 1965 (Geneva: Labor et fides).

5 Ibid.

6 Most translations use the phrase "and hated Esau." However, the Hebrew verbs for loving and hating do not refer to emotions but to actions, with the result that "passed over" is a better translation.

7 Jacques Ellul, *Apocalypse: The Book of Revelation*, trans. George W. Schreiner (New York: Seabury Press, 1977).

8 Some readers have erroneously concluded that Jacques Ellul is a proponent of the so-called doctrine of universal salvation. For him, there can be no such doctrine because it would essentially "mechanize" God and deny his sovereignty. God alone decides, but as is promised in many texts, he is reaching out to everyone with the good news in order to save humanity. This is a promise, not a doctrine. Those who believe in the doctrine of universal salvation are as mistaken as those who believe in the doctrine of predestination. God cannot be replaced by a "system" that ties him down. It is the problem of all systematic theologies, which take on the characteristics of a discipline. As I have shown elsewhere, such disciplines are incapable of dealing with life.

9 Jacques Ellul, *On Freedom, Love, and Power.*

Index